Advanced Mobility and Transport Engineering

Advanced Mobility
and
Transport Engineering

Edited by
Slim Hammadi
Mekki Ksouri

First published 2012 in Great Britain and the United States by ISTE Ltd and John Wiley & Sons, Inc.

ISTE Ltd
27-37 St George's Road
London SW19 4EU
UK

www.iste.co.uk

John Wiley & Sons, Inc.
111 River Street
Hoboken, NJ 07030
USA

www.wiley.com

© ISTE Ltd 2012

Library of Congress Cataloging-in-Publication Data

Advanced mobility and transport engineering / edited by Slim Hammadi, Mekki Ksouri.
p. cm.
Includes bibliographical references and index.
ISBN 978-1-84821-377-7
1. Transportation engineering. I. Hammadi, Slim. II. Ksouri, Mekki.
TA1145.A37 2012
629.04--dc23
2012008581

British Library Cataloguing-in-Publication Data
A CIP record for this book is available from the British Library
ISBN: 978-1-84821-377-7

Printed and bound in Great Britain by CPI Group (UK) Ltd., Croydon, Surrey CR0 4YY

Table of Contents

Preface

The main functions of the transport engineering field refer to the needs of users, the study and design of technical and industrial solutions, as well as their implementation and supervision.

The user of a transport system can be a network controller or a passenger who needs travel information. In any case, a client needs to be provided with advanced mobility services.

Transport engineering is a field of enquiry appealing to researchers worldwide. The purpose of their work is to improve existing solutions or to try to solve new functional problems in an effective manner.

New problem-solving methods are being developed in relation to the emerging needs of users as well as the latest communication and mobility technologies in an ergonomic, socioeconomic and ecological context.

Thanks to the meeting of the best teams of researchers and innovators in the Nord-Pas-de-Calais region within CISIT[1] – the International Campus on Safety and Intermodality in Transportation – many lasting partnerships have been developed with the contribution of industrialists, transport operators and international researchers who have been invited to join us. As a result of these fruitful partnerships, the idea of writing a reference work emerged.

These research endeavors are part of the "Multimodal Urban and Intercity Networks" action initiated by CISIT in order to accomplish the strategic objective of "optimal management of multimodal transport chains". This objective is associated with three other large strategic objectives:

---

1 www.cisit.org.

– new challenges for clean, lightweight and secure vehicles;

– safe, secure and intelligent mobility; and

– morpho-adaptive safety and human factors.

All of these objectives help to face the challenge of the sustainable mobility of people and goods.

The authors of this reference work offer the reader an overview of the latest techniques, approaches and methods used for identifying, designing, optimizing and carrying out advanced mobility services.

We express our sincere thanks to all those who have contributed to this work, members of CISIT, as well as researchers in various fields relating to transport engineering and advanced mobility services.

Slim HAMMADI
Mekki KSOURI
April 2012

Introduction

Given the constant reshaping of the mobility principles, concepts and individuals' preferences, the implementation of new services joining the context of intelligent mobility is becoming necessary. This reshaping is meant to address environmental, economic, and social problems and is part of a policy of incentives promoting clean, flexible and less costly modes of transportation. Furthermore, given the extension in distances and the duration of journeys , such services need to ensure full spatiotemporal coverage, attending to urban, peri-urban and extra-urban areas. Thus, besides ensuring continuity and security of all journeys, decreasing budget allocations for transport and combining efficacy with the need for the optimization of travel time, these are among the main objectives of these services. Competitiveness in this field has currently reached its highest peak: systems characterized by monomodality, intermodality, multimodality and recently co-modality, compete fiercely with one another. Therefore, following the example of CISIT – the International Campus on Safety and Intermodality in Transportation – in Nord-Pas-de-Calais, projects have been initiated in order to realize innovative ideas combining intelligence with transport. As for the latter, different systems including transport-on-demand, "eco-sharing" modes, travel assistance have been realized. Moreover, thanks to technological advancements, intelligent transport systems are now beyond the stage of mere ideas; they have become extremely significant, if not essential.

Within the framework of sustainable mobility, the time has arrived for minimum usage of the single car in favor of alternative modes of transport that are "soft" and collective: we need to promote a rational and suitable use of the best mode of transportation for a given journey. However, it is the transport information that must be central to both reflection and action.

Multimodal or passenger information is information that accompanies the passenger before and during his or her journey when using public transport. This travel assistance generally consists of a detailed description of available itineraries, arrivals and departures, duration of journeys, ticket prices for different modes of transport and sometimes even for different transport operators. In addition to this essential information, passengers can be provided with futher information called secondary (or approval) information that informs them about the weather, nearest restaurants, hotels and other local services. This secondary information is not necessary for describing the journey, but can be indispensable for transport users in order to choose the best mobility offer provided. Moreover, the quality of multimodal information in terms of availability and relevance has currently become a fundamental criterion in assessing the quality of services offered by transport operators.

Nowadays, researchers, industrialists and public communities are involved in a process of innovation in order to create multimodal and secondary information services, adapted to the needs of its users. Special attention to the industrial and commercial context of different transport operators is given.

Chapter 1

Agent-oriented Road Traffic Simulation

1.1. Introduction

The main objective of (computer) road traffic simulation is to recreate and understand the observed traffic phenomena. Road traffic can be defined as the phenomena resulting from the movement of road users within a road network of limited capacity. The "traffic system" is characterized by an endeavor consisting of road infrastructure that was designed in such a way as to accommodate a collective optimum, and by an ever-increasing demand on the part of users looking to achieve an individual optimum. The reconciliation between private and collective interests gave birth to a vast amount of research, especially in traffic supervision [HAL 97], the optimization of traffic flow [BAZ 05] and in road infrastructures [ESP 02].

One of the notoriously difficult theoretical problems in the development of simulation devices is the case study of an intersection. Traditional approaches, consisting mainly of traffic simulation devices, have so far relied on considerable simplifications. A problem-solving mechanism within an intersection allows vehicles to enter an intersection as long as their trajectories do not cross. Such solutions are sometimes satisfactory, but they are not always appropriate when it comes to recreating the behavior of real drivers. The precision of these simulations is very important, as the driver interferes with the overall flow of the road network.

Chapter written by RENÉ MANDIAU, SYLVAIN PIECHOWIAK, ARNAUD DONIEC and STÉPHANE ESPIÉ.

For our purposes, we propose to tackle this traffic simulation problem using an "agent-oriented" approach.

This chapter is divided into five sections. Section 1.2 briefly introduces multi-agent systems. Section 1.3 presents road traffic simulation devices. In section 1.4 we introduce the ArchiSim simulation device. Finally, in the last two sections we examine the model that was used as well as the results that were obtained in a few simulations.

1.2. The principle of multi-agent systems

This section is an excerpt from a document written for GdR I3 [GUE 10].

1.2.1. *Motivations*

In order to approach difficult problems, special efforts have been made in the area of distributed artificial intelligence and multi-agent systems. The latter offer some advantages [GAS 89, CHA 92, FER 95, BRI 01] and provide useful models for the study of complex distributed systems made of autonomous components capable of interacting with one other. These entities are called "agents". Breaking down the system into various agents allows for better responsiveness and a higher adaptability to the changing environment. Moreover, the interactions between agents may generate organized ("social") structures, which in turn constrain and coordinate agents' behavior.

The objective of multi-agent systems is to model complex, heterogeneous, nonlinear and evolving systems so that they bring about a type of intelligence and certain abilities that are different (and/or superior to) those of the agents that comprise them. This type of intelligence is born out of the coexistence and cooperation of autonomous agents.

Zambonelli and Van Dyke Parunak [ZAM 02] emphasize the fact that recent software systems have a very high degree of complexity, not only in terms of size but with regard to other factors as well. The agents of multi-agent systems offer multiple solutions to these problems:

– The environment that software systems are developed in is increasingly dynamic and subject to constant changes. Different systems (not necessarily software systems) coexist in the same environment, either collaborating or competing against one another. Their actions influence the environment and they generally act at the same time. Hence it is not possible to predict the results that an action will generate.

– An increasing number of IT components have been created in distributed environments, with different abilities and being linked to various networks, most of which are wireless. The systems that use these components need higher distribution levels, i.e. in the area of system entities management, in locating the center of control, as well as in the interactions between agents. The need for integration or for interoperability becomes crucial.

– There is a growing need for knowledge-based reasoning and knowledge-based service supply. New information-processing mechanisms are required and the interaction among system components needs a higher level of abstraction, with an additional need for semantic processing. In particular, using agent-oriented ontologies and an agent-oriented language can prove useful in dealing with these requirements.

– A higher level of customization becomes an equally important factor in the acceptance of a service (for example information retrieval or booking services). This implies that the systems should be reconfigurable and equipped with processing mechanisms based on the user's profile (i.e. using personal data).

The fundamental concepts of multi-agent systems are based on the "vowels" approach and they are presented below.

1.2.2. *Agents versus multi-agent systems*

A multi-agent system is a set of agents interacting with one another according to fairly varied patterns with the purpose of enriching collective behavior. These patterns can be:

– agent patterns;

– interaction patterns, inasmuch as the global features that are being examined are a result of inter-agent interaction;

– organization patterns, representing the global features of the society of agents; or

– environment patterns.

Figure 1.1 proposed by Ferber [FER 95] illustrates the main concepts and components of a multi-agent system as well as the relations between them.

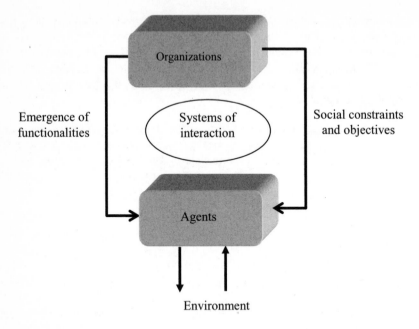

Figure 1.1. *The micro–macro relationship in multi-agent systems [FER 95]*

1.2.2.1. *Agents*

Multi-agent systems are comprised of agents and intended to model complex systems. Each agent possesses its own competences; however, it needs to interact with other agents in order to solve problems that fall into its area of expertise or to avoid conflicts that might follow from its decisions or actions towards the other agents. The objective of these systems is therefore to find a solution for global problems or simulating complex behaviors with the help of a set of entities having the following features:

– an agent is an autonomous entity: it acts without the intervention of humans or of other agents and it controls its actions according to its internal state as well as to the state of the environment;

– an agent is a proactive entity: in particular, the agent has its own purpose and pursues its own activities. As opposed to objects, the agent does not simply react to the messages it receives from other agents, but its actions are channeled by its goal;

– an agent is an adaptive entity: the agent is capable of adjusting its skills (communication skills, behavioral skills, etc.) according to the agent that it interacts with and/or the environment in which it evolves. Put another way, an adaptive agent has the ability to adjust the features of its tasks in order to satisfy internal as well as external demands.

This list is by no means exhaustive. Some researchers choose to invest in agents with different properties. Among these, we can mention expediency, anticipation, mobility and rationality.

Traditionally, agents are divided into two categories: reactive agents and cognitive agents. Reactive agents are uniquely defined within laws of stimulus/response association. They allow for the modeling of very refined behaviors, but they do not possess internal states (therefore they do not have the ability to build and update a representation of their environment). In contrast, cognitive agents are equipped with internal states, which can serve to represent the condition of their environment (in the absence of explicit signals). Each cognitive agent has the ability to reason on the basis of a fair amount of knowledge; it also has the ability to process different information with regard to the field of application as well as information regarding the management of interactions with other agents and with the environment. Cognitive agents are therefore capable of solving certain problems by themselves. The current tendency is to consider cognitive agents and reactive agents as part of a continuum rather than making a clear-cut separation between them.

1.2.2.2. *Environment*

The environment has oftentimes been considered a cardinal entity in multi-agent systems. Early work (see MACE (multi-agent computing environment) [BRA 87]) on multi-agent systems did indeed propose a representation of the environment.

Within MACE, the environment is represented by a set of system agents enabling the interpretation of commands, the management of user interfaces and interfaces with other machines as well as the management of storage memory. This environment allows for a real distribution of the agents among different processors. It also allows for the definition of demons, which inform the agents about the changes that have occurred in the MACE system. Thus, MACE produces an interesting representation of the environment. The majority of the other platforms, however, restrict the environment to the infrastructure that helps convey the messages.

Research in the field of located agents views the environment as the core entity. This entity is active and has its own dynamic. For example, studies of ants have shown that the environment models the dynamic of pheromones (density variation, dissipation, etc.). The dynamic of agents is founded on the dynamic of the environment. The latter also plays the role of collective memory for agents.

1.2.2.3. *Interaction*

In a multi-agent system, as soon as an agent finds itself confronted with its fellow agents, a series of actions may occur between these entities, provided that specific conditions are met – and that is when interaction takes place.

The study of interactions in multi-agent simulations extends the isomorphism between the subject under study in the initial discipline and its equivalent in the computerized model. This undertaking is clearly continuing the research carried out on classical MAS (multi-agent system).

Whereas a differential equation has nothing to do with the objects modeled (the macroscopic approach), in the agent-oriented approach we can stay closer to the initial domain (the microscopic approach). When these fields of study are more concerned with the relationship between entities rather than the entities themselves, the notion of interaction helps facilitate the dialog between field experts and computer specialists.

Relevant literature abounds with examples of such knowledge gaps in disciplines as varied as biochemistry, cellular biology, ecology, granular physical systems, social networks and financial markets. From this point of view, the fact that research has recently focused on interactions is merely a manifestation of this tendency to bring together computerized objects and natural systems.

Following in the footsteps of Ferber [FER 95] who divides interaction-based systems into two large categories, agent-centered interaction and environment-based interaction, the research community itself currently seems to be divided into two fields of study. The first category brings together the studies where interactions are used as a means of communication between agents. The researchers conducting these studies view interaction as a message that is part of a general interaction protocol between agents. This approach is used mainly in two domains, where frequent references are made to the concept of agent communication languages. The second category regroups the research studies where interactions are in themselves seen as actions involving several agents. There are, therefore, various approaches that seek to evaluate the actions carried out between agents.

One of the classic problems in the modeling of agents that must interact is coordination. Several definitions of coordination have been introduced in relevant literature [LES 98], each of them putting forward a specific point of view:

– Coordination can be defined as a series of meta-actions that authorize agents to interact with each other. Thus, for Malone [MAL 98], coordination is a set of "extra-activities" that need to be carried out for the interaction to take place.

– Coordination can also be compared to a research process that is devised within the framework of distributed problem-solving. In this context, the resolution of sub-problems, the mechanisms used for conveying interim messages or the dissemination of solutions towards sub-problems are all characteristics of this process.

– Coordination is also a way of resolving different types of conflict between agents, including conflicts over resources (between agents that must share a resource at a given time) or conflicts of interest (when agents have differing or, in extreme cases, antagonistic goals).

Coordination is the process that enables an agent to reason on the basis of its own actions and on the (anticipated) actions of other agents, thus attempting to guarantee that the group of agents acts as a coherent whole. Jennings also emphasizes that the process of reasoning should not only take into account the current state of the system, but also its future states [JEN 96].

1.2.2.4. *Organization*

An organization describes how the members interact and cooperate in order to achieve a common goal. One of the most complete yet concise definitions that we have at our disposal has been formulated by Edgar Morin: an organization is the "attribute of a system that is at once capable of maintenance and self-maintenance, of interconnecting different elements as well as holding itself together and of producing and producing itself" [MOR 86]. This definition shows that the structure is not constant nor is it independent of the system's activity. The representations of the organization are therefore dynamic.

Early research in distributed artificial intelligence was inspired by human metaphors. In fact, organizations were designed to resemble human organizations. The main problem was the coordination of different agents that were frequently designed as intelligent systems. Many studies have subsequently tried to define multi-agent organizational structures by combining concepts taken from various fields: sociology, biology, physics, chemistry, mathematics, computer science, etc. The proposed organizational structures may be either static, and therefore designed *a priori* by the programmer, or dynamic, as encountered in adaptive multi-agent systems. They depend on the environment in which they evolve, on available resources, and therefore on the problem they must solve or the system they must simulate.

These studies can be classified in three categories. The first category brings together all of the coordination mechanisms founded on metaphors taken from a variety of fields (biology, physics, etc.). The second category defines an organization as an abstract structure whose representation is shared among the members of the organization. The agents use this representation to coordinate their actions. These structures are often used to describe models and to explain existing organizations. They are particularly dependent on the type of multi-agent systems: reactive or cognitive. Finally, the third category defines an organization as a structure that is external to the agents. For this last category, the construction of a multi-agent system thus requires the design of the underlying organizational structure.

A synthesis of different organizations has been advanced in relevant literature, for example in the work of Horling and Lesser [HOR 04]. Numerous research studies focused their efforts on dynamic organizations that evolve in accordance with different parameters such as efficacy, the change in environmental constraints, etc. Recently, Serugendo has distinguished between the concepts of emergence and self-organization [SER 06]. Emergence is the global behavior of a system arising from local interaction, whereas self-organization is seen as a dynamic structure that can maintain itself without external interference.

1.3. General remarks on traffic simulation devices

1.3.1. *Granularity level*

One of the criteria that characterize traffic simulation is granularity, which is the level of detail it can offer. The devices available can be categorized according to three levels of granularity: microscopic, mesoscopic and macroscopic.

Simulations of the macroscopic type are concerned with traffic flow, which they seek to characterize according to measurable qualities such as flow rate, density, average speed, etc. These simulations allow for the description of traffic flow from a global perspective.

By contrast, microscopic simulations consider the different entities of traffic flow in an individual manner. The result is a much higher level of detail that permits a relatively accurate analysis of the interaction between simulated vehicles.

Mesoscopic simulations are a compromise between microscopic and macroscopic simulations. Vehicles are no longer considered individually, but they are joined together in a single unit that has similar and homogeneous features. For example, a group of vehicles driving on a freeway would be simulated as one single entity.

In what follows, we will analyze the policy of traffic scheduling and traffic volume as it is carried out in these different methods in greater detail.

1.3.2. *A centralized approach for traffic simulation*

Early models of traffic flow are either empirical or analytical. Empirical models use regression analysis based on data collected from real intersections. Analytical models are based on the parametric transformation of a vast number of variables, such as the geometry of the intersection, follow-up time, etc. [LIE 97].

Macroscopic simulations focus on vehicle flows, whereas the majority of microscopic simulations evaluate each vehicle individually. The devices enabling the simulation of crossroads that are not controlled by standard tricolored traffic lights (such as Vissim [VIS 03]) are based on a simplification of the problem. More specifically, conflict resolution in intersections is treated as a problem of centralized scheduling of different incoming flows. In these applications, every vehicle that is approaching the intersection is kept in a queue – one for every branch of the intersection.

The vehicle at the front of the queue is admitted in the intersection following a centralized process (the principle of gap acceptance) and with respect to different constraints. The first constraint regards the time passing between two vehicles: this needs to be long enough to allow for the insertion or the crossing of a traffic flow. For the driver, gap acceptance corresponds to an acceptable interval between vehicles (that is, between two consecutive vehicles in conflicting traffic flows), during which an operation can be performed.

This principle can easily be extended to include a sequence of intersections (i.e. an urban axis) by introducing impact supervision elements for the next intersections. Other constraints enable us to limit the number of possible combinations between different rotational movements on each axis (left, right and straight ahead) so that the vehicles' trajectories do not "conflict" at the center of the intersection. Finally, several simple rules may be added that can limit phenomena such as waiting or congestion at the center of intersections.

The scheduling policy (based on a centralized approach) of vehicles or flows of vehicles suggests that drivers' decisions depend on an external mechanism, much like a traffic agent who lets vehicles pass when their trajectories are no longer in conflict.

Using centralized scheduling techniques or vehicle-tracking laws, however, has several disadvantages. First, such approaches are not generic. For example, in the case of vehicle tracking laws that were obtained from measurements taken on actual roads, we can assume that the resulting equations are linked to features of actual road sections (length, number of routes, etc.) and that they only warrant re-simulations sections that have already been observed. Second, even though a scheduler can suffice for analyzing traffic flow in terms of entering/leaving an intersection, this mechanism is not suitable for analyzing phenomena inside the actual intersection. More specifically, the behaviors of individual drivers simulated by these mechanisms are not always realistic, and thus several phenomena cannot be simulated, such as the interference of traffic on consecutive intersections or traffic congestion inside an intersection. Therefore, tracking laws can only *ad infinitum* simulate a particular situation that was measured in reality.

Simulation devices that use these equations overlook the surrounding traffic so their adjustment proves to be quite tedious. Given these circumstances, it appears to be difficult to use such devices for assessing the impact of changes in road infrastructure, e.g. adding a roundabout or a traffic light. Moreover, in the case of complex traffic situations (such as an intersection), forming an equation of the movement of vehicles is difficult and requires several simplifications.

The use of a scheduler that centralizes the decisions of all the drivers in the intersection and all the simulated interactions moves away from real interactions between human drivers. A way of bypassing the limitations of the centralized approach involves using a behavioral approach for decentralizing traffic simulation.

1.3.3. *Behavioral approaches*

The so-called behavioral approach or "individual-oriented" approach brings a solution to the weaknesses that we have seen described in mathematical approaches. This approach is underpinned by the following postulate: the traffic is the resulting sum of all the actions and interactions of different actors in the simulation – users (motorists, pedestrians, vehicles with two wheels), signaling, road infrastructure, etc. [ESP 95].

The behavioral approach is thus linked to modeling and re-creating the behaviors and interactions of the different entities that are simulated as faithfully as possible in order to obtain life-like traffic phenomena. These phenomena are called emerging phenomena and they depend upon a distribution of behaviors (the heterogeneity of individual practices) among a set of vehicles simulated on a road network.

1.3.3.1. *Approaches based on cellular automatons*

Certain models based on cellular automatons were introduced in order to solve traffic simulation problems at intersections. For example, Ruskin [RUS 02] used a deterministic cellular automaton that splits the intersection in a grid where every cell can contain a vehicle or an empty space. Vehicle movement is facilitated by this formalism and the behavior of vehicles is considered a transition function of automatons. The representation of the environment, however, is too limited to faithfully render the dynamics of traffic situations in intersections. In fact, limiting the areas leads to limiting the speed of vehicles (there are only three authorized speed limits: 0 km/h, 25 km/h and 50 km/h).

1.3.3.2. *Approaches influenced by robotics*

The task of driving has always been modeled from the point of view of robotics. Certain models were advanced by researchers in robotics, with the aim of building an autonomous vehicle that is capable of evolving in road traffic, first in simulation and then in reality. For instance, Reece [REE 93] advanced a rule-based reasoning model specially designed for intersections. As a result, a robot became capable of driving without causing accidents. This model is not suitable for traffic simulation, however, since it is not capable of simulating all the possible behaviors of real driving.

1.3.3.3. *Current multi-agent approaches*

In relevant literature, besides the ArchiSim model (see section 1.4), only two other models provide actual alternatives to the classic ones.

The one advanced by Trannois [TRA 98] is an adaptation of a blackboard system for planning the actions of agents interacting in an urban environment. This approach is based on a model of the environment as well as on distributing the knowledge in a driving task. This knowledge is not included in the strategy for each event, but it is distributed among the entities of road infrastructure. This distribution means, for example, that a "Stop" sign brings some knowledge to the attention of different agents that want to cross the street. Every piece of information received by an agent is ranked according to its relevance for the given traffic situation.

The major inconvenience of this approach is the particularly strong connection between the behavior of drivers and road infrastructure. Consequently, it is very difficult to obtain autonomous agents that respect traffic regulations (normative behavior).

A different model was proposed by Paruchuri [PAR 02]. He introduced a model where every simulated driver is autonomous. In order to make their decisions, certain parameters are defined such as braking speed, acceleration, minimum inter-vehicle distance, safety margin for passing another vehicle, etc.

These authors maintain that their models authorize a realistic driving behavior. Agent autonomy remains restricted, however, given that certain traffic situations (i.e. deadlock) need to be supervised and controlled by an external centralized process.

1.4. ArchiSim simulator

1.4.1 *A distributed architecture*

The ArchiSim project, initiated in 1987, was instigated after carefully considering how to design a traffic simulation device that is capable of simulating the behavior of different actors in the traffic system as well as introducing a driving simulator [ESP 95].

The global architecture of ArchiSim is designed so that it can distribute a simulation throughout a set of machines that are interconnected through an Ethernet type of network. This way, the actors of the simulation can be calculated on different machines.

A server that aims to consolidate the current state of the simulated road network and that is updated thanks to the information sent by the different actors ensures the coherence of the whole. This server fulfills the role of the "vision server" – every actor in the simulation (be it a virtual or real driver placed inside the simulator) logs in order to retrieve information regarding its/his immediate environment as well as updating the information that concerns it/him.

1.4.2 *A behavioral model of agents*

The decision-making model of ArchiSim is founded upon principles of multi-agent systems. In what follows, we will describe it by detailing three of the four dimensions of the "vowel" paradigm (AEIO) described by Demazeau [DEM 01]: environment, agents and interactions.

1.4.2.1 *Environment and perception*

The environment consists of the road network, which is represented as a graph. In this graph, roads appear as a sequence of arches and the intersections are represented by nodes. Each entity of the simulation can be identified by: a route identifier, a milepost, its lateral distance in relation to the axial distance (determined by the direction of travel) and a heading relative to the axis of the carriageway. This choice of bench-marks for the environment allows the simulated vehicles to benefit from the entire space available on the road. This permits pre-calculated trajectories to cross each other (vehicle movement on rails that represent the center of routes) and for them to be frequently used in simulation devices.

The vision server described previously ensures environmental awareness. Every simulated entity can address a vision request to the server and retrieve symbolic and numeric information regarding its environment in exchange. For each element in the environment, the vision function specifies its type (vehicle, road sign, pedestrian, etc.), its position in the road network, and the different values of its kinematic variables when the element is a vehicle (speed, plus longitudinal and lateral acceleration).

A set of properties and qualitative relations between elements in the environment provides a spatial and symbolic description of the environment. For example a mobile device can know where vehicles are situated – in front of it, behind it, to its right, to its left – through the aid of a set of directional relations. This set is complemented by positioning relations that are appropriate for driving situations. These relations take into account the position of a mobile device in relation to road infrastructure and are defined from the perspective of the entity that perceives its environment: "vehicle X is located across my route/path", "vehicle Y is located beside me on the adjacent route", etc.

1.4.2.2. *Agents and interactions*

Every traffic actor (motorist, motorcycle policeman, pedestrian) is modeled in the form of an agent with:

– goals: desired speed, itinerary to be completed, etc.;

– its own abilities: the physical features of the vehicle (braking system, acceleration ability, size and wheel base of the vehicle on the carriageway), the level of driving experience, driving style, etc.;

– relative autonomy: in order to satisfy its goals, the agent is able to adapt, in time, by adjusting its trajectory and thus fully benefiting from the space available. It can also break traffic regulations according to the context, which proves a certain autonomy in relation to rules [CAR 05].

Drivable space is a common resource for all simulation agents. Several agents can thus covet the same space on the road at the same time, creating a conflict of resource use. Inter-agent interactions are therefore mainly conflicting and the decision-making algorithms used by ArchiSim are essentially algorithms of conflict-resolution. In reality, inter-agent interaction takes place without direct communication.

ArchiSim traffic simulation was developed and validated for different situations, among which are freeway situations (the case of driving in a queue) [ELH 00]. In what follows, we will focus particularly on our work in urban situations.

1.5. The issue of traffic simulation in intersections

An intersection is defined by a set of roads that intersect, thus making up a space for traffic (the center of the intersection) that allows vehicles to either change direction by entering a new traffic flow (flow-merge) or to change their direction on the same axis by crossing one or two antagonistic flows (what we call flow crossing).

1.5.1. *Behavioral model of agents*

1.5.1.1. *Normative model versus non-normative model*

In the general sense, a rule designates the set of principles and regulations that apply to an entity (an object, a person, etc.) and describes how this entity must be and how it must behave. In multi-agent systems, rules are generally used to specify what an agent must do. Put another way, rules provide a means of coordinating a set of agents through some form of regulation.

Shoham and Tennenholz [SHO 95] take the concept of social laws to mean the constraints placed on those actions that are motivated by antagonistic goals. The degree of influence that systemic norms have on individual decision-making constitutes one of the aspects of the autonomy of an agent [CAR 05] and several studies deal with breaking norms in a multi-agent system (for example [DIG 00]). We wish to use this concept in a traffic simulation context: the rules that constitute traffic regulations can be seen as a norm regulating the traffic system. A non-normative behavior, which is a behavior that does not observe the norms of the system, appears to be relevant within the framework of this application.

It seems *a priori* that the majority of applications only take into consideration those simulated agents that would rigorously follow the rules. We think it is also necessary to describe the non-observance of rules in the model of our agents. Our interest in this concept can be understood within the framework of road traffic simulation.

We can easily give examples where human drivers do not respect the rules (i.e. traffic regulations). For example, a well-known regulation maintains that a driver must not enter an intersection if they are not certain that they will be able to leave it. Several research studies in behavioral psychology show that a human driver does not always respect traffic regulations and that he/she will even develop his/her own informal driving regulations.

Another difficulty mainly relates to controlling the breaking of rules. If an agent decides to break the norm, it will be penalized according to context. In typical cases where this is applied by institutions, the penalty can easily be formulated. For example, it is always possible to penalize the agent on account of the accessibility of a resource, the accessibility of information or because time is wasted. As for driving, there are some examples of solutions forcing drivers to "behave" in France: fines, withdrawal of points (In France drivers start with a set amount of points on their license and have them deducted for driving offences; points can also be added to a license too.) and withholding the driving license. The penalties mentioned above seem less obvious to virtual agents in this type of application.

Therefore, we envisage a model that may require the violation of certain rules and that differs in certain respects from the literature written on the matter. In particular, we believe that each agent has a tendency to violate norms according to its objectives, but also according to its way of understanding the relative traffic priorities that are otherwise defined as traffic regulations.

1.5.1.2. *Anticipative model*

The initial idea consists of modeling the individual behaviors of drivers. According to their experiences, human drivers make predictions in order to avoid dangerous or critical situations. For example, Rosen [ROS 74] introduced the notion of preventive anticipation in order to control such situations and keep the agent in a desirable or stable situation (i.e. a non-critical situation) [DON 07].

Our aim was therefore to model this notion by adopting an approach based on constraints. A network of constraints is a set of variables with associated domains and a set of constraints: "Variables are objects or items that can take on a variety of values. The set of possible values for a given variable is called a domain. [...] Constraints are rules that impose a limitation on the values that a variable may be assigned" [DEC 03].

Every agent builds a representation of its environment and, more specifically, of the relations and interactions between the agents. The representation M_i of each agent i is made up of three elementary components $\langle A,D,R \rangle$:

– $A=\{a_1, a_2, ..., a_n\}$ is a sub-set of all the agents perceived by an agent x;

– $D=\{dom(a_1), dom(a_2), ..., dom(a_n)\}$ defines the domain of each agent in A;

– $R=\{r_1, r_2, ..., r_k\}$, where every r_i is a binary relation expressing an interaction between two agents of A.

It is worth noting that a domain may vary from an application to another, namely it can be spatial or temporal. Every action proposed by an agent is described by adding or eliminating a relation in R. The indirect effects are calculated using propagation techniques on the direct effects of actions; this limits the scope of the research. The classic AC-3 algorithm [MAC 1977] was adapted to our problem and Donniec [DON 08a] presents us with a detailed description of it.

1.5.2 *Illustrative example of the proposed model*

We will now explain how this model works in an intersection with three vehicles turning left. This traffic situation is illustrated in Figure 1.2. Agent x arrives in the intersection and needs to determine its priority in relation to the other vehicles y and z. The objective of all three vehicles is to make a left-hand turn. According to the Code of Regulations, we can ascertain that:

– x has the right of way over y and needs to give way to the vehicle coming from its right, namely z. However, z must let vehicle y drive up to its first point of conflict; and

– the vehicles should not enter the intersection because they are not certain they will be able to leave it.

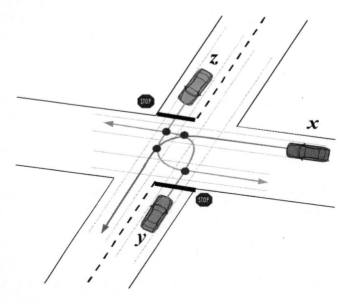

Figure 1.2. *Illustrative example of three agents at an intersection*

This example will be dealt with in two subsequent stages: the violation of the norm by the agents and the ability of the other agents to anticipate this.

1.5.2.1. *Norm violation by the agents*

We assume that the vehicles y and z have decided to break the rule and enter the intersection. In this example, breaking the rule consists of *not* stopping at the stop sign, and thus *not* giving way to *x*. In order to authorize this violation of the norm, we use a set of contextual rules [MAN 07]. We have defined the "if…then" type of rules that in turn allow us to define the dependencies between the right of way - as defined by the Code of Regulations (binary predicate *prioCode*) - and the priority as perceived by the agents (binary predicate *prio*). It is thus possible to regard the strict application of the Code of Regulations with a certain amount of tolerance.

In this primary stage, every agent evaluates the priority rules that it shares with the other perceived agents [MAN 08]. We can easily deduce the following:

– vehicle *x* has the right of way *a priori* over the other two vehicles *y* and *z*, formulated thus: prioCode(x,z)$\wedge$prioCode(x,y) ;

– prioCode(y,x)$\wedge\neg$prioCode(y,z) for vehicle *y* ; and

– prioCode(z,x)$\wedge\neg$prioCode(z,y) for vehicle *z* ;

In a normative behaviour, it is evident that vehicle *x* has the right of way over vehicles *y* and *z, i.e.* the predicate *prioCode* is directly defined by the predicate *prio*. The coordination mechanism is then applied in order to obtain the desired result.

Let us now suppose that vehicles *y* and *z* arrive at the intersection at high speed and they estimate at the same time that vehicle *x* is far enough from the intersection (the braking distance is sufficient). Let us suppose further that a rule taking into account braking distance can exist and that it can be applied to two vehicles, and that this rule might correct the understanding of priorities. By accepting this hypothesis, the relation defined by prioCode(x,y) $\wedge$ $\neg$prioCode(y,x) allows us to obtain *y's* perception at the expense of *x* : $\neg$prio(x,y)$\wedge$prio(y,x). Similarly, we can accept an identical reasoning for the vehicle *z*, the relation being thus modified prioCode(x,z) $\wedge\neg$prioCode(z,x) with the formulation :

$$prio(x,z)\wedge prio(z,x)$$

Let us now take the situation where agents *y* and *z* have decided not to observe the driving regulations (see Figure 1.3.). If *x* applied the reasoning scheme described earlier, it would move, thus causing a deadlock.

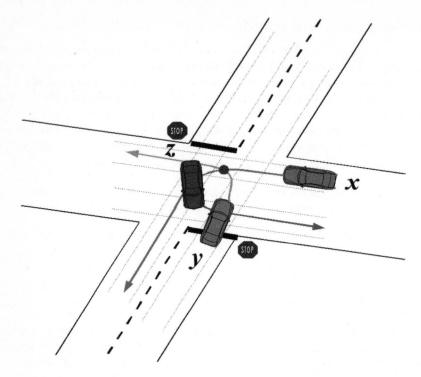

Figure 1.3. *Situation after the non-normative behavior of agents y and z*

As we have already mentioned, these rules of violating the norm express the idea that the simulated agent can act non-normatively (similarly to the behavior of a human driver), by estimating that there is no risk of collision. However, this behavior does not guarantee a coherent overall flow of road traffic. Let us bear in mind that the Code of Regulations was introduced not only for preventing collision between vehicles; but also for avoiding deadlock situations. Our idea aims to anticipate these deadlocks, and also to control the potential violation of rules by the agents.

1.5.2.2. *Deadlock anticipation*

For reasons of clarity, we will assume that the time needed for one vehicle to leave the trajectory of another vehicle is three seconds. In the model implemented, this calculation is obtained by the kinematic equation of restarting a vehicle. The time interval that agents anticipate is also limited, namely 10 seconds. In the ArchiSim model, this limit is a parameter (generated at random) that varies according to agents.

We have equally characterized the positioning of different agents by different relations. Simulations need to take the agents into account with their spatial as well as their time constraints:

– $bph_i(x,y)$ meaning that "agent x is physically blocked by y from the point of view of an agent i";

– $bpha_i(x,y)$ meaning that "agent i notices that agent x will be physically blocked by agent y";

– $bpr_i(x,y)$ meaning that "agent y has the right of way over x from the point of view of agent i".

The domains assigned to each agent define the time constraints and are represented as intervals. Every interval is a set of time horizons within which an agent will have the possibility to move. Thus, the presence of value i in the domain of an agent at a given time t indicates that this agent will be able to move at $t + i$. For example:

– vehicle x has the right of way in relation to the two vehicles y and z, formulated thus: prioCode(x,z)∧prioCode(x,y);

– $dom(z)=1,+\infty$ equals "z may act and move during the interval from $t+1$ to $+\infty$"; and

– $dom(z)=[1,4]\cup[8,10]$ equals "z will be blocked between $t+5$ and $t+7$".

Given that these relations have a particular semantics and that they are applied in a timeframe, we have defined specific data propagators for each relation. These propagators are based on the manipulation of intervals [MAN 07].

Agent x that has perceived the engagement of vehicles y and z in the intersection will make a reasoning presented as follows. Agent x had built its representation of the environment. We have proposed to use a mechanism that propagates constraints for each agent; this mechanism is defined by: $M_x=\langle A,D,R \rangle$. (For reasons of legibility, we will not indicate the index numbers representing the point of view of agent x in congestion relations that define set R. We should also note that only the information that has changed will be presented in what follows):

A={x,y,z}

$$D=\{dom(x)=[1,10],dom(y)=[1,10],dom(z)=[1,10]\}$$

$$R=\{prio(x,y)\land\neg prio(y,x),\neg prio(x,z)\land prio(z,x),bpha(x,z),bph(z,y)\}$$

It is worth noting that relation $\neg prio(x,z)\land prio(z,x)$ is redundant with congestion relations bph and bpha. In what follows, this relation will no longer be presented as part of set R. From the point of view of agent x, we obtain the following reasoning:

– *Propagation*: given the differing relations within set R, the domains associated with the three agents in A can be scaled down. The propagation can be carried out in two sub-stages. The first one consists of processing relation bph; while the second one seeks to exploit knowledge about the bpha relation. Agent z will be blocked until agent y is no longer on its trajectory. By estimating the necessary amount of time that z needs in order to pass the point of conflict equal to three seconds, domain $dom(z)$ is scaled down to the interval [4,10]. The processing of the second relation, bpha, enables us to scale down the domain of vehicle x so that it does not conflict with the resulting domain of z. If the entire time of conflict is two seconds, x will be able to move in the interval [1,2]. Vehicle z will be able to restart from $t+4$; and x will have to follow on its route starting at $t+5$, hence its domain is $dom(x)=[1,2]\cup[5,10]$. The domain is thus defined as:

$$D=\{dom(x)=[1,2]\cup[5,10],dom(y)=[1,10],dom(z)=[4,10]\}$$

$$R=\{bph(y,x),bph(x,z),bph(z,y)\}$$

– *Calculation*: of the effects of the actions of x: the coordination algorithm only deals with longitudinal acceleration. For the sake of simulation, let us take two possible actions for x: *Go* and *Stop*. If x decides to move forward (action *Go*) and thus to re-enter the intersection, blockage bpha becomes effective and relation bpha is replaced by bph; the priority relation between x and y becomes a blocking relation $bph(y,x)$.

– *Propagation*: the insertion of relation $bph(y,x)$ calls into question the domain of y which, on the first completed journey of a network, can be reduced to [7,10]. By way of consequence, this scaling down calls into question all of the other domains, which include that of z: $dom(z)=[9,10]$. Since domain z has changed, domain x can still be scaled down to $[1,2]\cup[10,10]$, this way inducing new domain-reductions for y and z. Vehicle x can move at iterations 1, 2 and 10; this implies that y will not be able to move before $t+11$. From this, we can infer that $dom(y)=\emptyset$. Since y cannot move in the interval examined, the same thing happens for z, and consequently $dom(z)=\emptyset$. At the next iteration, the impossibility of z to move in turn means that x cannot restart at $t+10$, hence we have a domain of x equal to [1,2]. At the end of these several iterations, we obtain:

$$D=\{dom(x)=[1,2]\cup[10,10],dom(y)=\emptyset,dom(z)=\emptyset\}$$

– *Researching undesirable states*: following this reasoning, x is capable of predicting that if it chooses to move forward it will be blocked starting with $t+2$ and it will also block y and z. From its point of view, this constitutes an undesirable situation. Agent x thus needs to eliminate the action of moving forward from its list of possible actions. It thus decides to stop and in this way it loses its right of way.

In this situation, the same reasoning from the point of view of y does not create an undesirable state of affairs. Agent x may consider itself as having the right of way in view of the partial braking performed by x in order to stop. Vehicle y can thus engage and unblock the other two vehicles, starting with z and then x.

1.6. Assessment of different scenarios

We will now introduce several validations as described in [DON 08a] and [DON 08b].

1.6.1. *Assessing the execution time of agents*

We have carried out measurements of the execution times of agents. We have described an intersection with priority to the right, where we have changed the density of vehicles per intersection branch. Figure 1.4 shows the curve that we have obtained.

It becomes evident that the more the density increases on each branch, the more time every agent needs in order to make its decision. For low densities of agents (less than 300 vehicles/hour), the necessary execution time for the entire set of agents is very reasonable, at below 0.1 second. For higher densities of simulated agents (800 vehicles/hour), the time needed in order to carry out the proposed model is 0.35 seconds of central processing unit (CPU) time on average. We can thus contend that this time is relatively low in view of the significant density of agents for the proposed simulations.

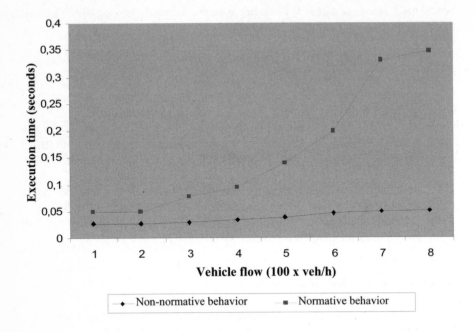

Figure 1.4. *Execution performance measurements in agent models*

1.6.2. *Reducing the number of deadlock situations*

We have also made simulations in order to study the number of deadlock situations. Deadlocks are to be found rather frequently in the following situations where there is:

– a high vehicle flow at the intersection entrance;

– a sequence of "double left-turns" (see Figure 1.5.);

– the presence of long vehicles (heavyweight vehicles or buses) in the intersection; and

– the re-forming of queues between two relatively close intersections.

Figure 1.5. *Example of deadlock at an intersection*

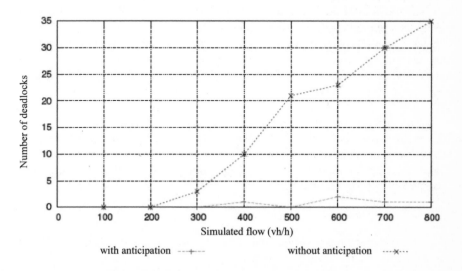

Figure 1.6. *Assessment of the number of deadlocks*

For every simulation, interlocking situations were counted via a supervising process (independent of the decision of every agent). With every iteration this supervisor verifies whether a deadlock has emerged (a deadlock is a situation of full congestion, where every agent is blocked). If a deadlock is found, the simulation is aborted and the situation is completely deleted (every agent in the simulated interaction is "killed"; then, the simulation is resumed).

Anticipation minimizes the number of deadlocks during the simulation of a non-signalized intersection. For a simulation stretching over a period of one hour using non-anticipating agents, as shown in Figure 1.6, the number of deadlocks varies from 0 to 35, depending on traffic flow. When agents are equipped with the ability to anticipate, the number is closer to 0, including for simulations with vehicle flows as high as 800 vehicles/hour and per axis.

1.6.3. *Real situations*

The intersection used for our validation is situated in the town of Reggio Calabria in the south of Italy. This intersection marks the junction between a main north–south axis heading to Rome and a secondary east–west axis heading to Zerbi. The latter is signalized by two "Stop" signs. Every branch of the intersection provides vehicles with the option to turn in two directions, and the space in the center is large enough to allow some vehicles to wait.

The traffic data measured by the University of Reggio Calabria was collected over a period of one hour between 12:30 and 13:30 on a regular weekday. For every branch of the intersection, we have at our disposal an incoming flow expressed by the number of vehicles per hour as well as the distribution expressed by the percentage of different turning movements performed in the intersection (right-turn, left-turn or straight ahead).

Starting from this data, we have generated a traffic demand that is equivalent to the one measured in the field and in the simulation; we have placed it in the virtual traffic detectors that were positioned at the same kilometer points as in reality. The simulated vehicles were created 200 m upstream of the intersection, with different parameters. These parameters are:

– the minimum waiting time at the "Stop" sign;

– the patience threshold (the minimum amount of time spent waiting in order for the driver to be considered impatient);

– the minimum distance at the time of conflict (the safety margin that an agent takes into account in order to calculate the distances within a conflict); and

– the anticipation distance and the time interval of the anticipation.

The minimum waiting time at the "Stop" sign had to be reduced to less than a second (contrary to the three-second rule imposed by the French Code of Regulations) in order to obtain behaviors that are representative of the "Latin" culture.

The values obtained by the root standard deviation for all three axes are lower than 0.1.This corresponds to an error rate of below 10%. In relevant literature, a good traffic simulation is generally considered to have an error rate below 15%.

The experiments that were carried out have shown that anticipation enables the prevention of congestion phenomena within the simulation. Furthermore, this allows us to insert more realistic individual behaviors without the risk of increasing the number of deadlocks. We were able to observe that, from a microscopic point of view, these individual behaviors improve the realism of the movement of simulated vehicles, especially by reducing oscillation effects. From a macroscopic point of view, the traffic that emerges from these individual behaviors can be considered realistic because in terms of traffic flow the gap between what is real and what is simulated is well below 10%.

We have also advanced simulations in a roundabout, thus revisiting American research [DON 08b]. Similarly, we have emphasized the fact that our results are better from the point of view of the gap between simulated and real traffic flows. Other studies were advanced in [DON 08c], especially the reduction of oscillations in local agent decisions, as well as a certain stability in the results of the simulation that are independent of the variation of the steps in this simulation.

1.7. Conclusion

In this chapter, we have advanced an original approach to road traffic simulation – an approach that is based on the emergence of realistic traffic situations starting from the local behavior of agents. The case study of traffic simulation at an intersection, which has proved to be a difficult and generally poorly dealt with problem, is hereby presented as a problem of multi-agent coordination. Every simulated vehicle tries to coordinate its movement with the other vehicles (be they present in the intersection of just approaching the intersection) in order to resolve the conflicts that arise on its trajectory.

Prior to the coordination mechanism briefly described in this chapter, we have focused on the way an agent perceives the surrounding traffic situation. In particular, we have shown that this acknowledgement of the situation influences the decision-making of agents and thus the behaviors obtained during the simulation.

In this framework, we have proposed the introduction of opportunistic (non-normative) behaviors that allow the simulated agents to occasionally bypass the Code of Regulations. The second point of interest involves the advancement of an anticipation mechanism that enables agents to reason on the effects of their actions and thus to avoid deadlock situations. This mechanism, tested on different scenarios, allows for a significant reduction in the number of deadlock situations caused by the opportunistic behavior of agents. Other results were equally highlighted.

This approach can therefore be generalized to other types of mobile devices, provided that the several primitive actions of the mobile device are accurately described and that the algorithm is applied within reasonable calculating times (we should keep in mind that the complexity of our approach depends on the number of perceived agents, the number of relations between these agents and the number of anticipated actions).

1.8. Bibliography

[BAZ 05] BAZZAN A.L.C., "A distributed approach for coordination of traffic signal agents", *Journal of Autonomous Agents and Multi-Agent Systems*, vol. 10, pp. 131-164, 2005.

[BRA 87] BRAGANZA C., GASSER L., MACE Multi-Agent Computing Environment, Version 6.0. Release Note 1.0, Technical Report CRI 87-16, University of Southern California, US, 1987.

[BRI 01] BRIOT J.P., DEMAZEAU Y., *Principes et architectures des Systèmes Multi-Agents*, Hermès-Lavoisier, Paris, 2001.

[CAR 05] CARABELEA C., BOISSIER O., "Coordinating agents in organizations using social commitments", *Proceedings of the 1st International Workshop on Coordination and Organisation (CoOrg'05)*, Namur, Belgium, April 2005.

[CHA 92] CHAIB-DRAA B., MOULIN B., MANDIAU R., MILLOT P., "Trends in distributed artificial intelligence", *Artificial Intelligence Review*, vol. , pp. 35-66, 1992.

[DEC 03] DECHTER R., *Constraint Processing*, Morgan Kaufmann, Elsevier, San Francisco, 2003.

[DEM 01] DEMAZEAU Y., Voyelles, Habilitation a Diriger des Recherches de l'INP Grenoble, Laboratoire Leibniz, Grenoble, France, April, 2001.

[DIG 00] DIGNUM F., MORLEY D., SONENBERG L., CAVEDON L., "Towards socially sophisticated BDI agents", *Proceedings of the 4th International Conference on Multi-agent Systems (ICMAS'2000)*, pp. 111-118, Boston, US, July 2000.

[DON 07] DONIEC A., MANDIAU R., ESPIÉ S., PIECHOWIAK S., "Comportements anticipatifs dans les systèmes multi-agents. Application à la simulation de trafic routier", *Revue d'Intelligence Artificielle*, vol. 21-2, pp. 185-223, 2007.

[DON 08a] DONIEC A., MANDIAU R., PIECHOWIAK S., ESPIÉ S., "Controlling non-normative behaviors by anticipation for autonomous agent", *Web Intelligence and Agent Systems: An International Journal*, vol. 6, pp. 1-14, 2008.

[DON 08b] DONIEC A., MANDIAU R., PIECHOWIAK S., ESPIÉ S., "A behavioral multi-agent model for road traffic simulation", *Engineering Applications of Artificial Intelligence*, vol. 21, pp. 1443-1454, 2008.

[DON 08c] DONIEC A., MANDIAU R., PIECHOWIAK S., ESPIÉ S., "Anticipation based on constraint processing in a multi-agent context", *Journal of Autonomous Agents and Multi-agent Systems (JAAMAS)*, vol. 17, pp. 339-361, 2008.

[ELH 00] EL HADOUAJ S., DROGOUL A., ESPIÉ S., "How to combine reactivity and anticipation: the case of conflicts resolution in a simulated road traffic", *Multi-agent-Based Simulation, Second International Workshop*, pp. 82-96, Boston, US, July 2000.

[ESP 95] ESPIÉ S., "ArchiSim, Multi-actor parallel architecture for traffic simulation", *Proceedings of the Second World Congress on Intelligent Transport Systems*, Yokohama, Japan, 1995.

[ESP 02] ESPIÉ S., "Multi-acteur dans la simulation de trafic automobile", in MANDIAU R., GRISLIN-LE STRUGEON E. and PÉNINOU A. (eds), *Organisation et Applications des SMA*, Hermès-Lavoisier, Paris, 2002.

[FER 95] FERBER J., *Les Systèmes Multi-agents, vers une Intelligence Collective*, InterEditions, Paris, 1995.

[GUE 10] GUESSOUM Z., MANDIAU R., MATHIEU P., BOISSIER O., GLIZE P., HAMRI A., PESTY S., PICARD G., SANSONNET J.P., TESSIER C., TRANVOUEZ E., "Systèmes multi-agents et simulation", in OGIER J.M. and SEDES F. (eds), *Assises du GDR I3*, Cepadues, 2010.

[GAS 89] GASSER L., HUHNS M.N., *Distributed Artificial Intelligence*, vol. 2, Pitman Publisher, London, 1989.

[HAL 97] HALL F., "Traffic stream characteristics", in GARTNER N., MESSER C.J. and RATHI A.K. (eds), *Traffic Flow Theory*, Oak Ridge National Laboratory, Oak Ridge, 1997.

[HOR 04] HORLING B., LESSER V., "A survey of multi-agent organizational paradigms", *Knowledge Engineering Review*, vol. 19, pp. 281-316, 2004.

[JEN 96] JENNINGS N.R., "Coordination techniques for distributed artificial intelligence" *Foundations of Distributed Artificial Intelligence*, pp. 187-210, Wiley, 1996.

[LES 98] LESSER V.R., "Reflections on the nature of multi-agent coordination and its implications for an agent architecture", *Autonomous Agents and Multi-Agent Systems*, vol. 1, pp. 89-111, 1998.

[LIE 97] LIEBERMAN E., RATHI A., "Traffic simulation", *Traffic Flow Theory*, Oak Ridge National Laboratory, Oak Ridge, 1997.

[MAC 77] MACKWORTH A.K., "Consistency in networks of relations", *Artificial Intelligence*, vol. 8, 99, pp. 99-118, 1977.

[MAL 98] MALONE T., "What is coordination theory", *National Science Foundation Coordination Theory Workshop*, Massachusetts Institute of Technology, Cambridge, MA, 1998.

[MAN 07] MANDIAU R., DONIEC A., PIECHOWIAK S., ESPIÉ S., "Anticiper pour maîtriser la violation de normes: application à la simulation de trafic routier", in CAMPS V., MATHIEU P. (ed.), *Systèmes Multi-agents – Modèles de Comportements, Actes des Journées Francophones sur les Systèmes Multi-Agents* (JFSMA, Carcassonne, France, October 17-19, 2007), Cepadues, pp. 87-96, October 2007.

[MAN 08] MANDIAU R., CHAMPION A., AUBERLET J.M., ESPIÉ S., KOLSKI C., "Behaviour based on decision matrices for a coordination between agents in urban traffic simulation", *Applied Intelligence*, vol. 28, no. 2, pp. 121-138, 2008.

[MOR 86] MORIN E., *La Méthode*, Tome 3 : La Connaisance de la Essais, Seuil, 1986.

[PAR 02] PARUCHURI P., PULLALAREVU A.R., KARLAPALEM K., "Multi agent simulation of unorganized traffic" *Proceeding of The International Joint Conference on Autonomous Agents and Multiagent Systems* (AAMAS'02), pp. 176-183, Bologna, Italy, 2002.

[REE 93] REECE D.A., SHAFER S.A., "A computational model of driving for autonomous vehicles", *Transportation Research*, vol. 27, no. 1, pp. 23-50, 1993.

[ROS 74] ROSEN R., "Planning, management, policies and strategies: Four fuzzy concepts", *International Journal of General Systems*, 1974.

[RUS 02] RUSKIN H.J., WANG R., "Modelling traffic flow at an urban unsignalized intersection", *Proceedings of International Conference on Computational Science*, pp. 381-390, 2002.

[SER 06] SERUGENDO G., GLEIZES M.P., KARAGEORGOS A., "Self-organization and emergence in MAS: an overview", *Informatica*, vol. 30, pp. 45-54, 2006.

[SHO 95] SHOHAM Y., TENNENHOLTZ M., "On social laws for artificial agent societies: Off-line design", *Journal of Artificial Intelligence*, vol. 1-2, no. 73, pp. 231-252, 1995.

[TRA 98] Trannois H., Lebrun A., Deleage J., "A multi-agent framework for car traffic simulation", *Proceedings of The Third International Conference and Exhibition on the Practical Application of Intelligent Agents and Multiagents*, London, UK, pp. 635-636, 1998.

[VIS 03] Vissim, VISSIM 3.70 User Manual, Technical Report, PTV Planung Transport Verkehr AG, Karlsruhe, Germany, 2003.

[ZAM 02] Zambonelli F., Van Dyke H., "Parunak: signs of a revolution in computer science and software engineering", *ESAW* (Engineering Societies in the Agents World III), pp. 13-28, 2002.

Chapter 2

An Agent-based Information System for Searching and Creating Mobility-aiding Services

2.1. Introduction

The satisfaction of clients who are looking for information services is significantly hindered – in terms of accessibility and reliability – by the constant and rapid increase in heterogeneous data that are distributed throughout large-scale networks. In particular, it is not easy to implement the applications on such extended networks, not only because of unexpected variations that might arise (bottlenecks, crashes, etc.) but also because of the limited bandwidth. This shortcoming is mainly explained by the fact that an increasing number of users access information simultaneously and is worsened by the increase in information demand (especially in the form of Web services).

In this chapter, we will focus on the field of mobility and transportation, trying to accompany and support the passenger throughout the journey in the most efficient and pleasant manner [ZGA 07]. This support is expressed by the availability of services, connected or related to transport, that correspond to reliable, interactive and instant information, which can be found on the so-called extended mobility-aiding services network (EMASN). For example, such a service can mean anything from the calculation of an itinerary in a multimodal transport network, to weather

Chapter written by Slim HAMMADI and Hayfa ZGAYA.

forecast information, cultural information, tourist information or availability of parking spaces (see Chapter 3).

In this context, the mobile agent paradigm [PHA 98, THE 99] is complementary to artificial intelligence, and particularly to distributed artificial intelligence (see section 1.2) since it can significantly reduce collision phenomena within the network [CAR 97]. Thus, a computerized agent equipped with mobility, henceforth called a mobile agent (MA), can migrate towards any node of the network that is able to receive and host mobile entities. The nodes that a mobile agent (MA) visits make up its itinerary, called a route plan (RP). Several research endeavors have focused on the advantages of the MA paradigm in relation to classic paradigms, such as the client/server paradigm. Such research has concluded that the MA paradigm is reliable in certain cases [PIC 97, BUS 03]. This reliability depends on the architecture of the system as well as on the methods and approaches that were used in carrying it out. We have demonstrated in our research [ZGA 06b] that using the MA paradigm in a largely distributed and heavily used information system is particularly appropriate if the paradigm is used within a framework of effective optimization. In this context, we have carried out a two-leveled optimization approach [AGA 05a, ZGA 05b] that calculates an actual number of mobile entities and builds the corresponding route plans throughout the EMASN.

Furthermore, in order to reinforce the robustness of the system in the face of random variations in the network, we have implemented a negotiation protocol between mobile entities and the system in order to find replacements for service providers affected by the fluctuation and thus reassign the non-attributed services to available nodes. In order to do this, we have designed a repository in the form of a flexible transport ontology to better manage and master the heterogeneous language of the interaction.

In the the next section, we will formally present the problem to be discussed. Then, we will reveal the general architecture of the system in the form of a multi-agent system (MAS). We will present a dynamic view of the system in section 2.4. The chosen optimization approach, which is integrated into the behavior of the system scheduling agent, will be detailed in section 2.5. We will put forward a negotiation protocol in section 2.6, followed by a flexible transport ontology. We will verify and justify the models that have been designed as well as the approaches chosen in section 2.8. Finally, the chapter ends with a conclusion and outlines some future perspectives.

2.2. Formulating the problem

Our aim is to design, optimize and implement an information system that aids mobility (ISAM), that enables us to offer users useful information during their travel (whether they travel on foot, by car, etc.), via any type of device, whether fixed or mobile (laptop, mobile phone, personal digital assistant, etc.) that is ultimately attached to the vehicle being used (Chapter 3). We aim to do this within the context of a network of competing information providers that market their services using various criteria (cost, response time, format, etc.). Therefore, our goal is to satisfy users at their earliest convenience, while minimizing provision costs. To do this, we advance a two-level optimization approach: the first level is carried out in non-real time, when the system starts or each time the state of the network varies significantly, while the second level is developed in real time, i.e. every time a set of user requests is available.

The first level of optimization corresponds to an actual set of MAS being assigned to all nodes belonging to the EMASN, thus creating an initial route plan (IRP) in order to explore the whole EMASN as efficiently as possible. This stage enables us to create a sort of intuitive "pattern", and to optimize it according to the state of the network.

The second level of optimization aims to find the best possible assignment of a subset of EMASN nodes to the services requested. These services have probably already been identified, comprising user requests that were received simultaneously. This stage allows us to generate definite route plans (DRPs) from the first level of optimization. These are the plans that will actually be followed by the MAs.

A service identified corresponds to the response to an acknowledged, independent sub-request, which is in turn connected to a single request or to a set of simultaneous user requests, formulated by one or more clients. More specifically, a single task may correspond to the request from a particular service, for example a multimodal transport service such as an end-point of an itinerary or a well-known geographical area, or it may correspond to a related service, such as a cultural event, weather forecast, available parking space or the nearest shopping mall.

Thus, simultaneous user requests can be broken down into independent services (T_i) whose potential providers (S_j) are being identified (see Figure 2.1). The set of information providers constitutes the EMASN nodes or servers that must be assigned to the requested services in order to satisfy the users who are connected to the system. Therefore, a node that is likely to be assigned to a specific service needs to be a potential provider of that same service.

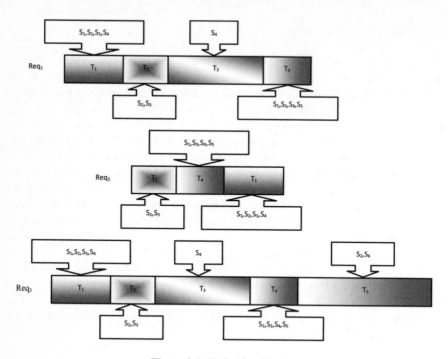

Figure 2.1. *Node identification*

A user is considered to be satisfied if his or her request is answered promptly and at a reasonable cost. We have named this the problem of assignment and distributed optimization of services and have defined it as:

– R simultaneous requests, waiting for a response at the same time t. The total number of these requests is R_t;

– the set of independent tasks I, representing all of the services available within EMASN, is marked as $T=\{T_1,\ldots, T_I\}$;

– every request $req_w \in R_t$ ($1 \leq w \leq R$) is broken down into a set of independent services. This is marked as $I_{t,w}=\{T_{w_1},T_{w_2},\ldots\}$ $I_{t,w}=\{T_{w_1},T_{w_2},\ldots\}$ with $1 \leq card(I_{t,w}) \leq$ and $I_{t,w} \subseteq T$;

– the set I' of the different requested services, comprising mainly of R_t, is marked as I'_t with $I'_t \subseteq T$ and $I'_t \bigcup_{w=1}^{R} I_{t,w} =I'_t$;

– every request req_w is characterized by an execution date D_w, a total cost C_w and an initially known deadline, d_w, corresponding to the response deadline to that request;

– the response to each service, $T_i \in T$, requires a resource that corresponds to an information provider, termed the "node", "server" or "service provider". This node will be selected from the set of J nodes registered in the system that makes up the EMASN. This set is marked as $S=\{S_1,\ldots, S_J\}$;

– the set of J' nodes (J' $\le$ J), selected from S in order to accomplish I'_t, is marked as S'_t ($S'_t \subseteq S$);

– we know the recovery time of each service starting from a particular server, so for a given node S_j and a given service T_i, the response time of the service T_i, using the resources of node S_j is defined and marked as $P_{i,j}$;

– the cost of the service T_i provided by node S_j is known and marked as $Co_{i,j}$;

– the quantity of data that need to be transferred in order to respond to service T_i starting from node S_j is known and marked as $Q_{i,j}$;

– the problem is characterized by a partial flexibility, which means that the response to each service T_i needs a node, which is selected from a set of nodes that offer the same service; but this offer differs according to the provider in terms of cost, response time and the amount of data transferred.

The three characteristics described above, namely $(P_{i,j};Co_{i,j};Q_{i,j})$, consecutively represent the terms that make up every element in the table of services (see Table 2.1).

	S_1	S_2	S_3	...	S_J
T_1	(0;0;0)	(0,2;5;3)	(0,4;3;3)		(0,2;5;3)
T_2	(0,2;4;5)	(0,1;5;2)	(0,4;5;1)		(0,3;8;3)
T_3	(0,1;0;3)	(0;0;0)	(0,2;0;3)		(0,4;2;2)
T_4	(0,3;2;1)	(0,3;1;1)	(0;0;0)		(0,0,0)
...					
T_I	(0,2;3;1)	(0,1;1;3)	(0,4;5;2)		(0,4;5;3)

Table 2.1. *Example of a table of services*

It is worth noting that when a provider does not offer a service for a given task (partial flexibility), the corresponding element in the table of services is (0;0;0); otherwise $P_{ij} \neq 0$, $Co_{ij} \neq 0$ and $Q_{ij} \neq 0$. It is nonetheless possible to have $P_{i,j} \neq 0$, $Q_{i,j} \neq 0$ and $Co_{i,j} = 0$ for information that is free of charge, for example in the case of a promotional offer.

2.3. The global architecture of the system

2.3.1. *Modeling based on communicating agents*

In order to solve the problem previously described, we advance a system that is based on the coordination of five types of computerized agents (see Figure 2.2):

– *Interface agent (IA)*: this agent interacts with the user thus enabling him or her to choose a form of response that is suitable to his or her demand; therefore the IA manages the request received and displays the appropriate result. This way, when a user accesses ISAM, an IA is charged with recovering his or her request and sending it to an available identifying agent.

– *Identifying agent (IdA)*: this agent is connected to a system that enables the management of user requests, which can be numerous and simultaneous. Thus, every time an agent receives a set of requests during a brief lapse of time Δ_ε (called simultaneous Δ_ε-requests), the agent is responsible for breaking them down and identifying their similarities. In so doing, the IdA decomposes the set of simultaneous Δ_ε-requests received in a set of independent services, acknowledging the potential similarities in order to avoid a redundant search for data in the EMASN. This process of decomposition generates independent sub-requests (which we have called services) corresponding, for example, to the end-points of an itinerary or to well-known geographical areas. A sub-request is therefore an elementary and independent service that can be offered, in different forms, by one or more information providers in the EMASN, called nodes or servers (section 2.2.). To do this, every node needs to be registered in the ISAM, thus recording all of the services it provides (section 2.3.2.), knowing that a particular service corresponds to the response to a sub-request defined by a fixed response time, cost and data packet size. The process of decomposition enables the identification of potential information providers for each service requested. Finally, the IdA cyclically conveys the result generated by this process of identification to a scheduling agent that is available.

– *Scheduling agent (SA)*: this agent must find the best information providers in order to respond to the services identified by IdA, given that a single service can be offered by several information providers, with different response times, costs and data sizes. Thus, this type of agent needs to find the best possible nodes-to-services assignment, while at the same time minimizing response times and provision costs. The goal is to observe the fixed response times and to provide users with responses within a good price–quality ratio according to their demands. The nodes that are thus selected generate DRPs from IRPs, which are then actually followed by information-collecting MAs. The SA needs to determine beforehand, in non-real time, the number of MAs and their IRPs; then, the SA assigns nodes to the services in real time (see section 2.5.).

– *Intelligent collecting-agent (ICA)*: this is a computerized MA that can travel "intelligently" from one node to another within the EMASN in order to collect the data that correspond to the requested information. At the end of its journey, this agent returns to its host node, marked as H. This particular type of agent is composed of data, a code and a state, and is characterized by rational behavior. In order to avoid overload, the size of the data collected by an ICA must not exceed a certain threshold; this problem is addressed in the first level of optimization. When it returns to the system, an ICA transmits the data collected to an available merging agent.

– *Merging agent (MgA)*: this agent needs to merge the data it has received so that it composes appropriate responses to the set of simultaneous Δ_ε-requests that have been kept in a queue. The merging procedure requires information from the IdA and SA and carries on depending on the availability of the data collected. The IdA needs to provide a matrix for decomposing the requests for independent services, so that it can later compose appropriate responses. The SA must specify the set of ICAs along the way, in order to clearly define the conditions for stopping the merging process.

The proposed system requires the integration of local databases in order to function. However, the data needed to satisfy system users are distributed throughout the EMASN in such a way that each information provider remains responsible for the age and reliability of its data.

In order to market its services, each information provider must register with the ISAM on a local database called a registering database; for each service, it needs to mention the necessary response time, the cost and the corresponding size of the data that need to be transferred. Furthermore, we considered implementing a separate local database in the ISAM, called an archiving database (ADB). An ADB would enable the optimization of the data flow transferred within the EMASN by using an approach that classifies data according to indicators; this way, an ADB can reduce the actual number of ICAs. The ADB is located in cache memory, enabling the dynamic data to be backed up; these data can be used locally as long as they are still reliable. As soon as a piece of information becomes "outdated", however, an ICA must go and look for it remotely, in order to update it.

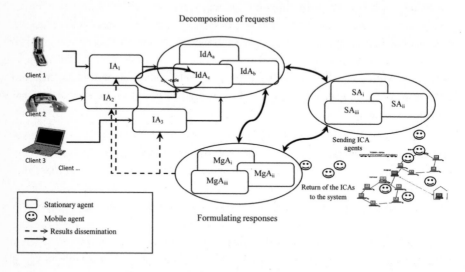

Figure 2.2. *Global architecture of the system*

2.3.2. *Local databases within the ISAM*

As we have mentioned previously, for an information provider to be able to market its data it must first register with the system to list or update the services it offers. A service corresponds to the response given to a task by an information provider, and it is characterized by a cost, a response time and the size of the data. A service is also characterized by a so-called reliability period; this means that it is possible to back up the information locally for a certain period of time with the aim of reducing the transmission of data. The system thus needs two local databases in order for it to function:

–*The registering database*: each provider that wishes to market its services through the ISAM must register with this database and list all of the services it offers. A provider must then provide a label for every service offered, stating its reference, the estimated response time, as well as the cost and size of corresponding data. It must also mention the address of the information system(s) that authorized the data collection. Several providers can therefore offer the same kind of service (and the same kind of label) but with different costs, response times and data sizes.

– *The ADB*: this database plays the role of a "buffer zone" in the sense that it contains static data and keeps it at a certain level. In other words, we have classified the data distributed throughout the EMASN according to their degree of stability, through the use of classification indicators. The aim of this method is to avoid searching unnecessarily for the same data that have not yet been modified, in the short term as well as in the long term.

The class diagram in Figure 2.3 illustrates the organization of the ISAM, integrating the local databases described above. The method of data classification as well as the implementation and usage of the ADB are integrated in the model we have proposed; we called this model "dynamic data archiving model".

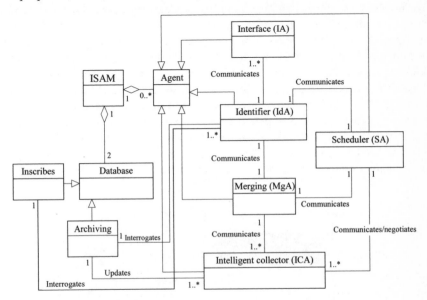

Figure 2.3. *ISAM organization*

2.3.3. *Dynamic data archiving model*

2.3.3.1. *Data classification and archiving*

A piece of information that corresponds to a multimodal transport service and/or to any other related service is represented by data that are located in distributed nodes; these nodes, in turn, represent the data servers of the information providers registered within the EMASN. Consequently, according to the architecture chosen and the optimization approach adopted (section 2.5.), the ICAs need to visit these nodes in order to collect the necessary data to satisfy system users. However, we can reduce the navigation of ICAs throughout the network in order to collect data that are occasionally static. It is therefore possible to optimize the data transferred within the EMASN by using an approach that classifies data according to their indicators. This approach helps reduce the actual number of ICAs calculated.

Previous research [KHA 05] has classified information according to four types of indicators: the localization indicator, the customization indicator, the time indicator and the update indicator. Thus, according to the values of these indicators, information may belong to the following categories: static, dynamic, event-driven, localized, non-localized, general or customized. We will focus on the classification that involves the time indicators and the update indicators, with the aim of classifying information in the static, dynamic or event-driven category for dynamic archiving of data. When an information provider offers a service, it must also mention the value of its time indicator, *TempInd*, as well as the value of its update indicator, *UpInd*. The time indicator of a piece of information represents its degree of stability, whereas the update indicator represents its period of reliability. Thus, as the value of the time indicator decreases, the information becomes more dynamic and as soon as the reliability period ends, the information is no longer valid and needs to be restored. These pieces of data, that are occasionally static, are archived in the ADB (see Figure 2.4) with the corresponding indicators *TempInd* and *UpInd*. The meaning of the values of these indicators is explained in Table 2.2.

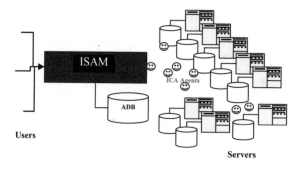

Figure 2.4. *Dynamic information archiving*

Indicators		Meaning
TempInd	*UpInd*	
0	Does not exist	The information is very dynamic
1	$\leq x$ hours	The information may change within less than x hours
2	$> x$ hours	The information may change within more than x hours
3	Does not exist	The information is static

Table 2.2. *Time indicator and update indicator for information classification*

When the information is very dynamic it is not archived in the ADB and the ICAs must look for it each time. This explains why, for this type of information, there is no update indicator. On the other hand, when the information is completely static, again there is no need for an update indicator because the information is fixed. In this case, if the information does not already exist within the ADB and if an ICA went looking for it, when it returns, the corresponding data will be archived once and for all in the ADB. In practice, however, the static data probably do not stay static forever and may change in exceptional circumstances. In this case, the information provider in question must inform the responsible IdA (that is responsible for the ADB). This procedure is mandatory for ensuring the reliability of information, which is the responsibility of providers. Finally, when they return to the system, the ICAs are responsible for updating outdated information.

2.3.3.2. *Functioning*

As soon as an available IdA receives a set of simultaneous Δ_ε-requests, it generates the set of tasks, I'_t, and composes them by identifying the information providers that are likely to respond to these tasks (services). Consequently, this agent must assess the *TempInd* indicator of each service identified; if the corresponding information is not very dynamic (*IndTemp* $\neq$ 0), then the IdA must verify whether this information had already been locally archived in the ADB. If this is the case, the IdA must then verify the value of the *UpInd* indicator. If the information is still valid, then the IdA can recover it directly from ADB and instantly send it to the available MgA. The SA responsible only entrusts the ICAs with searching for the information in the following situations:

– the information is very dynamic (*IndTemp* = 0);

– the information is not very dynamic (*IndTemp* $\neq$ 0) and it does not yet exist in the ADB; and

– the information is not very dynamic (*IndTemp* $\neq$ 0) and it already exists in the ADB, although it is no longer reliable.

In these last two cases, the information in the ADB needs to be updated. The dynamic archiving model is ensured by the IdAs, SAs and ICAs, and is thus illustrated by an activity diagram containing three data sets (see Figure 2.5), where each set of data is controlled by an agent.

In order to solve the problem described in section 2.2, we have proposed a dynamic and open system based on the interaction of five types of computerized agents: user IAs, IdAs, SAs, ICA and MgAs. The existence of each of these agents depends on the existence of user requests, i.e. their lifecycle is connected to the users' access to the ISAM. This "dynamic" aspect of the system is addressed in the next section.

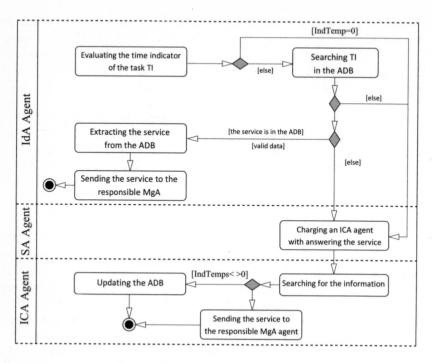

Figure 2.5. *Dynamic data archiving model*

2.4. Proposal of a resolution system with several interactive entities: a dynamic multi-agent system

At a given time t, the formulation of a user request needs the creation of an IA and triggers the creation of an IdA, an MgA, an SA and a certain number of ICAs. We call this set of IdAs, MgA, SAs and ICAs created at time t, the society of agents, P_t. Next, and for a short period of time (called the acquisition delay, Δ_ε, see section 2.3.), every new request formulated by a new IA is managed by the same society of agents, P_t, whose creation was triggered by the first request formulated at time t. If at time $t+\Delta_\varepsilon$ no societies of agents previously created are available, then the formulation of new requests triggers the creation of a new society $P_{t+\Delta\varepsilon}$ $P_{t+\Delta_\varepsilon}$ and so on. As soon as a society P_{t1} P_{t_i} created at time t_i is available, it becomes ready to generate a set of simultaneous Δ_ε-requests at a new time t_j with $t_i+\Delta_\varepsilon+\alpha \le t_j$ where α is the response time (which will be discussed later on). However, as soon as the availability of a society or of an IA reaches the period of inactivity Δ_∞, this society or agent is automatically destroyed.

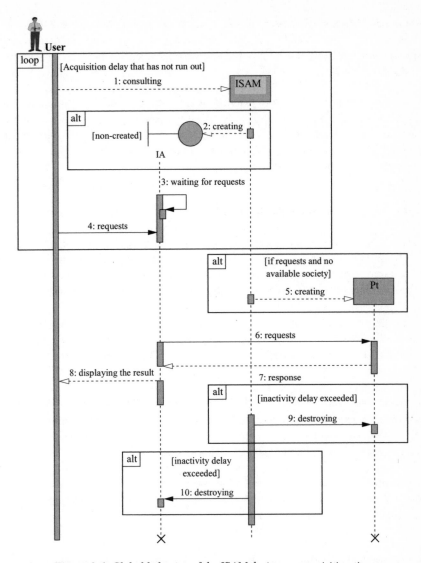

Figure 2.6. *Global behavior of the ISAM during an acquisition time*

Figure 2.6 represents a diagram of sequences that illustrate the global behavior of the system during a formulation period when a society interacts with an IA.

As we have mentioned previously, in order for the responses provided to be as satisfying as possible, they must be provided on time and at a reasonable cost, knowing that the data necessary for responding to these demands are distributed within the EMASN. However, if the system does not optimize the data flow throughout the network, and if the user requests are numerous and simultaneous, the responses will probably not be provided on time. Hence, it is necessary to adopt an optimization strategy.

The problem at hand is quite original: it is multidisciplinary in the sense that it introduces an OR dimension in a software engineering problem whose solutions have been strongly disputed. We have thus adopted a two-leveled optimization method that is founded on the mobile paradigm [ZGA 06a, ZGA 05b] that corresponds to the behavior of an SA.

2.5. The behavior of a scheduling agent

The behavior of an SA is composed of two sub-behaviors that function at the same time. The first one is triggered in non-real time, at the start of the application or each time the state of the network varies considerably. The second one is triggered in real time upon the receipt of a set of simultaneous Δ_ε-requests.

The first behavior enables the transfer of data flows in the EMASN and thus prepares the IRPs of ICAs by accepting the existence of a module that systematically provides the ISAM with the latest network variations. This module is called a network administration module.

The second behavior is Δ_ε-cyclical, and it creates the DRPs for the ICAs. This behavior is triggered with more precision upon the receipt of data generated by the IdA, namely the set of services required and identified by the requests received as well as the set of nodes that could provide these services.

The choice of separating these two processes is explained by the basic need to make the best use of the calculations made in real time in order to minimize response delays.

2.5.1. *First level of optimization: building initial route plans for mobile agents*

The cost-effective algorithm for building route plans for MAs – cost-effective mobile agent planning – suggested by [BAE 01] is the most appropriate plan for our problem. The dynamic BYKY2 algorithm that Baek proposed optimizes the number of MAs, by taking into account the state of the network and thus reducing the total execution time. In our early research [ZGA 05a], we drew on this approach, considering the state variations of the MAs and more specifically of the data that they carry. We have also implemented the CoJPa algorithm for constructing journey patterns. We address the problem of route plans for MAs in what follows by considering the following hypotheses:

– the collection of data on a node previously visited by an MA needs an execution time. We assume that the size of data to be collected from a particular node of the EMASN is equal to the average size of all data that need to be collected from that same node;

– initially, an ICA is not completely "void" because it contains an initial quantity of data, at least corresponding to its source code. This quantity of data, even if minimal, is taken into account and marked as Q_0;

– we estimate that the minimal latency between each pair of nodes within the EMASN is available thanks to the pre-existing network administration module; and

– the data can be too large to be carried by the MAs, especially when this information is in multimedia form. Thus, we admit that the transmission of a quantity of data from one node to another via EMASN depends on current latency.

2.5.1.1. *Description*

The problem of building route plans for MAs starts when the ICAs are created and launched from the original node of the system (the host node). The other nodes in the EMASN represent remote information providers that the ICAs may visit in order to collect the data corresponding to the information necessary to satisfy the services demanded by users. These information providers are "concurrent" nodes, distributed within the EMASN that "market" services that are similar or different. Different nodes can thus offer the same service but in different formats, with different costs and different response times. "The response time of a service starting from a node" is the time needed to complete the task that corresponds to this service on a particular node. Hence, we can deduce that the response time in the host node is null. Given that the network latencies are supposedly known and can affect the navigation time of the ICAs, our goal is to minimize the number of these agents as well as their navigation time. Thus, at this stage of optimization we seek to calculate the actual number of ICAs by creating their IRPs with the aim of exploring the whole of the EMASN, while taking into account its state. Let us bear in mind that during this first optimization stage, an agent collects the average (in terms of quantity and response time) of all the data that needs to be collected from that same node. For a formal description of this problem, we introduce several definitions below using the variables described in Table 2.3.

Variable	Description
m	Number of ICA's
AC $ICA_1, ..., ICA_m$	ICA's identifiers
H	Host node
W_k	Sequence of nodes representing the route plan of the ICA_i: $W_k = (S_{k_1}, S_{k_2} ...)$ with $1 \leq card(W_k) \leq J$
$T(W_k)$ or T_k	Journey duration for W_k of the ICA_k (definition 2.4)
$Qte_{k,u}$	The quantity of data carried by the ICA_k up to node S_u inclusively (definition 2.2)
$Tr(Qte_{k,u}, S_u, S_v)$	Transmission time for $Qte_{k,u}$ starting from node S_u up to node S_v (definition 2.3)
CT_j	Execution time at S_j necessary for the extraction of the Qt_j quantity of data
Qt_j	Quantity of data at S_j (definition 2.1)
Qt_{k_r}	Quantity of data at S_{k_r} to be extracted by the ICA_k from node S_{k_r} belonging to its route plan, W_k
$d(S_i, S_j)$	Data transmission flow between nodes S_i and S_j

Table 2.3. *Notations*

DEFINITION 2.1.– Qt_j (quantity of data in node S_j) is the average quantity of data that need to be extracted from S_j.

T_i represents a service proposed by S_j. We recall that $P_{i,j}$ represents the time needed to respond to service T_i by using the resources of node S_j, and $Q_{i,j}$ represents the size of the data packet to be collected from node S_j that corresponds to service T_i according to the appropriate table of services (Table 2.1). Therefore:

$$Qt_j = \frac{\sum_{i=1}^{I} a_{i,j} \times Q_{i,j}}{\sum_{i=1}^{I} a_{i,j}}$$

[2.1]

$$CT_j = \frac{\sum_{i=1}^{I} a_{i,j} \times P_{i,j}}{\sum_{i=1}^{I} a_{i,j}}$$

[2.2]

where $a_{i,j}$ is a Boolean variable so that $a_{i,j} = 1$ if node S_j offers the service T_i and otherwise $a_{i,j} = 0$ (following the corresponding table of services).

DEFINITION 2.2.– $Qte_{k,u}$ (quantity of data carried by ICA_k up to S_u inclusively) is the quantity of data collected and transported by ICA_k throughout its journey, starting from the host node (H) up to the node S_u inclusive.

$Qte_{k,u}$ is calculated as follows:

$$Qte_{k,u} = Q_0 + \sum_{r=1}^{u} Qt_{k_r}$$

[2.3]

DEFINITION 2.3.– $Tr(Qte_{k,u}, S_u, S_v)$ (transmission time) is the time necessary for the migration of the ICA_k from node S_u to node S_v carrying the quantity of data $Qte_{k,u}$.

$Tr(Qte_{k,u}, S_u, S_v)$ is calculated as follows:

$$Tr(Qte_{k,u}, S_u, S_v) = \frac{Qte_{k,u}}{d(S_u, S_v)}$$

[2.4]

DEFINITION 2.4.- $T(W_k)$ (journey duration W_k) is the time needed for ICA_k to visit the network node sequence $(S_{k_1}, S_{k_2} ...)$ with $1 \leq card(W_k) \leq J$ before returning to the host node.

Based on Table 2.4, $T(W_k)$ is calculated as follows:

$$T(W_k) = T_{departure} + T_{journey} + T_{return}$$

[2.5]

$p = \text{card}(W_k)$	W_k	$T_{\text{departure}}$	T_{return}	T_{journey}
1	(S_{k_1})			CT_{k_1}
[2..J]	$(S_{k_1}, \ldots, S_{k_p})$	$Tr(Q_0, H, S_{k_1})$	$Tr(Qte_{k,k_p}, S_{k_p}, H)$	X_k

Table 2.4. *Journey duration*

with:

$$X_k = \sum_{i=1}^{p} CT_{k_i} + \sum_{i=1}^{p-1} Tr(Qte_{k,k_i}, S_{k_i}, S_{k_{i+1}}) \qquad [2.6]$$

2.5.1.2. *Route plan representations*

Our aim is to find a minimal number of ICAs needed to explore the entire network, by reducing their navigation time.

It is evident that the movement of an ICA towards every node of the network (m = J) ensures the best response time because, in this case, the agents are launched at the same time starting from the host node towards all the other nodes in the network. Thus, every agent operates on independently and returns to the host node as soon as its work is completed. In this case, the best response time is maintained as a threshold marked as δ that corresponds to the journey time of the last agent that returns to the system.

Starting from this threshold, we will divide the network into different parts according to node aggregation so that the journey time for each part does not exceed the threshold, δ. The main goal here is to respect δ by reducing the number of ICAs (m ≤ J) in order to reduce resource consumption within the system. For this optimization stage, we rely on the size of the data transported and the execution times without taking into account the cost of services. Given that that $d(S_i, S_j)$ is known, i.e. we know the flow between each pair of network nodes, S_i and S_j, we will now elaborate a brief description of the algorithm explained in [ZGA 05a].

Description of the algorithm for the construction of journey patterns (CoJPa):

– stage 1: arranging the nodes in the descending order of journey time, $T(W_i = S_i)$ $\forall 1 \leq i \leq J$, and establishing the threshold, δ, corresponding to the journey time from the first node of the list:

$$\delta = \max_{1 \leq i \leq J}(W_i = S_i) \qquad [2.7]$$

– stage 2: dividing the network into different parts so that the journey time of every part does not exceed the threshold δ previously established.

In order to build an IRP, this algorithm searches for the next node to be visited starting from the current position of the ICA, by recalculating the new journey time. A node is selected if the time necessary for completing the itinerary that is being created does not exceed the threshold, δ. If the threshold is exceeded, an IRP is ready to be assigned to an ICA and the algorithm ends if each node is part of an IRP that has already been attributed. The algorithm thus distributes all the nodes of the network to a set m of ICAs, each agent becoming a potential patrol agent for the part of the network to which it was assigned.

As soon as a set of user requests appears, the DRPs are deduced from these pre-established IRPs so that the ICAs only patrol the nodes that were chosen to offer the services demanded, in real-time. The clearly combinatorial aspect of the problem means that the choice of these nodes is made through an evolutionary approach that we shall describe in the next section. A subset S' of S will be chosen in order to optimize the management of information flows in the case of request acquisitions. This way, the number of ICAs decreases everytime the nodes composing the IRP of an ICA have not been selected by the optimization approach. In this case, the new number of ICAs is marked as m' and the new number of nodes is marked as J' with J' = |S'|. We thus obtain m' ≤ m, J' ≤ J and S'⊆S. Thanks to this second level of optimization, the information necessary to respond to the services demanded will be disseminated in the most effective manner possible in terms of response time and total provision cost.

2.5.2. *Second level of optimization: creating services using an evolutionary framework*

Evolutionary algorithms represent the research techniques used to carry out global and robust research. They draw from biological evolution in order to solve complex problems. These are stochastic research methods that rest upon the principle of competition between individuals and that operate upon a mass of potential solutions. The principle of survival is thus only applied to keep those results that are most convenient and to obtain the best possible approximations of the optimal solution. In other words, with each generation, a new set of approximations (individuals) is identified by a process of selection according to their level of fitness in the current population. This set, once identified, will be replicated with the help of evolutionary operators, such as crossover and mutation. The set of the elite individuals can then be updated, and so on and so forth. In this section we will consider the important characterstics of evolutionary algorithms and their validity in solving difficult problems that aim to research and compose distributed mobility services. Therefore, we adopt an evolutionary approach that is characterized by:

– genetic representation (a code) tailored to our problem so that it determines possible optimization solutions;

– genetic operators that transform the composition of infants in the course of reproduction. We recall that a service (a sub-request) must be provided by a single information server selected from the set of servers that provide the same service with different offers. Therefore, we seek to correct the decisions that are generated and do not observe this constraint;

– parents are selected at random from the current population for crossover and mutation, with a probability for crossover p_c ($0 < p_c < 1$) and a probability for mutation p_m ($0 < p_m < 1$);

– we adopt a non-elitist replacement technique in order to obtain a heterogenous population and to avoid premature convergence; and

– fitness functions evaluate the solutions according to two criteria: cost and response time.

2.5.2.1. *Solution modelling*

The most appropriate choice of a representation for a solution to a global problem is fundamental for the success of the evolutionary algorithm's applications. In previous research [ZGA 05b], we have designed effective coding for a possible solution by respecting the constraints of the problem. We have thus proposed a flexible representation of the chromosome, called the flexible tasks assignment representation (FeTAR).

The chromosome is represented by a matrix $CH(I' \times J')$, which has lines that represent the set of services demanded, which globally compose the simultaneous requests; the columns represent the different nodes identified. Every element in the matrix indicates the assignment of a node S_{c_j} ($1 \leq j \leq J'$) to a service T_{c_i} ($1 \leq i \leq I'$) as follows:

$$
CH[C_i, C_j] = \begin{cases} 1 & \text{if } S_{c_j} \text{ is assigned to } T_{c_i} \\ * & \text{if } S_{c_j} \text{ can be assigned to } T_{c_i} \\ X & \text{if } S_{c_j} \text{ cannot be assigned to } T_{c_i} \end{cases}
$$

If, for a given solution, every service is assigned to a single node, then the solution is feasible. Table 2.5 shows an example of a possible solution, an occurrence of FeTAR. For example, service T_{32} is proposed by several information providers: S_5, S_{18}, S_1, S_{14} and S_{10}; but it is node S_{14} that was chosen to provide this service. For service T_6, however, server S_{50} is the only possible information provider, in which case the system does not decide but is assigned because it has no other choice. The flexible aspect of a FeTAR solution enables us to modify the assignment of nodes to services thanks to genetic operators that will soon be presented. These operators enable the generation of child chromosomes from parent chromosomes, thus inheriting the characteristics of the latter.

2.5.2.2. *The adopted genetic operators*

2.5.2.2.1. Crossover operator with external control

In genetic algorithms, crossover is a genetic operator used to vary the programming of a chromosome or chromosomes from one generation to the next. The role of crossover is to generate an offspring that is determined by a combination of traits from the parents. We propose a crossover operator that combines two parent chromosomes in order to create two child chromosomes, by using an algorithm called *CrossFeTAR*.

	S_5	S_{18}	S_1	S_{14}	S_{201}	S_{50}	S_8	S_9	S_{10}	S_3
T_{12}	*	*	*	1	*	*	*	*	*	*
T_3	*	*	*	*	x	*	*	*	*	1
T_5	1	*	*	*	x	*	*	*	*	*
T_6	x	x	x	x	x	1	x	x	x	x
T_{27}	x	1	*	x	x	x	*	*	x	*
T_{10}	x	x	*	*	x	x	x	*	1	x
T_{32}	*	*	*	1	x	x	x	x	*	x
T_{13}	*	*	*	*	x	x	*	*	*	1

Table 2.5. *Example of a FeTAR ocurrence*

The correction of a chromosome at stage 4 of this algorithm occurs with non-feasible solutions. A non-feasible solution can either be a solution that assigns a service (or several services) more than once, or a solution that does not assign a service (or several services) at all. We can correct a non-feasible solution by using the *CorrectFeTAR* algorithm.

CrossFeTAR algorithm

The creation of E_1 (E_2 resp.) representing infant 1 (infant 2 resp.) is given by:
- Stage 1 : choose randomly two parents and a node: P_1, P_2 and $S_{c_j}(1 \leq j \leq J')$
- Stage 2 : the assignments of services for S_{c_j} in E_1 (E_2 resp.) must correspond to the same assignments of S_{c_j} for P_1 (P_2 resp.)
- Stage 3 :
  For every $(1 \leq k \leq J')$ and $(k \neq j)$
      The assignments of services for S_{c_k} in E_1 (E_2 resp.) correspond to the same assignments of S_{c_k} for P_2 (P_1 resp.)
- Stage 4 : if E_1 (E_2 resp.) does not correspond to a feasible solution then E_1 must be corrected (E_2 resp.) : CorrectFeTAR(E_1(respE_2))

CorrectFeTAR algorithm

The correction of an ocurrence CH FeTAR is given by:
For every $1 \leq i \leq I'$
   initialize to zero :
   the vectors IndexAssigned[] and IndexNotAssigned[] with dimensions J'
   $k_1 \leftarrow 0$
   $k_2 \leftarrow 0$
   For every $1 \leq j \leq J'$
    If CH[c_i, c_j]= 1 then
      Increment k_1 with 1
      IndexAssigned[k_1]$\leftarrow$j
      Else
          If CH[c_i, c_j]=* then
            Increment k_2 with 1
            IndexNotAssigned[k_2]$\leftarrow$j
        EndIf
        EndIf
      EndFor
      If k_1=0 then
      Choose randomly a subscript p with $1 \leq p \leq k_2$

```
          s←IndexNotAssigned[p]
        CH[c_i, c_s]←1
      Else
        If k_1>1 then
          Choose randomly a subscript p with 1≤p≤k_1
          s←IndexAssigned[p]
          For every 1≤x ≤J' and x≠s
              If CH[c_i, c_x]=1 then CH[c_i, c_x]←*
                  EndIf
                EndFor
        EndIf
        EndIf
  EndFor
```

For example, starting from two parent chromosomes P_1 and P_2, the crossover processs generates two infant chromosomes E_1 and E_2 as follows:

P_1	S_{12}	S_6	S_3	S_{24}
T_1	X	*	*	1
T_5	*	*	1	*
T_3	1	X	*	*
T_9	*	*	1	X
T_2	*	*	1	*

P_2	S_{12}	S_6	S_3	S_{24}
T_1	X	*	1	*
T_5	*	*	1	*
T_3	*	X	*	1
T_9	*	*	1	X
T_2	*	*	1	*

E_1	S_{12}	S_6	S_3	S_{24}
T_1	X	*	*	*
T_5	*	*	1	*
T_3	*	X	*	1
T_9	*	*	1	X
T_2	*	*	1	*

E_2	S_{12}	S_6	S_3	S_{24}
T_1	X	*	1	1
T_5	*	*	1	*
T_3	1	X	*	*
T_9	*	*	1	X
T_2	*	*	1	*

Here, we notice that the two generated infant chromosomes are not feasible solutions. In particular, E_1 does not assign service T_1 at any time and E_2 assigns the service T_1 twice through the servers S_3 and S_{24}. The correction should randomly transform E_1 in E_{11}, E_{12} or E_{13} and E_2 in E_{21} or E_{22} as follows:

E_{11}	S_{12}	S_6	S_3	S_{24}
T_1	X	1	*	*
T_5	*	*	1	*
T_3	*	X	*	1
T_9	*	*	1	X
T_2	*	*	1	*

E_{12}	S_{12}	S_6	S_3	S_{24}
T_1	X	*	*	1
T_5	*	*	1	*
T_3	*	X	*	1
T_9	*	*	1	X
T_2	*	*	1	*

E_{13}	S_{12}	S_6	S_3	S_{24}
T_1	X	*	1	*
T_5	*	*	1	*
T_3	*	X	*	1
T_9	*	*	1	X
T_2	*	*	1	*

E_{21}	S_{12}	S_6	S_3	S_{24}
T_1	X	*	*	1
T_5	*	*	1	*
T_3	1	X	*	*
T_9	*	*	1	X
T_2	*	*	1	*

E_{22}	S_{12}	S_6	S_3	S_{24}
T_1	X	*	1	*
T_5	*	*	1	*
T_3	1	X	*	*
T_9	*	*	1	X
T_2	*	*	1	*

2.5.2.2.2. Mutation operator with integrated control

Mutation is another important genetic operator besides crossover. This operator introduces a certain variation in the genes of the population of individuals. Typically, the mutation is applied to a chromosome in order to create a new, modified chromosome. Here, it applies to a chromosome that represents a feasible solution. The controlled mutation algorithm that we propose is described by the following *MuteFeTAR* algorithm.

MuteFeTAR algorithm
– Stage 1 : choose randomly a chromosome CH, a service T_{c_i} ($1 \le i \le I'$) and a node S_{c_j} ($1 \le j \le J'$)
– Stage 2 :
If CH[i,j]= * then
find j_1 with $1 \le j_1 \le J'$ and CH[i,j₁]=1
CH[i,j₁] ← *
CH[i,j] ← 1
Else
If CH[i,j] = 1 and $\exists\, j_1 / 1 \le j_1 \le J'$ with CH[i,j₁]=* then
CH[i,j₁] ← 1
CH[i,j] ← *
EndIf
EndIf

For example, if the chromosome E_{11} suffers a mutation, it can transform in E'_{11} as follows:

E'_{11}	S_{12}	S_6	S_3	S_{24}
T_1	X	1	*	*
T_5	*	*	1	*
T_3	*	X	*	1
T_9	*	*	1	X
T_2	1	*	*	*

Mutation of the chromosome E_{11}

2.5.2.3. *Generating definite route plans*

The selected occurrence of *FeTAR* transforms equations [2.1] and [2.2] according to the corresponding table of services (section 2.2) as follows:

$$Qt_{c_j} = \sum_{i=1}^{I'} (a_{c_i,c_j} \times Q_{c_i,c_j})$$ [2.1']

$$CT_{c_j} = \sum_{i=1}^{I'} (a_{c_i,c_j} \times P_{c_i,c_j})$$ [2.2']

with a_{c_i,c_j} a Boolean variable being evaluated as follows: if CH[c_i,c_j] = 1 ($1 \le i \le I'$ and $1 \le j \le J'$) then $a_{c_i,c_j} = 1$ else $a_{c_i,c_j} = 0$. The definite duration T_k of an ICA_k, and the DRPs are then deduced by using equations [2.1'], [2.2'], [2.3], [2.4], [2.5] and [2.6].

2.5.2.4. *The functions of evaluation*

With each iteration, the individuals in a current population (the occurrence chromosomes in *FeTAR*) are evaluated according to the same fitness measurements. In our case, the function "objective" seeks to maximize the number of satisfied clients, i.e. to minimize response time and provision costs. However, the response time is considered to be much more important than the total cost, since it is more useful to have a service that is "a bit more costly" than not having any service at all during an authorized period of time. In other words, a possible solution is first evaluated according to its response time (number of requests answered during an authorized period of time) and then according to the average cost of all the requests. Thus, a chromosome must express the response dates of all of the requests as well as the average information cost [ZGA 05a].

According to the chromosome-occurrence generated by *FeTAR*, the evaluation functions fitness_1 and fitness_2 calculate the response time and total cost for every user request. A chromosome will therefore be illustrated by an evaluation vector generated by these two fitness functions that for every request, req_w, express the cost (C_w) as well as the calculated response time (D_w) and the authorized response time (d_w).

Fitness_1 algorithm

FR_w: the final execution time for the request $req_w \in R_t$

$\forall$ $ICA_k / 1 \le k \le m$:

U_k: a set of tasks to be accomplished by the agent $ACI_k / 1 \le k \le m$

FU_k: total time necessary for accomplishing U_k

B_k: Boolean mark up value for the movement of the ICA_k

1. Initialization:
   $\forall ICA_k / 1 \le k \le m$: $U_k \leftarrow \varnothing$, $FU_k \leftarrow 0$
   $\forall$ $req_w \in R_t$: $FR_w \leftarrow 0$
2. Build U_k and calculate $FU_k \forall ACI_k / 1 \le k \le m$:
       For every $T_{c_i} \in I'_t$:
           Find k/ ICA_k achieve T_{c_i} (after the DRP_k and $CH[c_i,c_j]$)
           $U_k \leftarrow U_k \cup \{T_{c_i}\}$
       For every ICA_k: $FU_k \leftarrow T_k$ (formulas [2.1'], [2.2'], [2.3], [2.4], [2.5] and [2.6])
3. Calculate $FR_w \forall$ $req_w \in R_t$:

For every $req_w \in R_t$:
    $B_k \leftarrow$ false
    For every $T_{c_i} \in I_t'$:
        If $T_{c_i} \in req_w$ then
            Find $k / T_{c_i} \in U_k$
            If $B_k =$ false then
                $FR_w \leftarrow \max(FR_w, FU_k)$
                $B_k \leftarrow$ true
            EndIf
        EndIf
    EndFor
EndFor

Fitness_2 algorithm

C_w the total cost of the request $req_w \in R_t$
1. Initialization:
For every req_w R_t
    $C_w \leftarrow 0$
EndFor
2. Calculate the total cost for each request:
For every $I_{t,w}$ that composes req_w
    For every $T_{c_i} \in I_{t,w}$
        Look for $j / CH[c_i, c_j] = 1$
        $C_w \leftarrow C_w + Co_{c_i, c_j}$
    EndFor
EndFor

2.5.2.5. *Generating solutions*

In order to determine the best solutions, we have adopted an elitist evolutionary approach [AGA 08] using external storage limited to the size of the current population, with the aim of storing the most well-adapted individuals (see Figure 2.7).

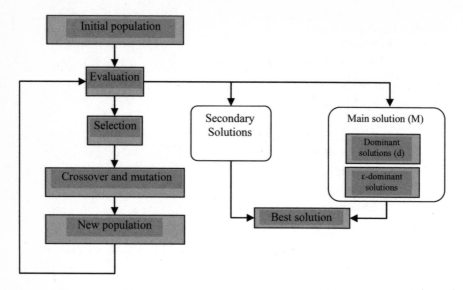

Figure 2.7. *The evolutionary approach adopted*

We differentiate between the solutions generated according to the observance of authorized response delay, since the user will not be satisfied if they do not receive their answer in time (the priority of the time criterion). Thus, the solutions generated are classified first according to time and second according to cost. Knowing that $d_{max}=max(d_w)_{1\leq w\leq R}$, we will then distinguish between two categories of solutions:

– the set of main solutions (M) represents the best solutions observing all of the response times that will be authorized. In other words, a chromosome $CH\in M$ if and only if $\forall w$ $(1\leq w\leq R)$, $D_w\leq d_w\leq d_{max}$. This set of solutions is split into two archives: dominant solutions (d) and ε-dominant solutions $(\varepsilon - d)$; and

– the set of secondary solutions (M') represents the best set of solutions with the minimum number of occurrences when the authorized response time has been exceeded. In other words, chromosome $CH\in M'$ if and only if $\exists w$ $(1\leq w\leq R)$ with $d_{max}<D_w$.

At this level, the solution founded on the MA paradigm that we have presented should integrate an infrastructure that is intolerant to errors. Unfortunately the networks, especially those extended to a large scale and have heavy traffick, are very frequently subject to errors, such as system crashes and bottlenecks. In this context, we propose an interaction solution between the SAs of the system and the ICAs in motion, so that the latter change their itinerary, in real time, finding the best possible replacements for the information providers that are affected by the current disruption. SAs must ensure the feasibility of the newly found solutions, in terms of response time and total service cost.

2.6. Managing system robustness when dealing with disruptions: advancing a negotiation process between stationary and mobile entities

As we have previously mentioned, we have adopted the MAs paradigm for collecting information inside the network. Our goal is to optimize the management of responses to user requests formulated in real time, especially when they are numerous and simultaneous. The problem arises when the EMASN is affected by a disruption. In these cases, the ICAs must avoid the nodes that are no longer available in the network by changing their itineraries (DRP) in real time. These agents must also find effective replacements in order to offer the services whose providers, which were initially chosen for the selected solution, were affected by the disruption. This change must take place under the supervision of the SA, which needs to ensure the feasibility of the new solution in terms of cost and response time.

In order to achieve this, we have implemented a negotiation protocol between the ICAs (the negotiation participants) and the SA (the negotiation initiator) issued from the same society of agents (section 2.4). This protocol draws from the well-known Contract-Net-Protocol [SMI 80].

In the solution we have proposed, we enable partial contractual aggreements with the aim of reaching mutual solutions as quickly as possible that depend on the current position of the ICAs on their DRPs as well as their priorities, preferences and constraints. The priorities represent the sequence of nodes of the EMASN that are programmed within the remaining DRP and that are thus already optimized in terms of network latency as well as service costs and response time. The preferences represent the sequence of the EMASN nodes that are preprogrammed in the remaining PRI and are optimized only in terms of network latency. Finally, the constraints represent the sequence of EMASN nodes whose access is ill advised (for example bottlenecks) or even prohibited (for example, a list of nodes that were affected by the disruption). Rounds of negotiations must take place as long as there are still services that do not have a provider and the authorized response time has not yet run out. In what follows, we will describe the different members of the proposed protocol.

2.6.1. *Initiators and participants*

The initiator of the negotiation is an SA that has itself created the ICAs and has launched them in the EMASN according to a well-defined plan. This agent triggers the negotiation as soon as it acknowledges the list of non-functional nodes provided by the network administration module (section 2.5) by proposing a new DRP contract for the ICAs still in motion. In this case, every ICA participant sends its opinion (refusal or agreement, full or partial) to the initiator who, upon receipt of this opinion, provides the final update of the list of non-assigned services to the servers. The SA must not wait for all the responses each time in order to make a decision, since the waiting delay is clearly limited. Consequently, it asks the participants to propose assignement possibilities for the services according to their current position and their priorities, preferences and constraints. These three characteristics are dynamic and they depend on the state of the network and the current position of the agent.

2.6.2. *The proposed protocol*

A protocol defines a structured language that is used by the agents of a MAS with the aim of exchanging information in order to better interact, and cooperate or negotiate. The protocol proposed (see Figure 2.8) is a negotiation protocol characterized by a sequence of messages exchanged between an initiating agent (SA) and the participating agents (ICA) issued from the same society. The main goal is to find new providers for the services whose servers that we initally chose according to our optimization approach were affected by the disruption.

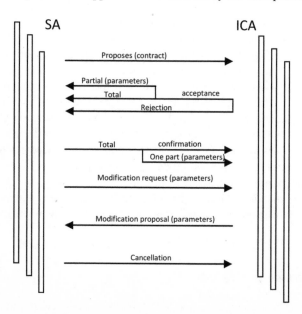

Figure 2.8. *The proposed negotiation protocol*

This set of services is marked as Φ_t and it is updated during the confirmation phase, i.e. every time that the SA decides "who will do what" according to the propositions it receives from the participating agents. Furthermore, the protocol could operate between several initiators and several participants, for example in the case of overlap between several sets of simultaneous Δ_e-requests. In this chapter, we are focusing on negotiations between a single initiating agent and several participating agents that relate to the initiator through the same society.

The negotiation starts with the proposal of a contract describing the nodes proposed to the ICAs using a genetic operation applied directly to the chromosome (*FeTAR* occurrence), which corresponds to the current solution [ZGA 05a, ZGA 05b]. Every agent can totally or partially reject or accept the proposed contract depending on the state of the nodes and can in turn propose a modification of its trajectory, in order to assign as many services as possible from Φ_t according to its priorities, preferences and constraints. This decision is made with the help of an algorithm that dynamically reconstructs the itineraries of the ICAs, named *ARDyCA* [ZGA 06a]. A renegotiation corresponds to a new round of negotiations triggered by a request to change the contract, a part of which had not been accepted in the previous round. The proposed negotiation protocol is founded on high level semantics that exceeds the limits of classic communication. This difficulty challenged us to design a scalable library of specialized vocabulary and semantics for the negotiation protocol proposed for inter- and intra-system interaction. The library is conceived in the form of a dedicated dynamic ontology.

2.7. The usefulness of a dedicated dynamic ontology

Our goal is to define a repository in the form of a vocabulary suitable for agents on the ISAM platform, called a flexible ontology multiservice system (FOMS), in order to automate the different possible interactions (see Figure 2.9).

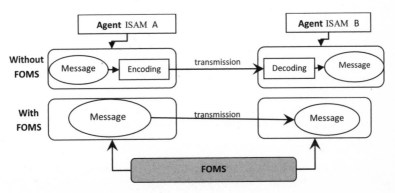

Figure 2.9. *Usefulness of the FOMS within the ISAM*

The main idea is to facilitate, i.e. automate, the understanding of messages exchanged between the agents. However, we propose to delve further into this aspect by producing scalable ontology packages that can adapt to all interaction situations, thus ensuring a perfect understanding between the systems, particularly in the case of the heterogeneity of data issued by different remote sources [SAA 08].

In this framework, information providers are completely free to choose the indentifiers of their services, which allows them to keep their own referencing without being forced to adapt to a repository chosen by the system. The main goal here is to allow total freedom for providers to update their data without disturbing the interaction with the system. The ISAM must then guarantee the consistency (an expression has the same meaning for all agents) and compatibility (a concept is designated by the same expression for all agents) of information throughout the system.

In this context, FOMS is based on a three-levelled knowledge-management system (see Figure 2.10). First, an interaction level that represents the exchanged messages, triggering, second, a semantic level in the case of incomprehension. This level is based on a semantic translator that interacts with the knowledge-management level, in order to find the best possible interpretation according to an identified level of translation. The last level, see Figure 2.11, represents the kernel of the knowledge-management system, allowing access to the data exchanged as well as their translations and updates in an intelligent knowledge database where the packages of scalable ontologies are ordered.

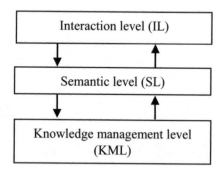

Figure 2.10. *Three-levelled architecture of the knowledge-management system*

In order to guarantee the flexibility of FOMS, a particular ontology domain (DOnto) must be derived from a generic ontology that contains all of the fundamental concepts for creating a particular universal set of references. The flexibility of FOMS enables us to implement a knowledge-management system in whichever field we desire. For example, in the field of transport every operator can build its own knowledge-management system knowing that the different ontologies can reassemble in the same domain without overlapping. Moreover, the implementation of a universal semantic set in a particular domain that the agents in the ISAM can rely on for communication needs all possible elements in the domain of discourse used by the interacting agents to be classified. This classification is derived from the FIPA-ACL (Agent Communication Language) that accords semantics with the content of a given ACL message, thanks to a performative message [CAI 04]. Thus, we need to distinguish between predicates and terms.

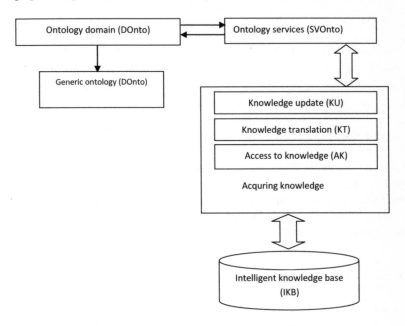

Figure 2.11. *Knowledge management level*

2.7.1. *Terms*

Terms are the expressions that identify the (abstract or concrete) entities that "exist" in the world and upon which agents found their reasoning. We distinguish between two types of terms: the concepts and the actions of the agents:

– *the concepts*: these are the expressions that represent entities with more or less complex structures, that can be defined in terms of slots. In this case, the generic ontology defines the concept of the "element" that represents each consituting part: information server, service, request/sub-request, agent route plans, etc.; and

– *the actions of the agents*: these are special concepts that indicate actions that can be carried out by the agents.

2.7.2. *Predicates*

Predicates are Boolean expressions indicating facts of the environment (the real world) such as: availability of an information provider; the identification of a provider as a constraint/priority/preference of a particular agent; etc.

2.8. Simulations and results

In order to implement the whole of the ISAM (agents behavior, interactions, etc.) we have choosen to use the JADE platform[1] (Java Agent Development framework). This choice was made because of the different characteristics of this platform that correspond to the waiting states of the ISAM.

In particular, JADE is a middleware[2] that enables a flexible implementation of MASs, which can communicate through an effective transfer of ACL messages, complying with FIPA (Foundation of Intelligent Physical Agents) specifications. JADE is written in Java[3] language. It supports mobility, evolves rapidly and is part of the multi-agent platforms that offer the possibility of integrating web services [GRE 05]. Furthermore, JADE tries to facilitate the development of agent applications by optimizing the performances of distributed agent systems.

2.8.1. *Intra-system communication*

Thanks to the "yellow pages" system provided by JADE, the different agents in the ISAM are able to publish their different services. This technique enables the localization of all available agents, providing a particular service in order in real time so they can be contacted. The conversations between the different agents of the ISAM can be debugged via one of the JADE graphic tools: the Sniffer Graphical Tool (see Figure 2.12). In the left window of the Sniffer, we can see the different container applications located on remote servers in the EMASN, where the ICAs can move to collect information according to the developing contract.

---

1 http://jade.tilab.com.

2 Enables communication between clients and servers that have different structures and a different implementation.

3 www.java.sun.com.

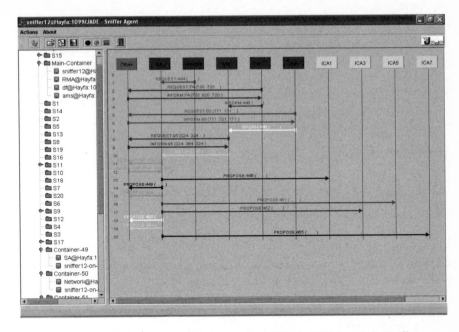

Figure 2.12. *Debugging an agent interaction within the ISAM using the Sniffer tool in the JADE programming language*

2.8.2. *The validity and assessment of the mobile agent paradigm*

In the context of the applications dispatched to large-scale networks, the emergence of the "mobile agent" paradigm in 1994 was an overwhelming invention that promised industrialists attractive solutions for better access to randomized and bulky information. Over time, the advantages of this paradigm have been discussed at great length and it was eventually proven that this paradigm was only useful in certain cases [PIC 977, BUS 03]. In particular, the effectiveness of the MA paradigm depends significantly on the acrchitecture of the system adopted [LU 03, BUS 03].

In this section, we justify the use of this paradigm within ISAM by comparing it to the classic client/server paradigm [ZGA 06b, PIC 07, KET 05]. For the client/server paradigm (CS), η_{CS} ($\tilde{\eta}_{CS}$ respectively) represents the function of the data transmission costs corresponding to the sending of a request message (response respectively) T_{CS} and ρ_{CS} correspond to the maximum response time for a given request and to the total transmission costs, and they are calculated as follows:

$$T_{CS}= \sum_{j=1}^{J'} \left(\frac{\sum_{i=1}^{I'} (\eta_{CS} I_{c_i,c_j} + \tilde{\eta}_{CS} Q_{c_i,c_j})}{d(H,S_{c_j})} \right)$$

$$\rho_{cs}= \sum_{j=1}^{J'} \left(\sum_{i=1}^{I'} a_{c_i,c_j} (\eta_{CS} + \tilde{\eta}_{CS}) \right)$$

where:

– I_{c_i,c_j} and Q_{c_i,c_j} correspond to the size of the request message and the size of the response message for the task T_{c_i} on the server S_{c_j};

– T_{c_i} and S_{c_j} represent the service and the node that correspond to the i^{nd} line and to the j^{nd} column of the matrix that symbolizes the chromosome FeTAR CH generated by a SA with $1 \leq i \leq I'$ and $1 \leq j \leq J'$; and

– a_{c_i,c_j} is a Boolean variable so that if $CH[c_i,c_j] = 1(1 \leq i \leq I'$ and $1 \leq j \leq J')$ then $a_{c_i,c_j}=1$ else $a_{c_i,c_j}=0$.

For the MA paradigm, when an ICA moves towards a given node, it brings along all of the responses collected from nodes it had already visited. Thus, when an ICA finishes collecting the data from the last node in its itinerary, it returns to its host node in the system with all of the collected results. For this paradigm, η_{AM} ($\tilde{\eta}_{AM}$ respectively) represents the function of the transmission costs of data, which corresponds to sending a request message (response, respectively). As a consequence, the total transmission cost ρ_{AM_k} for an ICA_k is calculated thus:

$$\rho_{AM_k}= \sum_{j=1}^{J'} b_{c_j,c_k} \eta_{AM} + \tilde{\eta}_{AM}$$

with b_{c_j,c_k} as a Boolean variable so that if S_{c_j} belongs to the DRP of the agent ACI_{c_k} ($1 \leq j \leq J'$ and $1 \leq k \leq m'$) then $b_{c_j,c_k} = 1$ else $b_{c_j,c_k}=0$. The maximum response time for a given request corresponds to the maximum navigation time of all theactive ICAs involved:

$$T_{AM}= \max_{1 \leq k \leq m'} (T(W_{c_k}) + \rho_{AM_{c_k}})$$

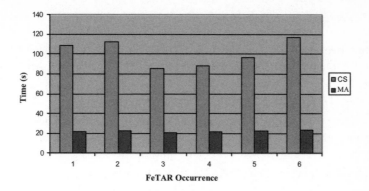

Figure 2.13. *Comparing MA and CS paradigms
for a single FeTAR occurrence*

We are interested in open, heavily trafficked and distributed systems, however, and such systems are composed of a significant number of nodes with an intensive flow of user requests. In this case, ρ_{cs} is likely to be larger than ρ_{AM_k}, so we will not take into consideration the transmission costs of data in the simulation results. We have selected an optimized occurrence of *FeTAR* in order to respond to a set of 10 requests received simultaneously through 2s (2s-simultaneous requests) globally broken down into 54 services requesting access to 17 remote providers. The simulation results show that this solution took 21.86 s within the MA paradigm and 108.95 s within the CS paradigm (see Figure 2.14). We then generated other *FeTAR* occurrences for the same example and the results are formal (see Figure 2.13); using the MA paradigm, which is founded on an optimization approach within ISAM, is a lot more effective than the CS approach.

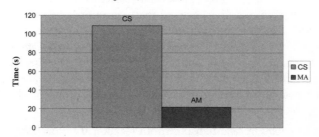

Figure 2.14. *Variation in results according to FeTAR occurrences*

2.8.3. *Example of a mobility-aiding services demand scenario*

During two seconds ($\varepsilon = 2$ s), we have a number of users connected to ISAM at $t = 11$ h via their respective substrates. Each of them formulates their request as follows:

– request 1: "travel at a time t from location B to location C";

– request 2: "travel next weekend from location A to location B with a minimum cost; enquire about the weather forecast and cultural events for the next weekend in location B";

– request 3: "travel at time t from location A to location C";

– request 4: "enquire about current disruptions in public transportation from location B to location C";

– request 5: "find the best connection service with the train X, foreseen in location A at 12h00 for going to location C";

– request 6: "travel at time t from location A to location B";

– request 7: "find the best value hotel in location D for next weekend and make reservations, find the best route and departure time for going from location B to location D by car, according to road traffic";

– etc.

We place our example in an EMASN, making 100 services ($I = 100$) proposed by 20 information providers ($J = 20$) available. For reasons of clarity, we suppose that the IAs send their Δ_ε-requests to a single available IdA that breaks down the set R_t of these requests in a set of $I' = 64$ independent services: $I'_t = \{T_1, T_2, T_3, T_6, T_9, T_{13}, T_{16}...\}$.

The process of breaking down requests is not discussed in this chapter, but it is worth noting that a task can represent several services with different constraints. A service is identified thanks to a keyword that corresponds to a specified "action" according to the constraints mentioned. For example, T_{19} represents three services corresponding to the same task: "travel from location A to location B" with the constraints "at time t", "next weekend with the best price", "best connection service with train X at 12h00". Knowing that there is no direct connection between points A and C for this example, the IdA decomposes R_t in a set of independent services as follows:

– T_1 = "disruptions in road transport from location B to location C (at the time t)";

– T_2 = "weather forecast in location B (next weekend)";

– T_3 = "find the best value hotel in location D during next weekend and make reservations";

– T_6 = "find the shortest route for travelling by car from location B to location D";

– T_9 = "find the best departure time for travelling from location B to location D by car according to road traffic predictions during next weekend";

– T_{13} = "cultural events in location B (next weekend)";

– T_{16} = "travelling from location B to location C (at a given time t, starting from12h00)";

– T_{19} = "travelling from location A to location B (at a time t or next weekend with the best value connection service with train X at 12h00)";

– etc.

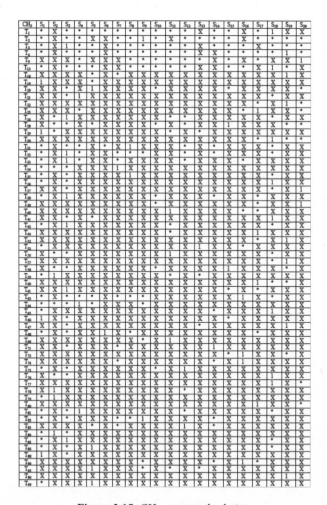

Figure 2.15. *CH₃ generated solution*

In response to user requests formulated at time t, the MgA provides reliable information that satisfies the services demanded by the users, and will be disseminated towards the corresponding substrata. The solution generated by the system, enabling the dissemination of this information, is illustrated by chromosome CH_3 (see Figure 2.15). This solution observes all execution times at the latest of requests ($d_w = 25$ $\forall$ $req_w \in R_t$) with a maximum time $d_{max} = 23.46$ s and an average total cost equal to 30.5 cost units.

2.8.3.1. *Initial route plans and definite route plans of ICAs*

– m = 5, the IRPs are: $IRP_1 = (S_{20}, S_{15}, S_1, S_3)$; $IRP_2 = (S_{18}, S_7, S_{10}, S_{17})$; $IRP_3 = (S_2, S_{13}, S_{19}, S_6)$; $IRP_4 = (S_{16}, S_{14}, S_5, S_{12}, S_4)$; and $IRP_5 = (S_{11}, S_8, S_9)$;

– m' = 5, the DRPs are:

- $DRP_{t,1} = (S_{20}\{T_9,T_{37},T_{39}\},S_{15}\{T_{28},T_{58}\},S_1\{T_{19},T_{29},T_{66},T_{88}\},S_3\{T_3,T_{26},T_{32}, T_{33},T_{38},T_{42},T_{61},T_{85}\})$,

- $DRP_{t,2} = (S_{18}\{T_1,T_{13},T_{30},T_{36},T_{41},T_{65},T_{76},T_{77}\},S_7\{T_{34}\},S_{17}\{T_{25},T_{44},T_{60},T_{80}\})$,

- $DRP_{t,3} = (S_2\{T_{59},T_{78},T_{79},T_{84}\},S_{13}\{T_{53}\},S_{19}\{T_6,T_{16},T_{22},T_{52},T_{57},T_{67},T_{96}\}, S_6\{T_{68}\})$,

- $DRP_{t,4} = (S_{16}\{T_{63},T_{73},T_{74},T_{90}\},S_{14}\{T_{71}\},S_5\{T_{20},T_{86},T_{95},T_{99}\},S_{12}\{T_{75}, T_{83}\},S_4\{T_{21},T_{64},T_{81}\})$, and

- $DRP_{t,5} = (S_{11}\{T_{40},T_{56},T_{69}\},S_8\{T_{31},T_{35}\},S_9\{T_2,T_{82}\})$.

2.8.3.2. *Applying the negotiation process*

Taking the following set of unavailable nodes:

$$Ind_t = \{S_1,S_3,S_7,S_{14},S_5,S_{17},S_{12},S_9,S_{13},S_{19}\},$$

we deduce that the following tasks need reassigning:

$$\phi_t = \{T_{19},T_{29},T_{66},T_{88},T_3,T_{26},T_{32},T_{33},T_{38},T_{42},T_{61},T_{85},T_{34},T_{71},T_{20},T_{86},T_{95},T_{99}, T_{25},T_{44},T_{60},T_{80},T_{75},T_{83},T_2,T_{82},T_{53},T_6,T_{16},T_{22},T_{52},T_{57},T_{67},T_{96}\}$$

and we thus obtain 34 services that need reassigning.

In this example, the negotiation process allows us to reassign a larger part of the set ϕ_t (see Figure 2.16) thanks to the priorities of the ICAs, then thanks to their preferences and finally thanks to their constraints. For this simulation scenario, each stage of the proposed *ARDyCA* algorithm (see section 2.6.2) corresponds to two rounds of negotiation by iteration. In conclusion, thanks to this negotiation process between the ICAs and the SA from the same society, the system found new providers for the services that had been cancelled and allowed the minimization of expenses by best satisfying the users in favour of the disruption.

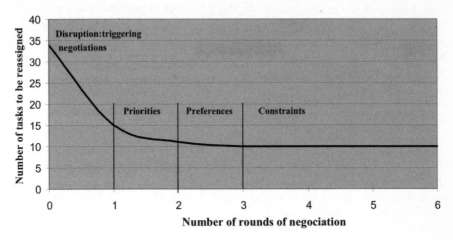

Figure 2.16. *Applying the negotiation protocol*

The work that we have presented in this chapter represents a model as well as the optimization and implementation of a global system that provides services for its users in the most effective way possible. As we have mentioned previously, these services can be a provision related directly to transport, such as itinerary demand, or indirectly related to transport, such as any information requested during the journey, e.g. a weather forecast or cultural information. However, the itinerary demand is an independent research problem [KAM 07]. The goal is always the same: removing the passenger's need to consult different sites to come up with a response to their request that can involve different services.

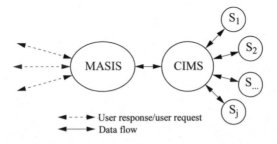

Figure 2.17. *Integration of a cooperative mobility system*

In the particular case of an itinerary demand, the goal is to avoid the situation where the passenger consults several sites from different public transport operators in order to plan his or her journey. In this particular case, namely when a request from an ISAM client contains an itinerary demand service, the response will not be provided directly by the transport operators but by a cooperative information mobility service (CIMS) allowing the best possible itinerary involving one or more operators to be compiled (see Figure 2.17).

2.8.4. *Case study of an itinerary service [KAM 07]*

Our objective is to create a CIMS capable of accessing transport operators' different information systems and then integrating the search results generated by their corresponding itinerary calculators. These results must be optimized according to user criteria, hence by resorting to distributed algorithms that calculate the shortest route, and adapting them to dynamic time graphs. Given the contribution of MAS in distributed information system engineering, a multi-agent approach was adopted that took into account the distribution as well as the heterogeneity of data within the network. Furthermore, multi-agent modeling of CIMS guarantees flexibility, enabling a versatile evolution in time and space, which fits well with its distributed and evolving character.

2.8.4.1. *The organization of cooperative information mobility service*

As mentioned previously, the CIMS must be capable of ensuring access to different transport operators' various information systems. An operator corresponds to an independent travel aiding information system that is connected to a transport network. Thus, for the design of CMIS, a transport information agent (TIA) was associated to each travel aiding information system in order to retrieve the information necessary for responding to a travel request. The latter is of the "go from A to B" type, where A and B are the departure and the arrival points of an itinerary that can be found through the means of transport of the same operator. However, when a user requests an multimodal service itinerary (which can be a combination between different modes of transport issued by different networks), the idea is to question the TIAs responsible in order to retrieve the necessary information to respond to local itinerary offers, this way composing a global offer. This task was entrusted to a mediating agent, called a broker agent. This agent will have to search for local responses in a field of search identified by a yearbook selecting agent. Thus, according to the itinerary service requested, the yearbook selecting agent will have to identify the TIAs responsible as well as the stations in common (see Figure 2.18). The stations in common are the intersecting nodes that are relative to the common stations called "exchange poles", and they enable passengers to change between transport operators. Each TIA will thus calculate the optimal local itinerary issued by its network so that the broker agent can finally calculate a global itinerary that is optimized starting from these local calculations.

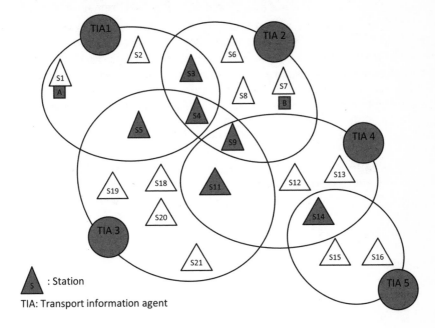

Figure 2.18. *Identifying information agents*

Every TIA calculates the end of the itinerary issued by its network with the aid of an algorithm that shows the shortest route, such as the Dijkstra algorithm [DIJ 59].

Then, the composer agent (CA) calculates the global itinerary thanks to another algorithm of the shortest distributed route, inspired by the work of Wang and Kaempke [WAN 04]. These authors developed the first algorithm of the shortest distributed route, which enabled the composition of a shorter global route starting from several networks represented by static graphs. However, the CIMS is characterized by dynamic graphs because the local itineraries calculated by the TIAs are not known beforehand as they are being created in real time and they change online according to user requests.

Consequently, for the needs of the CIMS, we have adapted this algorithm to our problem and implemented an algorithm of the shortest distributed route (SDR).

2.8.4.2. *The shortest distributed route algorithm*

This algorithm allows us to find a shorter route $P_G^*(A,B)$ from node A to node B in the G(N,E) graph that is an aggregation of $G_i(N_i,E_i)$ representing exchange poles (see section 2.8.4.1). N_i and E_i are, respectively, the set of nodes and the set of edges relative to a class C_i that we associate to a TIA_i. A node of class C_i symbolizes a station relative to the transport network of a particular operator delineated by the TIA_i; and an edge represents a round trip carried out by a means of transportation managed by the same operator. An edge (a,b) has a weight marked as d(a,b) with $(a,b) \in E_i$ if and only if $a \in N_i$ and $b \in N_i$ and the end of the route between a and b is ensured by a means of transport managed by C_i.

Consequently, G corresponds to the graph associated with the whole of the distributed environment defined by n classes C_i (see Figure 2.19) thus making G(N,E) an aggregation of $G_i(N_i,E_i)$, as previously mentioned, with:

$$N = \bigcup_{i=1}^{n} N_i \quad E = \bigcup_{i=1}^{n} E_i$$

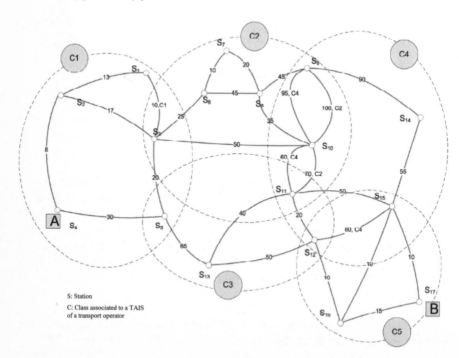

S: Station
C: Class associated to a TAIS
of a transport operator

Figure 2.19. *Example of a G(N,E) graph in a distributed environment*

The shortest distributed route algorithm allowing us to calculate the shortest global route $P_G^*(A,B)$ between two nodes A and B in a G(N,E) graph can be summed up in five main stages:

– stage 1: build the G_{cint} associated with G(N,E) knowing that $G_{cint}(N_{cint},E_{cint})$ is the complete intersection graph corresponding to the distributed G(N,E) graph and:

- the nodes in G_{cint} are the intersection nodes of the n classes of G(N,E):

$$N_{cint}= \bigcup_{i=1,j=1}^{n} (N_i \cap N_j)$$

- an edge (a,b) of E_{cint} must have $a \in N_{cint}$, $b \in N_{cint}$ and $\{a,b\} \subseteq N_i$ with N_i being the set of nodes in a class C_i;

– stage 2: build the $G_{eint}(A,B)$ associated with G(N,E) knowing that $G_{eint}(N_{eint},E_{eint})$ is the extended intersection graph corresponding to the distributed G(N,E) graph and:

- the nodes in G_{eint} are the nodes of G_{cint} to which we add nodes A and B if they are not already included in G_{cint}, thus:

$$N_{eint}=N_{cint} \cup \{A,B\}$$

- the edges of G_{eint} are all the edges of G_{cint} to which we add the set of edges relative to the shortest local routes enabling us to link A and B to the intersection nodes of relative classes to those arrival and departure nodes;

– stage 3: determine $P_{G_{eint(A,B)}}^* = \{s_1,...,s_m\}$ by carrying out a Dijkstra on $G_{eint}(A,B)$ with s_1-...-s_m being the intersection nodes of $P_{G_{eint(A,B)}}^*$;

– stage 4: for every k ($1 \leq k \leq m-1$):

- for (s_k,s_{k+1}) determine class C_i relative to the edge (s_k,s_{k+1}),

- for (s_k,s_{k+1}) determine the detail of $p_i^*(s_k,s_{k+1})$,

with $p_i^*(a,b)$ being the shortest local route associated with class C_i allowing us to move from A to B knowing that $d(p_i^*(a,b))=\min_{k=1,2,...,n_{p_i(a,b)}}\{d(p_i^k(a,b))\}$ so that:

- $n_{p_i(a,b)}$: the number of possible local routes between a and b relative to class C_i,

- $p_i^k(a,b)$: the k^{nd} local route in class C_i allowing us to go from a to b;

– stage 5: the $p_i^*(s_k, s_{k+1})$ make up the optimal global route $P_G^*(A,B)$.

As we have mentioned previously, we can calculate the shortest local route with the help of a classic algorithm dedicated to this type of problem, namely the Dijkstra algorithm [DIJ 50]. This point is studied more carefully by Zidi [ZID 06], who seeks to minimize the waiting times of passengers at exchange poles, especially in a degraded mode, by reassuring them, as much as possible, of the continuity of jouneys in multimodal networks.

2.9. Conclusion and perspectives

In this chapter, we have presented an ISAM equipped with optimization algorithms. The main goal is to provide mobile users (travelling on foot, using public transport, etc.) with the best possible response to their requests in terms of cost and delay. In order to do this, we have advanced a two-levelled optimization solution that enables us to build the journeys of MAs as effectively as possible so that the latter can move on a distributed network when needed and search for the information relating to these services.

Furthermore, the itinerary demand services are specific services that, by themselves, require us to carry out a MAs equipped with distributed algorithms of the shortest route. We have also ensured the robustness of an ISAM in the face of random variations in the network thanks to the implementation of a negotiation process between optimizing the stationary agents and MAs of the system. In order to limit expenses and try to provide the services demanded despite these random variations, this protocol is triggered every time a disruption is detected. However, the complexity of the interaction between the different entities in the system require the generation of a common, universal set of references, in the form of a flexible and dynamic ontology that enables systems to communicate with each other. Our main goal is to solve problems of heterogeneity, where each system can use different terms with the same meaning or the same term with different meanings.

In view of this work, it would be useful to generalize the proposed protocol in order to control the interaction between several initiators and participants, for example in the case of overlap between sets of user requests.

2.10. List of abbreviations

– ADB: Archiving Database

– ADiRICA: Algorithm of Dynamic Reconstruction of ICA Agent Routes

– CoJPa: Construction of Journey Patterns

– CIMS: Cooperative Information Mobility Service

– DRP: Definite Route Plan

– EMASN: Extended Mobility Aiding Services Network

– FOMS: Flexible Ontology Multiservice System

– IA: Interface Agent

– IdA: Identifying Agent

– ICA: Intelligent Collecting Agent

– IRP: Initial Route Plan

– ISAM: Infomation System that Aids Mobility

– MgA: Merging Agent

– MA: Mobile Agent

– MAS: Multi-Agent System

– RP: Route Plan

– SA: Scheduling Agent

– TemInd: Time Indicator

– TIA: Transport Information Agent

– UpInd: Updating Indicator

2.11. Bibliography

[BAE 01] BAEK J.W., YEO J.H., KIM G.T., YEOM H.Y., "Cost effective mobile agent planning for distributed information retrieval", *Proceedings of the 21st International Conference on Distributed Computing Systems*, pp. 65-72, School of Computer science and Engineering, Seoul National University, US, 2001.

[BEN 05] BEN KHALED I., KAMOUN M.A., ZIDI K., HAMMADI S., "Vers un système d'information voyageur multimodal (SIM) à base de système multi agent (SMA), "*REE*, no. 1, pp. 41-47, 2005.

[BUS 03] BUSE D.P., FENG J.Q., WU Q.H., "Mobile agents for data analysis in industrial automation systems", *Proceedings of the IEEE/WIC Int'l Conf. on Intelligent Agent Technology (IAT'03)*, pp. 60-66, Halifax, Canada, October 2003.

[CAI 04] CAIRE G., CABANILLAS D., "JADE tutorial applications-defined content languages and ontologies, *Tutorial JADE*, TILAB (formerly CSELT), November 2004.

[CAR 97] CARZANIGA A., PICCO G.P., VIGNA G., "Designing distributed applications with mobile code paradigms", *Proceedings of the 19th International Conference on Software Engineering*, pp. 22-32, New York, US, July 1997.

[DIJ 59] DIJKSTRA E.W., "A note on two problems in connection with graphs", *Numerische Matematik*, vol. 1, pp. 269-271, 1959.

[GRE 05] GREENWOOD D., "JADE Web Service Integration Gateway (WSIG), Whitestein Technologies", *Tutorial JADE*, AAMAS, 2005.

[KAM 07] KAMOUN M.A., Conception d'un système d'information pour l'aide au déplacement multimodal: une approche multi-agents pour la recherche et la composition des itinéraires en ligne, doctoral thesis, Ecole Centrale de Lille et Université des Sciences et Technologies de Lille (LAGIS)/ESTAS de l'INRETS, 2007.

[KET 05] KETEL M., DOGAN N.S., HOMAIFAR A., "Distributed sensor networks based on mobile agents paradigms", *System Theory, SSST'2005*, pp. 411-414, Department of Computer Science, North Carolina A&T State University, Greensboro, US, 2005.

[LUB 03] LUB X., MORI K., "Autonomous information services integration and allocation in agent-based information service system", *Proceedings of the IEEE/WIC International Conference on Intelligent Agent Technology (IAT'03)*, pp. 290-296, Halifax, Canada, October 2003.

[PHA 98] PHARM V.A., KARMOUCH A., "Mobile software agents: an overview", *IEEE Communication Magazine*, vol. 36, no. 7, pp. 26-37, 1998.

[PIC 97] PICCO G.P., BALDI M., "Evaluating the tradeoffs of mobile code design paradigms in network management applications", *Proceedings of the 20th IEEE International Conference on Software Engineering (ICSE'97)*, pp.146-155, Kyoto, Japan, April 1998.

[SAA 08] SAAD S., ZGAYA H., HAMMADI H., "Novel ontology model for communicating heterogeneous negotiation mobile-agent in a transport environment", *Studies in Informatics and Control Journal (SIC)*, vol. 17, no. 4, pp. 333-352, 2008.

[SMI 80] SMITH R.G., "The Contract Net Protocol: highlevel communication and control in a distributed problem solver", *IEEE Transactions on computers*, vol. 29, no. 12, pp. 1104-1113, 1980.

[THE 99] THEILMANN W., ROTHERMEL K., "Efficient dissemination of mobile agents", *Proceedings of the 19th IEEE International Conference on Distributed Computing Systems Workshop (ICDCSW')*, *IEEE Computer Society*, pp. 9-14, Austin, US, May 31-June 4, 1999.

[WAN 04] WANG J., KAEMPKE T., "Shortest route computation in distributed systems", *Computers and Operations Research*, vol. 31, pp. 1621-1633, 2004.

[ZGA 05a] ZGAYA H., HAMMADI S., GHÉDIRA K., "Workplan mobile agent for the transport network application", *Proceedings of the 17th IMACS World Congress Scientific Computation Applied Mathematics and Simulation (IMACS'2005)*, pp. 11-15, Paris, July 2005.

[ZGA 05b] ZGAYA H., HAMMADI S., GHÉDIRA K., "Evolutionary method to optimize Workplan mobile agent for the transport network application", *Proceedings of the International Conference on Systems, Man and Cybernetics (IEEE SMC'2005)*, pp. 1174-1179, Hawaii, US, October 2005.

[ZGA 06a] ZGAYA H., HAMMADI S., "Dynamic approach to reassign tasks when servers breakdown in a multi-modal information system", *Proceedings of the 2006 IMACS Multiconference on Computational Engineering in Systems Applications (CESA'2006)*, pp. 985-991, Tsinghua University Press, Beijing, China, October 2006.

[ZGA 06b] ZGAYA H., HAMMADI S., "Assignment and integration of distributed transport services in agent-based architecture", *Proceedings of the IEEE/WIC International Conference on Intelligent Agent Technology (IAT'06)*, pp. 96-102, Hong Kong, China, December 2006.

[ZGA 07] ZGAYA H., Conception et optimisation distribuée d'un système d'information d'aide à la mobilité urbaine: une approche multi-agents pour la recherche et la composition des services liés au transport, doctoral thesis, Ecole Centrale de Lille (LAGIS), 6 July 2007.

[ZGA 08] ZGAYA H., HAMMADI S., GHÉDIRA K., "Combination of mobile agent and evolutionary algorithm to optimize the client transport services", *RAIRO-Operations Research Special Issue on Cooperative methods for Multiobjective,* vol. 42, no. 1, pp. 35-67, 2008.

[ZID 04] ZIDI K., HAMMADI S., "CGOMFP Control Genetic Operators with Management of the Final Population to optimize a multimodal transport moving", *IEEE SMC 2004*, The Hague, Netherlands, October 10-13, 2004.

[ZID 06] ZIDI K., Système Interactif d'Aide au Déplacement Multimodal (SIADM), doctoral thesis, LAGIS de l'Ecole Centrale de Lille et l'Université des Sciences et Technologies de Lille, December 2006.

[ZIT 98] ZITZLER E., THIELE L., "Multiobjective optimization using evolutionary algorithms: A comparative case study", *Lecture Notes in Computer Science*, vol. 1498, pp. 292-301, 1998.

Chapter 3

Inter-vehicle Services and Communication

3.1. Introduction

The context of transport-related applications has been widely dissociated from actual modes of transport. In fact, mobile terminals with fairly high processing capabilities as well as an acceptable size have only recently become popular (the first Pocket PC was created at the beginning of 2000). In the first step, the notion of transport-related applications was logically connected to a set of services that were accessible from a static machine (servers, workstations, and calculators) and that sought to simplify, for instance, the implementation of freight transportation or the management of a fleet of vehicles. As we have mentioned previously, the optimization of these means of transport and of vehicles in general was and continues to be the motivation behind many applications that seek to improve vehicle rounds, minimize costs or improve the services on offer.

An increasingly significant part of transport-oriented applications, however, is being specifically targeted at vehicles themselves, with the final goal of embedding these applications in the actual vehicles. The objective is to advise the user, as accurately as possible, according to his or her needs. These new applications offer a wide range of services. For instance, one application can guide the driver towards an available parking space. A different application can inform drivers in the case of specific events (accidents, improvement works, etc.). Yet another application can offer the driver information related to the environment in which his or her vehicle is

Chapter written by Sylvain LECOMTE, Thierry DELOT and Mikael DESERTOT.

based. These applications, which are varied yet complementary, seek to make the driving experience safer, more efficient and more economical (limiting the number of miles travelled to reach the final destination).

In this context, it becomes evident that vehicles must adopt a new kind of equipment that enables them, in real time, to connect to and execute several services, but also to communicate and interact with their environment. These materials can come in many forms, from cell phone terminals, still largely used for calling people, to all-inclusive platforms incorporated directly into the vehicle. The latter have already emerged on certain car models[1], but they are also being integrated by different vehicle manufacturers, though this has been recent.

We can mention, for example, the integration of a "green wave" calculation mechanism by Audi that enables the driver, via communication between the car and the infrastructure, to arrive at the traffic light precisely when the light turns green (with the aim of reducing CO_2[2] emissions). Similarly, Peugeot has incorporated a Wi-Fi environment and remote 3G access in its 5008 model with the *Wifi On Board*[3].

This chapter presents the field of services and communication technologies in an inter-vehicle context. The new transport-related services that we are about to present are limited by a number of domain-specific characteristics. In particular, whereas in the field of transport the constraints that are identical to those in the field of ambient computing can easily be identified, additional constraints will require new, tailor-made solutions. Among these constraints, the main ones concern:

– *Using the services*: given the set of data and available services at a given time *t*, according to the context [DEY 00, GRI 08, GRA 09] we need to choose which data are reliable enough to be processed or which services need to be released, connected or updated.

– *The diversity of various stakeholders*: a first type of exchange obviously regards the vehicles. Exchanges can, however, also occur between vehicles and fixed points (parking pay stations, wireless access points, etc.). Finally, if the constraints are still too strong in the context of two mobile systems that are too different from each other, it is still possible to instigate communication between a pedestrian with a communicating mobile device and a vehicle.

---

1 www.osgi.org/wiki/uploads/Congress2003/OSGiWorld_BMW_AutomotiveTrack_Day2.pdf.
2 www.newspress.co.uk/DAILY_LINKS/arc_sep_2008/190908aud.htm.
3 www.edmunds.com/insideline/do/News/articleId=157327.

– *Grand mobility*: a vehicle, whether a car or a truck, moves at different speeds. Thus, the information exchange, or the exchange of services or data, quickly becomes a challenge with regards to the coherence and integrity of that data.

– *The multitude of communication media*: if personal services in the context of home automation are mainly based on Wi-Fi networks in infrastructure mode or on Bluetooth networks, the context of other vehicles requires other means of communication, such as *ad hoc* Wi-Fi communication between different external stakeholders or 3G communication for remote services in environments without Wi-Fi coverage. The connection can even become wired in cases where the processing is carried out by the vehicle manufacturer in the service garage (analog-to-digital converting bus, Ethernet).

– *Deployment*: the deployment as well as the updating of services is problematic in a mobile system whose connectivity is not guaranteed over time. The challenges of administering these environments have only recently begun to be resolved by the platform intermediary, with the help of dynamic services. These specificities as well as the additional constraints make up one of the most actively emerging fields. This chapter, with the help of examples, approaches the different possible solutions that could be implemented. The works of research that we present were carried out at the University of Valenciennes and Hainaut-Cambrésis/LAMIH[4], within the SyME (Mobile and Embedded System) research theme carried out by the DIM team (Decisional and mobile computer Science, Decision, Informatique et Mobilité in French). The examples and results of the experiments that illustrate this chapter were started with the VESPA (*Vehicular Event Sharing with a mobile Peer-to-peer Architecture*) prototype, a vehicle-oriented event-sharing application that relies on an *ad-hoc* peer-to-peer mobile architecture. This chapter will equally rely on other research, carried out by the IFSTTAR (French Institute of Science and Technology for Transport, Development and Networks) or by the LIG (Grenoble Computer Science Laboratory)[5].

Particular attention will be paid to the implementation and choice of communication media, to the management of data reliability and to deployment and connectivity issues. Thus, having the execution baseware already available, we have opened the door to an entire set of services, whether free or otherwise, that are being offered by several providers. The combinations of available services will also rapidly increase. A strong interaction between different stakeholders will result in significant service improvement for drivers. The challenge now consists more in the way in which these services will be created, maintained, deployed or assembled, rather than in the way in which they will be incorporated.

---

4 www.univ-valenciennes.fr/LAMIH/.

5 www.liglab.fr/.

Throughout this chapter we will start by describing the specificities of services and inter-vehicle communication. Next, we will focus on the specificities of inter-vehicle communication. The later sections will present the implementation of inter-vehicle services in different projects, and the problems related to the deployment and maintenance of this type of embedded mobile application. Finally, the chapter will end with some predictions on the future of services and inter-vehicle communication technologies.

3.2. The specificity of inter-vehicle communication

As we have mentioned in the introduction, inter-vehicle services inherit the same characteristics as the services related to ambient computing. This field was always associated with a well-defined and static environment (such as a building, a house, a factory, etc.) filled with data captors and stakeholders capable of communicating with each other. Communication is generally achieved via a centralized controller or a piece of mobile equipment that one of the users in that environment has at his or her disposal. Depending on the information collected and on the services available, the user is presented with many choices regarding his or her environment or the information he or she can obtain. Mobile terminals are becoming more widely used at the moment and it is a widely acknowledged fact that most people usually have at least one means of communication (e.g. a cell telephone) on their person.

This kind of equipment has recently been upgraded with increasingly advanced functions. Among these, the ones most relevant for our purposes are the geo-location functions that allow the user to define itineraries starting from his or her position or to find the nearest services and the large panel of available technologies (EDGE, 3G, Bluetooth, Wi-Fi). These new models of mobile terminals help to bridge the gap between vehicular services (the global positioning system [GPS] and other position-determination technologies) and personal services, which can be accessed by anyone anywhere. It is now possible to benefit from an entire set of services, not only in a traditional pervasive context but also in an inter-vehicle context, by using the same equipment we once used solely for making phone calls.

For example, a pedestrian walking in the town center (see Figure 3.1) could use services such as online shopping, geo-location, telephony, social networks, advertising, etc. He or she can also access the usual Internet services via his or her network connection (weather forecast, news, e-mail, etc.).

This same pedestrian, once in his or her vehicle, may wish to continue using the same service panel (see Figure 3.2). Here, too, he or she can be assisted by a set of environment-specific services, which we will call inter-vehicle services. Such services provide useful traffic-related information, such as information about improvement works or accidents.

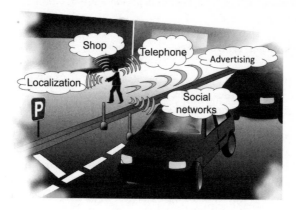

Figure 3.1. *A pedestrian connecting to different services*

Starting from this observation, looking at the continuity between services and communication technologies in a pervasive environment on the one hand and the context of vehicles on the other hand, it becomes evident that the constraints related to the first field will extend to the field of transport. This continuity means that the same devices and the same principles can apply to vehicles. The applications designed for ambient computing environments must handle the activity of their new environment and rely on flexible and dynamic architectures. The same goes for inter-vehicle services, although additional constraints define this specific domain.

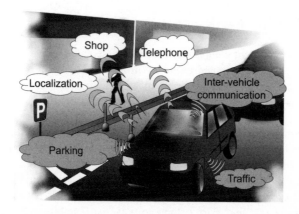

Figure 3.2. *The services and data that can be used by a vehicle*

The remainder of this section presents the definition of an inter-vehicle service, details the differences between ambient computing and inter-vehicle computing, and finally identifies the different types of stakeholders involved.

3.2.1. *What is an inter-vehicle service?*

The term "inter-vehicle service" designates the set of capabilities that a means of transport must have in order to interact with its environment. This interaction and communication can be carried out in various ways:

– by sharing the information a vehicle has. This information may have been directly collected by the vehicle that transmits it (for example a vehicle that has just vacated a parking space and chooses to send this information) or the vehicle might have in its turn collected some information and wishes to convey it even further (for instance a vehicle was informed of the existence of an accident and continues to pass this information on to other vehicles);

– by downloading and installing applications. These resources facilitate the users' experience while driving; and

– by connecting to remote services, whether they are proposed by peers (other vehicles), whether they are offered by the nearest providers or even if they are accessible via the Internet (see section 3.2.3.)

The field of transport for which inter-vehicle services were originally conceived involves certain specificities that will have an impact on the way in which these services will be carried out (see section 3.3.1).

3.2.2. *Inter-vehicle services versus ambient computing*

The notion of ambient computing is already associated with a set of technologies and equipment that is distributed in the environment. This term can also be found in relevant literature and is also referred to as the "Internet of things", "pervasive computing" [HAN 03], smart space or even "ubiquitous computing".

This equipment has computing as well as storage capabilities that offer its users complementary services in their own environment. In practice, the equipment used to implement ambient computing is characterized as embedded, distributed and non-invasive. Most of the time these three are interconnected and they are highly significant in relation to the problem of communication. What is more, they are dynamic in the sense that they belong to a type of mobile equipment that must respond to certain self-adaptability criteria in order to be able to run in different contexts.

Ambient computing can be found everywhere – in a house, a hospital, a public space, a building, in the street, etc. Inter-vehicle computing is similar to the notion of ambient computing.

On the one hand, ambient computing is placed in the continuity of the services provided to a user. This implies that the same properties will be shared. The difference comes from the constraints of the environment in which this computing is executed. On the other hand, the problems related to the field of transport need to be overcome, and although they are specific to transport most of their solutions will be the same as those available for ambient computing.

Certain specific aspects of the environment (see section 3.3.1) require solutions to be adapted to every need. These same specific aspects are the ones that require complementary solutions in order to respond to constraints. These solutions thus complement those that are available in ambient computing (see Figure 3.3).

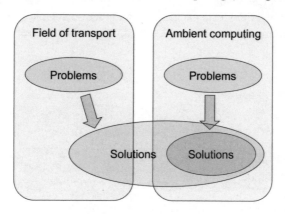

Figure 3.3. *Problems and solutions in ambient computing and inter-vehicle computing*

Finally, the usual problems related to distributed systems and the data handling are the same in ambient and inter-vehicle computing. Distributed systems introduce certain boundaries in terms of reliability, architecture and fault tolerance. Data manipulation, however, is subject to different obstacles regarding the processing and dissemination of personal information that can harm users. These constraints, far from being solved, are common to various domains related to identification and they first go through a set of legal solutions and solutions related to the evolution of mentalities, before actually being solved from a technical point of view.

3.2.3. *What type of stakeholders are involved?*

Different types of stakeholders may come into play. We can distinguish between two main categories of stakeholders:

– *mobile stakeholders*: these include peers (other vehicles) and also other remote communication stakeholders (for example a pedestrian having access to a communicating mobile device) who are in the vicinity; and

– *static stakeholders*: these are mainly communicating infrastructures that can be found in a city, such as parking spaces, information points, shops or in specific places such as freeway toll points.

The main differences between these two categories are the mode of communication as mobile stakeholders will favor *ad hoc* communication modes; and the type of exchanges made. The connection with static stakeholders will be more stable, and possibly allow data exchange at a higher rate. Such connection will thus enable the implementation of more evolved, more complex services that use up more resources.

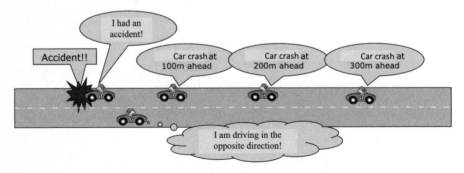

Figure 3.4. *Application of vehicle-to-vehicle communication*

Figure 3.4 shows an example of an application that enables the communication between two vehicles (vehicle-to-vehicle or V2V communication). The different stakeholders are all identical here: they are cars that run in both directions on the road. If the car at the head of a queue of vehicles spots an accident, it is capable of transmitting the information to a restricted zone around it (the limits of this zone depend on the equipment used or on the constraints of the software chosen). This information can be used by the vehicles that follow, in order to inform the driver and thus lead to greater safety. The vehicle that is travelling in the opposite direction can, in turn, be a transmission vector for this information – even if the information does not directly concern it. This may enable the data to travel farther than the actual place of the accident, reaching the vehicles concerned in the case where there is no relaying vehicle running in the same direction. The main problem here is deciding what information should be conveyed, how far away it should travel, whether the driver should be notified or not, etc. In the example of the application presented in section 3.3.2.1, VESPA proposes that the information be processed and characterized according to the reliability of the data collected.

Figure 3.5. *Vehicle–environment interaction*

Figure 3.5 presents the interactions that are possible between a vehicle and static stakeholders (or the infrastructure, V2I, "vehicle to infrastructure"). The so-called static stakeholders are communication bases – which are usually wireless – and are situated near roads. The different stakeholders that want to exhibit data or services deploy them. Several types of applications are being presented:

– A communication and an information exchange can take place between a vehicle and an underground parking lot. The parking lot offers a detailed plan of its several levels. The driver is thus guided directly towards an available parking space. Information of such precision was not originally available on embedded GPS terminals (we can imagine how difficult it would be to index all the parking lots in France). However, thanks to this communication technology, the information can travel easily, although temporarily. It can be erased as soon as the driver finds the available space.

– When entering a town or a city, a driver can be informed of cultural activities available, and also particularly congested locations. In order to do this, a communication base could be set up in a tourist office and spread this type of information. For larger dissemination within a city, the bus stops, which are currently being equipped with more means of dissemination, could easily extend coverage in terms of communication and information exchange.

– Besides disseminating information and services relating to the town where they are located, these same bus stops can also offer driving aid services, such as locating parking lots near public transport.

– The shops that can be found while driving in a commercial area can also be vectors for the dissemination of data and services. They can signal the products offered, or the current promotional offers. If this type of information is more likely to disturb the driver rather than to help him or her drive, the data can be stored in order to be used later when the driver becomes a pedestrian, once his or her vehicle is parked. Using this type of service may, however, be useful if the driver knows what kind of product he or she is looking for. By configuring a search for the desired item, the driver will be notified when a nearby shop offers that item. This helps to avoid slow driving and unexpected or sudden stops and prevent dangerous driving behaviors that could be caused by a visual scrutiny of the shops.

This proposed service panel could go as far as highly evolved applications, but is still difficult to implement at the moment. For example, a fast food restaurant that offers drive-through services could set up a service whereby the order is placed straight from the vehicle. Taking the order would thus be easier, since the restaurant can insist on certain items by means of data that it exposes and this could reduce waiting times.

Finally, certain stakeholders should rely on specific connection modes. For example, the car dealer that is responsible for maintenance will, for example, want to connect to a wired network in the car. If the data he or she is looking for is technical, this can be an effective way of carrying out updates on large pieces of software. In cases where a mobile terminal is used, such updates are cut out from the car maintenance and only deal with updating an application on the mobile.

However, as we have mentioned in the introduction, platforms are increasingly being integrated, to the point of being almost fully embedded in the vehicles. A mobile terminal, such as the telephone, will become a new type of external stakeholder; communication with this stakeholder will be possible to provide useful data for the driver for when he or she gets out of the vehicle.

The multiplication of stakeholders, whether static or mobile, brings a whole new set of problems that will have to be approached in order to carry out inter-vehicle services and enable communication between different technologies.

The first of these problems regards the deployment of resources, services and the computing components that are necessary to aid the driver. It must be possible to add these modules on to the platform in a dynamic way, without having to reboot so that the services that are being used remain available. This constraint is coupled with the fact that the set-up will need to be implemented while the vehicle is still in motion. The task is facilitated when the vehicle is travelling slowly but can become very complicated at higher speeds.

A second problem arises when several stakeholders wish to deploy services or components in the same environment, i.e. the environment embedded in the vehicle. It thus becomes necessary to isolate the different applications, to manage the different versions of services, etc. Yet, at the same time, complete isolation of the different applications takes up space in the storage memory (with a potential multiplication of similar software components). Hence, there must be a compromise between re-utilization and isolation.

Finally, different safety issues are related to these domains, whether they concern the deployment or collection of data. Not everyone should be capable of deploying whatever resource they want to vehicles; similarly, an application must make sure that the service it uses does not compromise the data it must process. These problems are classical in all domains seeking to link multiple stakeholders together; there are solutions for these problems, although they depend on the choice of environment chosen for execution.

The diversity of these stakeholders thus influences the architecture of a vehicle-oriented application. A consequence of this diversity is a different way of interacting, according to the context in which the vehicle evolves and the kind of stakeholder the vehicle could be connected to. In fact, ways of connecting services or transferring data will become increasingly important in what follows. They are described in detail in section 3.3.3.

3.3. Inter-vehicle communication

Over the past few years, numerous research endeavors have focused on inter-vehicle communication networks. Several protocols were thus created in order to enable vehicles to exchange information via wireless networks. In this section, we will present the constraints imposed by inter-vehicle communication and the different solutions that we can consider or will soon materialize.

3.3.1. *What constraints?*

3.3.1.1. *The dynamic aspect*

The most restrictive characteristic of inter-vehicle networks is undoubtedly the considerable mobility of the information-exchanging nodes. Not only does the travelling speed of vehicles make the transmission of information to vehicles more difficult, but it also causes the data received to quickly become outdated.

3.3.1.2. *Networks*

Various research efforts have so far explored the use of short-range networks (for instance IEEE 802.11, ultra large band, etc.) to create driving assistance services. These networks enable two vehicles in close proximity (i.e. a few hundred meters away from each other, at most) to exchange information when they are within communication range. Cell phone networks (for example 3G networks) can get around this constraint, but in turn they require the use of an intermediary service for the transmission of information. Hence, they can increase communication times to the point where they are not helpful in certain cases (e.g. communicating emergency braking to the vehicles behind).

3.3.2. *Can we do without communication architecture?*

We can distinguish between two modes of communication in the context of inter-vehicle services. The first mode, called the *ad hoc* mode, consists of exchanging data directly with nearby vehicles by using short-range networks. The second solution consists of exploiting a communication infrastructure, thanks to which the vehicles can disseminate and/or receive information. Whereas such infrastructures generally enable us to greatly simplify the channeling of information to vehicles, they cannot be envisaged in the short term throughout entire routes. Direct communication between vehicles thus provides an interesting alternative for the deployment of the first inter-vehicle services. Eventually, the two solutions may turn out to be complementary.

The example of VESPA that will be described in the next section proves that it is possible to bypass the architecture, especially when having to notify the driver of events taking place near the user. The absence of such architecture allows a better system reactivity (because this reactivity works without the use of a server, it is more difficult to update). However, in the case of more remote services, using fixed elements in the architecture entails a better management of information and it allows for the information to be channeled with greater ease.

3.3.2.1. *The example of VESPA*

In this section, we will focus on VESPA (*Vehicular Event Sharing with a mobile Peer-to-peer Architecture*), a system that we have designed to enable the sharing of information between vehicles by using *ad hoc* inter-vehicle networks. The unique contribution of our VESPA system is that it proposes a generic approach that enables various kinds of information to be shared.

Nowadays, the solutions available in the context of inter-vehicle communication are dedicated to a particular type of event: sharing information about available parking areas [XU 04], exchanging information related to emergency braking [MOR 03, DEB 04], and other solutions regarding the exchange of traffic-related information in real-time [ZHO 08].

Currently there are several events that it might be useful to inform other vehicles of (such as accidents, traffic jams, emergency braking, parking areas, emergency-response vehicles, etc.) and it is inconceivable that a driver should use a different system for every information type that he or she is interested in. Our contribution thus enables information to be shared between vehicles about any type of event, including mobile events (for example a vehicle whose rear lights are faulty) – and this is something that other solutions do not currently provide.

A prototype of this system was created at the LAMIH at the University of Valenciennes (see Figure 3.6).

One of the main functions of VESPA is the assessment of the validity of an event experienced by a vehicle, i.e. determining the probability of a vehicle encountering the event, especially in order to warn or inform the driver if needed [DEL 08]. A dissemination protocol enables the dissemination of information about generated events to vehicles that may be concerned, at the same time as ensuring that the network will not be spammed [CEN 08].

Figure 3.6. *The VESPA application*

3.3.2.2. *The EasyRide example*

EasyRIDE is a project developed by engineering students at the University Joseph Fourrier in Grenoble, that offers a dynamic car pooling service (which means that the request for information is made precisely when it is needed and not in a predicted manner). This service is based on the use of mobile technologies and the use of servers, see Figure 3.7[6].

Figure 3.7. *Dynamic car-pooling with EasyRIDE*

EasyRide uses a server to manage the registrations and thus to facilitate the fiscal aspects of charging and tax relief (fiscal aids for using services that reduce CO_2 emissions), but also to facilitate contact between a driver and a "client", who may be far and away from each other at the time of the car pooling agreement.

3.3.2.3. *The example of RouveCOM*

RouveCOM [GRA 04] is a project that involves two stages: first, the work is carried out on the inter-vehicle communication (V2V communication), but there is also a second step that seeks to offer a communication architecture between vehicles and a fixed infrastructure (V2I communication) that can be found along the entire road (and that uses the emergency stop terminals, which can be found along the freeway, for this purpose).

The vehicle thus equipped is presented in Figure 3.8. The wireless connections serve a double purpose (V2V and V2I).

---

6 http://ricmnfc.free.fr/public/index.html.

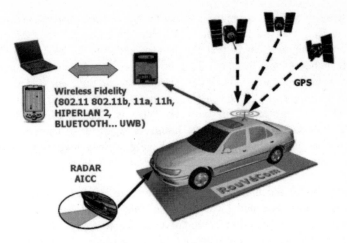

Figure 3.8. *Vehicle equipped with a RouveCOM*

3.3.3. *Data exchange or service invocation?*

In order to assist drivers by the transmission of useful information, two approaches can be used. The first one consists of diffusing the data towards the vehicles, where the data will be processed in order to inform the driver if necessary. The second approach consists of invocaking remote services from the vehicle in order to obtain this information by using cell phone networks, for example. The first solution is currently the most widespread. However, access to remote services offers the possibility of accessing other sources of information for drivers that might prove especially valuable (for example, Web services providing traffic-related information or the price of motor fuel). These two approaches are not conflicting, but they complement each other. The "data" approach, being the most convincing in the context of *ad hoc* communication, is complemented by the service approach where we can fully benefit from the possibility of using remote servers when a communication infrastructure is being used.

3.4. Deployment and maintenance

The constraints related to vehicular environment make the deployment process, as well as the updating and maintenance of the deployed applications, particularly complex. This problem becomes crucial, however, when we need to handle evolving protocols, safety updates or to enable stakeholders to be able to dynamically deploy software components.

In the case of ambient computing, every mobile terminal that is used for driving or for interacting with the environment is frequently connected to a static terminal, usually for the simple reason that the battery needs to be recharged. It is thus possible to benefit from this period of time when the device is connected to a network in order to update or install new applications. In the context of vehicles, this principle is no longer valid. The vehicle does not need to be recharged and so it does not need to be connected to any network. What is more, it can be situated at a reasonable distance from its owner's house or apartment. Therefore, it is not possible to rely on the fact that we will benefit from a high flow, durable and reliable connection in carrying out the set of operations desired.

The deployment and maintenance must therefore rely on specific architectures that are specifically designed for evolving in this kind of environment, which is really dynamic, while ensuring competitive access to the platform. This section presents the needs and different solutions for this problem. A concrete example of implementing such a solution is described using the VESPA applications presented in section 3.3.2.1.

3.4.1. *What are the deployment needs?*

There are two types of needs relating to the deployment of applications and vehicular environments:

– It is necessary to be able to update every system that can be found in the vehicle. In particular, certain basic software building blocks have to be embedded in order to achieve a minimum bootstrap for the entire set of applications and services. These basic building blocks are usually accompanied by a set of basic services that will in turn facilitate the implementation of future applications. They must be able to benefit from software developments and so it must be possible to dynamically update them.

– Inter-vehicle communication allows the stakeholders to exchange information, services and resources. This exchange includes the transfer, but also the installation and release of these stakeholders. It must, therefore, be possible to add new parts to the application. Furthermore, this addition must be possible as a hot-patch and it must be able to withstand fluctuations in the quality of connection. For instance, if vehicles running in opposite directions are sharing certain resources, the active connection time is short and so it is unlikely that the entire transfer will be completed. The ability to restart this transfer when another source becomes available is the responsibility of the platform. For instance, the next available vehicle that possesses this resource will finish the transfer.

These two needs involve a certain number of problems, some of which have already been addressed in other fields. Thus, it is possible to benefit from "off-the-shelf" solutions in order to solve most of these problems.

The management of different versions of the elements is one of the main problems that need to be addressed. Knowing whether an element needs to be updated is indispensable, on the one hand in avoiding useless transfers and on the other hand in avoiding the risk of destabilizing the system by inserting an incompatible element. The management of these versions thus introduces a new need – that of knowing which versions of the modules are necessary. Inter-vehicle application consists of a set of modules that interact with one another. However, assembling these modules remains subject to rules of interface design and strict combinations, dictated by the characteristics of each component.

Therefore, another difficulty resides in the possibility of defining the dependencies in terms of resources and the versions required for the different modules to be deployed. If a software service is deployed and it requires a third service in a specific version, it must be able to:

– specify these dependencies and identify the versions necessary for creating a deployment plan;

– know at every moment the state of the software embedded in the vehicle in order to avoid redundant deployment; and

– know where and how to retrieve the correct versions of each element.

This problem has already been considered for the deployment of applications in distributed environments, but it must be adapted to the vehicular context. In fact, the environmental constraints dictate the ability to manage partial deployments. However, this type of need cannot be found in an environment where the network connection is supposedly reliable and continuous. What is more, it is important for our context to be able to fully benefit from every service or piece of data as soon as it is available. The deployments can become competitive in the case where two services depend on the same module and demand the installation of that module. This event must be managed and the system must be able to respond to this type of request.

Offering every stakeholder the possibility of deploying resources or sending the data on a vehicular applicative platform reveals new complexities. Such a deployment must not be harmful to the applications already running. The arrival of new data or new services has to be made in a reliable way or it should not be carried out at all. This reliability can be breached unintentionally or it can be the result of a malicious behavior on the part of a stakeholder. This is why safety is required in order to guarantee such architecture, as it is necessary in all distributed systems. It is important to be able to certify that trustworthy stakeholders produce the collected data retrieved. We must also ensure that the service user is able to transmit sensitive information without being afraid of his or her details being captured and that the services used do not have any malicious code.

Different solutions can be used to solve all of these problems, with the aid of the different deployment mechanisms available at the moment.

3.4.2. *Available deployment mechanisms*

Deployment can be broken down into four different notions:

– formulating the needs in relation to deployment. For every resource or service to be deployed, we must know its needs in terms of third-party services or execution environment;

– the putting together or the dynamic processing of the different data and services deployed;

– conditioning the elements to be deployed. In order to be able to transmit and retrieve the information necessary for deployment, the different data must be wrapped up in a format that can be understood by all; and

– the deployment itself, namely the actual transfer from the deployment unit of the transmitter towards the receiver.

The first two points should be provided by the platform architecture, so the final two points depend on the model used by the platform. The following two sections introduce the architecture and the model retrieved for inter-vehicle computing.

3.4.2.1. *Platforms with dynamic services*

A service-oriented architecture rests on three fundamental entities, common to all architectures. These entities are: the service provider, the consumer and the registry. The interaction between them is made thus: the service provider specifies a service and enables consumers to discover it. In order to do this, it registers the service in a service registry (also called a directory). This registry presents the specification to every consumer in search of a precise service. Once the negotiation with the registry is completed, this consumer obtains one or more references towards the service implementation according to the researched contract. The user is able from this moment on to use this service.

The service architecture is called dynamic architecture when the providers and service consumers can join and leave the architecture in the course of its execution. The connections between the services are created as needs evolve.

Given the dynamic environment in which services are usually performed, one of the challenges frequently addressed in the relevant literature[7] proposes an effective and reliable way of assembling an application.

The definition of the architecture of an application is one of the inherent properties of models with different components. The latter generally facilitate the assembly and reuse of different components by relying on dependency descriptors and on the naming of the different components used. This naming of components is opposed to the negotiation carried out when the references are towards the services being retrieved. Thus, the execution environment of the components is less dynamic because of these strong connections, which are fixed before the instantiation of an application.

In the domain of services, an assembly is created from elements provided by different organizations. Each of these elements thus has a lifecycle that is independent from the others; this characteristic justifies the introduction of lifecycle management, assemblies' management and evolved dynamic behavior.

In order to benefit from the definition of model architecture with different components and from the dynamic properties of service platforms, researchers have developed service-oriented models with different components. These models present a fine and precise architecture, while maintaining a large amount of flexibility. Such architecture offers different possibilities for adaptability. The service-oriented architecture brings a response to the reduction in coupling between the different elements of a system, and responds to the needs identified for dynamic assembly and the expression of those needs.

3.4.2.2. *Execution environments and available models*

The choice of execution environments is currently narrowed down to the Net or Java environments. Both are increasingly widely deployed on mobile devices (perhaps awaiting new standards along with the democratization of computing systems embedded in vehicles). They run on "virtual" machines, so they remain portable and adapted to the environment. Even if they share different models that facilitate the carrying out of distributed applications (JINI, CORBA, etc.), few of them respond to the same characteristics as the service-oriented models with different components.

---

7 www.iona.com/devcenter/sca/SCA_White_Paper1_09.pdf.

Among the different standards available, the OSGi platform seems to be the closest one to the specified needs. It is Java-oriented, relies on an event-driven model, has a registry of services and is easy to administer. Although these properties can be found on other architectures, OSGi has an advantage that makes this platform stand out from the rest. It handles the physical level (conditioning and loading) as well as the logical level (service layer). Additionally, it is designed in order to evolve in constrained environments.

3.4.2.3. *OSGi*

The OSGi Alliance is a non-profit independent organization. It brings together a large number of people working in the industry, including members and contributors. It proposes a set of specifications that offer service-oriented environment-based components, enabling the management of the lifecycle of software programs in a standard manner. This environment is based on Java, see Figure 3.9.

The core specification of the platform has not evolved significantly throughout the course of its updates. It is gradually expanding, but this is mainly done by enlarging the range of standard services provided. These services may be used on top of the main platform but are not mandatory for its execution. This allows us to guarantee a certain minimalism for the platform and to ensure that this platform is easy to run on embedded equipment. In fact, OSGi initially targets platforms such as the set-top-box, the network or residential gateways, etc. This equipment has limited storage and running capabilities. It has increasingly strong constraints regarding the lifecycle of software components, since in these fields new components have to be deployed and dynamically assembled during the execution of the gateway without interrupting the services that are already running. With the emergence of new fields, such as mobile telephony and embedded computing, the specification offers particular types of behavior tailored to these specific environments. Teams of dedicated experts propose these additions to the specifications[8]. The OSGi platform has become the standard building service-oriented dynamic Java platform.

OSGi thus has all of the notions related to service-oriented architectures. The platform proposes a registry where the services are registered when they start up. They are indexed by the service contract (in this context, a Java interface) and a set of properties (version, seller, language, etc.) that facilitates the refinement of the search for a service thanks to LDAP (lightweight directory access protocol) filters. The platform is also based on an event-driven system. It enables the notification of the components running on OSGi in order to dynamically manage their lifecycle according to the actions carried out on the platform.

---

8 It should be noted that an expert group exists for vehicle context (www.osgi.org/VEG/HomePage).

OSGi facilitates the deployment, execution, administration and withdrawal of remote software services. OSGi is composed of two different layers: a physical layer that is concerned with deploying the execution units and code dependencies, and a logical layer that facilitates the description of the components of services, their assembly and the management of their dynamic behavior.

OSGi is thus a layer of abstraction, on top of the virtual Java machine that offers an execution environment with dynamic services. This architecture displays all of the properties that permit us to maximize the modularity and manage the dynamic connection between components.

Although this platform offers the basic functionalities necessary for the implementation of services and of inter-vehicle communication, it does not respond to all the needs expressed and thus needs to be customized. Its design based on extensibility and dynamism means that it is possible to achieve this customization task quite easily. In fact, as will be illustrated in the next section, it is possible to deal with the limits encountered by extending the framework.

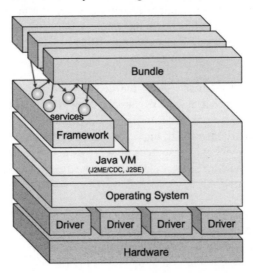

Figure 3.9. *The OSGi platform*

3.4.2.4. *Limits and alternatives*

Despite the advantages introduced by the OSGi platform, this platform still has a number of limitations. However, recent research efforts have focused on these obstacles.

One of the problems resides in isolating the execution of applications. OSGi provides a level of isolation for the simultaneous execution of different versions of the same service. If the different resources deployed can be marked as different signs and thus be clearly identified, and if it is possible to rely on the classical Java mechanism as far as security is concerned, the isolation of different applications running on the same platform cannot be guaranteed. Thus the work carried out by Gama [CAM 09], for example, provides the basic mechanisms that assist with the implementation of competitive execution, but this execution remains isolated from the various software application programs created from the assembly of the components.

Another difficulty relates to the management of such architecture. Adapting execution times or facilitating the dynamic composition of applications requires a strong management of the framework. This management takes place both at the level of deployment, but also at the instantiation level of the necessary services. In the given environment (i.e. a vehicle), it is impossible to imagine that the decisions related to different evolutions of the environment will be constantly controlled by an administrator. The platform itself must provide auto-configuring capabilities, as well as external management facilities with the aim of supervising the system. These two needs are addressed by the OSGi community [ROY 07, DIA 08] and can easily be implemented in the field of transportation.

Finally, one last limitation regards the deployment properties of the platform. OSGi has already proposed a set of dynamic deployment capabilities that can be coupled to external devices in order to manage dependencies[9]. However, the strong mobility of the environment introduces particular difficulties. For example, the integrity of the deployment of resources or services is not guaranteed and does not yet support partial transfers. Researchers have nonetheless recently started to show interest in the problem [PAR 07].

The proposed architecture with dynamic services in the OSGi specification is thus a solid background for the creation of vehicle-oriented applications. It is also enhanced by the existence of different component-based models that improve the assembly of the building blocks of an application [CER 04, ESC 07]. Moreover, in relation to competing platforms such as .Net, OSGi benefits from the functioning characteristics of the Java class loader. It allows a dynamic loading of fine granularity. .Net enables downloading with coarser granularity, thus making the updating of applications less flexible. The granularity is the domain application in the Microsoft environment, whereas in the OSGi environment the granularity is the conditioning unit, the JAR (the equivalent of a .Net Assembly or of a Java class loader).

---

9 www.osgi.org/download/rfc-0112_BundleRepository.pdf.

All these advantages mean that OSGi is increasingly being used in the industry, in application servers (Websphere, Weblogic, Geronimo, etc.) [DES 06], *plugin* applications (Eclipse), and even cell phone environments (Nokia).

This confirms the relevance of this kind of platform. Also, the future versions of Java will integrate concepts similar to those that are being inserted in OSGi for the modularity, conditioning and assembly of services.

3.4.3. *Application of the VESPA example*

The implementation of an architecture relying on SGi was experienced with VESPA, as we described in section 3.3.2.1. The work that was carried out brought about two complementary results:

– a generic framework was created for the development of vehicle-oriented applications; and

– based on this framework, an adaptable and evolving version of VESPA was built.

3.4.3.1. *A dynamic platform for the field of transport*

In a classically pervasive environment, even if the system must adapt to its environment, the evaluation of each request takes place in a stable context. In the field of vehicles, however, the environment will evolve even as the request is being evaluated. Therefore, the reaction to the changing context must be fast and effective. These needs, to easily change the context, are generally orthogonal to the other functionalities of the application. For instance, a vehicle-oriented application developer does not want to handle these changes in the context, be it the adaptation or connection of services. Moreover, the majority of the applications in this field share certain needs. It is thus useful to be able to propose a platform that provides these services in a generic and non-functional manner. The main needs involve:

– *geo-localization*, which is crucial in the field of transport. It is a basic service, and the majority of adaptations depend on it. It is usually based on the GPS. However other technologies, such as Wi-Fi, can substitute for the GPS in areas with no coverage, such as underground parking lots for example;

– *time*, which is an indispensable variable for the synchronization or marking of data in every distributed system. It can be retrieved by the GPS (thus avoiding synchronization issues) information or by the remote time server; and

– *communication technologies*, whose different modes and protocols will be implemented over time, according to the stakeholders and the availabilities of different technologies.

In order to abstract the management of these unavoidable services in the field of vehicles by as much as possible, we can add extensions to the OSGi platform in order to offer a basic framework for the various vehicle-oriented applications. This is one of the objectives of our works [DES 09]. This extension consists of different basic services conditioned in a modular way by the OSGi host environment. The unit of delivery is called a bundle. A bundle is a JAR enhanced with meta-information. This meta-information mainly describes the code dependencies (in a manifest.mf file) and possibly the architecture of the services required and provided by the bundle (in an XML file) that also describes the logical layer. The bundle also contains Java classes that implement service components, as well as an Activator class used to manage the lifecycle of the bundle. Finally, it encloses different resources (configuration files, native libraries, images, etc.) that can later be used to configure or provide various services.

Figure 3.10 presents the transport-oriented platform that we have proposed. It is composed of at least three services depending on the context (i.e. localization, time and communication). It can be extended by different classic non-functional services (e.g., persistence, log, etc.), instantiated according to needs. This way, an application deployed in this environment benefits from the different services offered. Then, depending on the situation, the platform becomes responsible for the substitution of basic services in order to pass from one mode of communication to the other or from one positioning service to another.

Furthermore, the application may interact with third-party applications or services which are deployed in that environment. For example, an application that seeks to share data between vehicles may collaborate with an application that provides real-time traffic information. An application can even connect third-party services that are initially unavailable in the environment. The decision to move the connection of one service towards another service depends on the availability or unavailability of the different components. Expressing the needs of the applications deployed is thus essential for making sure that the assembly is correct.

This basic platform, supported by OSGi, brings a certain number of answers to the problems related to the field of transportation. For example, conditioning and deployment are taken into account by the OSGi. The assembly can be extended and realized at execution time. This allows the addition of new functionalities by providers according to the different services encountered as vehicles move. To sum up, this extension of OSGi for basic inter-vehicle services simplifies the creation of applications dedicated to the field of transportation.

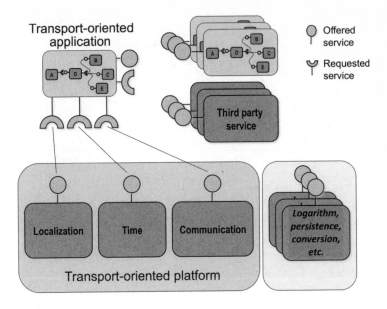

Figure 3.10. *Transport-oriented dynamic platform*

3.4.3.2. *A dynamic inter-vehicle communication application*

The platform for transport-oriented services was implemented within VESPA. First, the architecture of VESPA must be rethought in order to benefit from the different services (i.e. localization, time or communication). Moreover, VESPA must benefit from the functionalities of the platform in order to be extensible and must be able to adapt throughout the displacements of the vehicle in which it is embedded.

Figure 3.11 presents the general architecture of VESPA that has been optimized with the aim of exploiting the properties of the model and applying them to services. The management of basic transport-oriented services is delegated to the platform. VESPA connects the time services or positioning services that it finds suitable according to availabilities. The different modes of communication will also adapt and evolve depending on different needs. Different services that facilitate the collection and transmission of information create a layer of adaptation that enables the pre- or post-processing of raw data. These components can be updated in order to benefit from new functionalities.

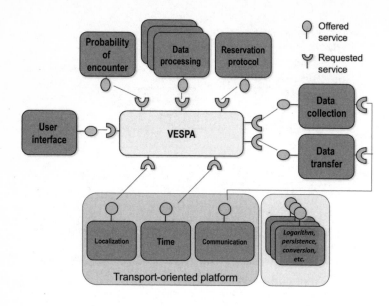

Figure 3.11. *Adaptable and dynamic VESPA engine*

At the heart of VESPA is a component that will manage collected data and will make appropriate decisions according to the context. We can extract the different basic building blocks that regulate its behavior. A component can manage the protocol for reserving parking spaces (i.e. processing the information received by the various stakeholders looking for a free parking space). Another component can estimate the probability of an encounter. Starting from the data received, it allows us to estimate reliability in relation to the context of the vehicle. Finally, different services allow us to manage and process each type of data collected. These services can evolve and be updated. Moreover, new services that handle new types of data can be added dynamically. Thus, if the vehicle arrives in a specific environment, it is capable of receiving the software building blocks required for it to extend its capabilities and interact with its new environment.

Finally, VESPA connects a graphic interface service in order to send the information collected and processed to the driver, such as the directions towards a parking space or the signaling of an accident.

VESPA is the first application that uses this platform. It seeks to expand to incorporate new applications, such as the examples described in section 3.3.2. It is suitable for the context of communication technologies and inter-vehicle services, because of its adaptability and its ability to evolve.

3.5. What kind of future can we envisage for inter-vehicle services and communication technologies?

As we have seen in the introduction to this chapter, a number of car manufacturers offer communication services in their models (for example Peugeot, Volkswagen and BMW). At the same time, several projects have started to reflect on what the services offered will look like in the near future (for example the set of projects carried out by CISIT that have already been presented in this book).

Progress is still needed at the level of communication (i.e. we need new regulations that take into account the constraints of V2V communication), sensors (costs, contained data) or radars. However, current technology facilitates the deployment of services in vehicle fleets. They mainly seek to improve the safety of users and to improve sustainable development via the improvement of traffic flow and the guiding of drivers towards desired resources (e.g. a parking space that is close by). Other services, based on the same solutions, are also available to improve the comfort of public transport users (e.g. notifications at bus stops and proximity applications).

These services have a future if they can adapt to the evolution of modern transportation and if we can easily facilitate their development. That is why in this chapter we have emphasized the deployment and updating methods for these services, as they evolve according to both time and the other services provided. Similarly, these services will have to adapt to certain constraints, such as user preferences, or even the characteristics of the urban environment where they are running.

3.6. Bibliography

[CEN 08] CENERARIO N., DELOT T., ILARRI S., "Dissemination of information in intervehicle ad hoc networks", *IEEE Intelligent Vehicles Symposium (IV'08)*, Eindhoven, The Netherlands, June 2008.

[CER 04] CERVANTES H., HALL R.S., "Autonomous adaptation to dynamic availability using a service-oriented component model", *International Conference on Software Engineering (ICSE)*, Edinburgh, United Kingdom, May 2004.

[DEB 04] DE BRUIN D., KROON J., VAN KLAVEREN R., NELISSE M., "Design and test of a cooperative adaptive cruise control system", *Intelligent Vehicles Symposium (IV'04)*, Parma, Italy, 2004.

[DEL 08] DELOT T., CENERARIO N., ILARRI S., "Estimating the relevance of information in inter-vehicle ad hoc networks", *MDM International Workshop on Sensor Technologies for Information Explosion Era (SeNTIE'08)*, IEEE Computer Society, Beijing, China, April 2008.

[DES 06] DESERTOT M., DONSEZ D., LALANDA P., "A dynamic service-oriented implementation for Java EE servers", *SCC'06 IEEE International Conference on Service Computing*, pp. 159-166, Chicago, United States, September 2006.

[DES 09] DESERTOT M., LECOMTE S., DELOT T., "A dynamic service-oriented framework for the transportation domain", *ITST'09, 9th International Conference on ITS Telecommunication*, Lille, France, October 2009.

[DEY 00] DEY A.K., ABOWD G.D., "Towards a better understanding of context and context-awareness", *Workshop on The What, Who, Where, When, and How of Context-Awareness, as part of the 2000 Conference on Human Factors in Computing Systems (CHI 2000)*, The Hague, The Netherlands, April 2000.

[DIA 08] DIACONESCU A., BOURCIER J., ESCOFFIER C., "Autonomic iPOJO: towards self-managing middleware for ubiquitous systems", *1st International Workshop on Social Aspects of Ubiquitous Computing Environments (SAUCE 2008)*, Avignon, France, December 2008.

[ESC 07] ESCOFFIER C., HALL R.S., LALANDA P., "iPOJO An extensible service-oriented component framework", *IEEE International Conference on Service Computing (SCC'07)*, Salt Lake City, United States, 2007.

[GAM 09] GAMA K., DONSEZ D., "Towards dynamic component isolation in a service oriented platform. Component-based software engineering", *12th International Symposium, CBSE2009*, East Stroudsburg, PA, United States, June 24-26, 2009.

[GRA 04] GRANSART C., HEDDEBAUT M., RIOULT J., "Communications sans fil entre véhicules: une aide à la conduite", *1ᵉ Conférence Nationale sur le Multimédia Mobile, MCUBE*, Monbéliard, France, March 30-31, 2004.

[GRA 09] GRANSART C., LECOMTE S., "Utilisation du contexte dans l'adaptation d'applications dédiée aux transports", *Atelier sur la Gestion des Données dans les Systèmes d'Information Pervasifs (GEDSIP'09)*, Toulouse, France, May 2009.

[GRI 08] GRINE H., LECOMTE S., "Self-adaptation of a query service using reconfigurable components", *1st International Workshop on Data and Services Management in Mobile Environments (DS2ME) In conjunction with the 24th International Conference on Data Engineering (ICDE'08)*, Cancun, Mexico, April 2008.

[HAN 03] HANSMANN U., MERK L., NICKLOUS M.S., STOBER T., *Pervasive Computing: the Mobile World*, Springer, New York, 2003.

[MOR 03] MORSINK P., HALLOUZI R., DAGLI I., CSEH C., SCHAFERS L., NELISSE M., DE BRUIN D., "Cartalk 2000: Development of a cooperative adas based on vehicle-to-vehicle communication", *10th World Congress on Intelligent Transport Systems and Services*, Madrid, Spain, 16-20 November, 2003.

[PAR 07] PARREND P., FRENOT S., "Supporting the secure deployment of OSGi bundles", *International Symposium on a World of Wireless, Mobile and Multimedia Networks (WoWMoM2007)*, Helsinki, Finland, June 18-21, 2007.

[ROY 07] ROYON Y., PARREND P., FRNOT S., PAPASTEFANOS S., ABDELNUR H., VAN DE POEL D., "Multi-service, multi-protocol management for residential gate-ways", *BroadBand Europe*, Antwerp, Belgium, December 2007.

[XUB 04] XU B., OUKSEL A.M., WOLFSON O., "Opportunistic resource exchange in intervehicle ad-hoc networks", *5th International Conference on Mobile Data Management*, Bekerley, United States, 2004.

[ZHO 08] ZHONG T., XU B., SZCZUREK P., WOLFSON O., "TRAFFICINFO: An algorithm for VANET dissemination of real-time traffic information", *15th World Congress on Intelligent Transport Systems*, New York, United States, November 2008.

Chapter 4

Modeling and Control of
Traffic Flow

4.1. General introduction

In the *White Paper – European Transport Policy for 2010: Time to Decide*[1], we are told that:

"Because of congestion, there is a serious risk that Europe will lose economic competitiveness. The most recent study on the subject showed that the external costs of road traffic congestion alone amount to 0.5% of Community GDP (gross domestic product). Traffic forecasts for the next 10 years show that if nothing is done, road congestion will increase significantly by 2010. The costs attributable to congestion will also increase by 142% to reach 80 billion Euros a year, which is approximately 1% of Community GDP.

With respect to sustainable surface transport, the following actions were envisaged… increasing safety, and avoiding traffic congestion (in particular in urban areas), through the integration of innovative electronics and software solutions and by means of the use of advanced satellite navigation systems and telematic solutions."

The European Commission's white paper emphasizes the fact that the limited capacity of road infrastructures available to users, and constantly increasing

Chapter written by Daniel JOLLY, Boumediene KAMEL and Amar BENASSER.
1 www.senat.fr/europe/textes europeens/e1818.pdf.

demands with regard to traffic[2], goods, and people, are the source of numerous problems encountered by highly industrialized societies. These problems, related mainly to recurring or non-recurrent congestion phenomena in large metropolitan areas in particular, are an obstacle to the socioeconomic evolution of our societies and are resulting in ever-growing direct and indirect costs for the population. The solution to the phenomenon of congestion has become one of the main concerns of transport centers.

One of the most natural solutions is the building of new infrastructures. This is not an easy solution, however, as it requires a considerable financial investment. Public authorities are often faced with a lack of space available for the construction of new roads, or are confronted with resistance from the people directly affected by these building projects.

The necessity to create traffic flow models has quickly become apparent in order to better manage these situations. A wide range of simulation tools has been developed on the basis of these models, aimed at helping road network operators ensure better traffic management. Indeed, dynamic simulation tools allow us to evaluate the impact of an operation's action on traffic conditions and to propose effective management strategies in order to optimize infrastructure yield. These tools aid in stochastic and operational decision-making.

4.1.1. *Different models of road traffic flow*

Lighthill and Witham [LIG 55] presented the first flow model, based on the similarity between road traffic flow and the circulation of fluids in conduits. This analogy gave rise to a group of macroscopic models. Generally speaking, macroscopic models are dedicated to the prediction and assessment of traffic and to the regulation at the overall network level. However, their aggregate character prevents them from taking into account the movement of individual vehicles and the interaction of these vehicles with their environment.

Other types of models are able to address the individual behavior of vehicles and their interactions. These are called microscopic models. This class of model is used more frequently in traffic simulation. However, the large number of variables and parameters to be taken into account makes their use in the representation and simulation of a large-scale road network very difficult and costly.

---

2 In France, in 2000 there were 72% more cars than there had been in 1985. Source: CCFA and CSIAM, available at: http://ec.europa.edu/transport/strategies/doc/2001_white_paper_lb_texte_complet_en.pdf.

There is also another category of models that studies the behavior of vehicles without explaining their interactions. These are called mesoscopic models. In this category of models, vehicles are grouped into batches, the movements of which are calculated using a macroscopic model.

The main difficulty encountered in traffic modeling has to do with problems of scale. If we consider an urban network, it is generally made up of quick routes, which necessitate macroscopic modeling, and crossroads, which usually require microscopic modeling. Problems of scale are related to space and time. They can be simply illustrated by considering a large road network in which the fluidity of traffic is diversely represented according to the part being considered. A very long section of road can be in a state of congestion with travel times being measured in hours, while another, shorter section of road is in a fluid state characterized by travel times measured in seconds. This situation cannot be effectively represented using the aforementioned models, which cannot simultaneously take these different particularities of traffic into account.

To resolve these problems of scale and make up for the insufficiencies of the traffic models cited above, hybrid models have recently appeared. This type of representation must, however, guarantee the preservation and continuity of flow during changes from one model to another.

4.1.2. Classification criteria for road traffic flow system models

Road traffic flow models offer an effective method for describing the phenomena and behavior of the flow of vehicles within urban and interurban networks. The variety of models developed to date requires categorization in order to best judge their ability to adapt to the problem being addressed. Several criteria have been proposed to distinguish traffic models from one another [HOO 01]:

– *representation of variables*: traffic flow models describe dynamic and complex systems in which time is the main variable. Two categories of models exist side-by-side, depending on whether time is taken as a continuous or discrete variable;

– *representation of the process*: modeling is based on the utilization of a group of variables and parameters that may be random. Representation models can thus be stochastic or deterministic; and

– *level of detail*: the degree of granularity plays an essential role in the classification of traffic models. This criterion is generally used to distinguish between the different models. A high level of detail allows us to describe the individual behavior of vehicles, a characteristic of microscopic models. An intermediate level of detail corresponds to mesoscopic models. Finally, macroscopic models are characterized by a low level of detail.

Traffic models are interesting because they allow us to represent the behavior and phenomena of traffic flow, yet they also constitute an incontrovertible support in the creation of simulators for the study and evaluation of traffic system performance. The reader can find additional information in [LIE 02].

Below, we will present these models according to their level of detail: first microscopic models, and then macroscopic ones. Mesoscopic models are not addressed in this chapter; however, the reader can find additional information in [PRI 61, BUC 68, PRI 71, PAV 75, BRA 76, HEL 97, HOO 98, HOO 99, HOO 00].

4.2. Microscopic models

Road traffic is a complex system by nature. It is very difficult to establish a model that will precisely describe the behavior of each of the vehicles in circulation in a road network. Generally, the models proposed in the literature are relatively simple. They can be grouped into two main categories. The first category includes car-following models; the second includes cellular automata models. We will describe each of these categories below.

4.2.1. *Car-following models*

There are four types of car-following models: the safety distance model; the optimal speed model; the stimulus-response model; and the psychological model.

4.2.1.1. *Safety distance model*

The model based on safety distance describes the dynamic of a vehicle with regard to the behavior of the vehicle in front of it. The simplest model was conceived on the basis of the following rule: "The safety distance of a vehicle n driving at a speed of 16.1 km/h must be equal to or greater than the length of this vehicle" [PIP 53]. Using this rule, we can deduce the safety distance that separates the nth vehicle driving at speed v from the $(n-1)^{th}$ vehicle in front of it:

$$D_n(v) = L_n(1 + \frac{v}{16.1})$$ [4.1]

where L_n is the length of vehicle n. In the Pipes model, the safety distance is proportional to speed. The same principle was proposed by Forbes [FOR 58].

Another formulation was proposed by Leutzbach [LEU 88], who introduced the idea of overall reaction time τ_g. This parameter has to do with:

– perception time, which is the time necessary for the driver to collect information about the environment, and more precisely, information about the obstacles facing him or her;

– decision time; and

– the braking time necessary for the driver to slow down or stop.

Leutzbach defined braking time in terms of a sufficient distance for a vehicle to come to a complete stop. This definition takes into account the driver's reaction time and the maximum deceleration of the vehicle, which depends on a friction variable μ and gravity g. The safety distance is defined in terms of the maximum braking distance, which is defined by the following relationship:

$$D_n(v) = L_n + \tau g v + \frac{v^2}{2\mu g} \qquad [4.2]$$

The Forbes model was improved by Jepsen [JEP 98], who introduced the idea of the minimum distance d_{min} that a vehicle must respect, and a risk factor due to speed v. The risk factor translates a driver's capacity to avoid a collision, or at least to limit its impact. This capacity is shown by the increase in the security distance by a linear factor f in relation to speed v.

$$D_n(v)=L_n+d_{min}+v(\tau g+vf) \qquad [4.3]$$

The minimum distance d_{min} is the distance that separates two completely stationary vehicles during a traffic jam.

4.2.1.2. Optimal speed model

Proposed by Newell [NEW 61], this model supposes that a driver adapts his/her speed to an optimal speed v_0 depending on the distance separating him/her from the vehicle in front. This model is expressed by the following relationship:

$$v_{i+1}(t+\Delta t) = v_0(x_i(t) - x_{i+1}(t)) \qquad [4.4]$$

In equation [4.4], the reaction time is replaced by the braking time Δt of the driver. Initiating a limited first-order development, Bando [BAN 95] proposed an extension of the Newell model, described by the relationship:

$$\frac{dv_{i+1}(t)}{dt} = \frac{v_0(x_i(t) - x_{i+1}(t)) - v_{i+1}(t)}{\Delta t} \tag{4.5}$$

$$v_0(x_i(t) - x_{i+1}(t)) = \frac{v_0}{2}(\tanh(x_i(t) - x_{i+1}(t) - d_c) + \tanh(d_c)) \tag{4.6}$$

In equation [4.6], v_0 and d_c are two optimal speed parameters. Note that, in this model, small disturbances may arise in certain conditions that can lead to traffic congestion.

4.2.1.3. Stimulus-response models

This type of model is based on the existence of a relationship between an action (the driver's behavior) and a stimulus in the following form:

action = sensitivity * stimulus

In general, a stimulus can be the distance that separates two vehicles or the relative speed of two vehicles when one is following the other, and the response can be the braking or acceleration of the following vehicle after a certain amount of time Tp. One of the first models of this type was proposed by Chandler [CHA 58], which supposes that the acceleration of a vehicle n at position $x_n(t)$ following vehicle $n-1$ is given by the following relationship:

$$a_n(t + Tp) = \gamma * (v_{n-1}(t) - v_{i+1}(t)) \tag{4.7}$$

where $v_n(t)$ and $a_n(t)$ are the speed and acceleration, respectively, of vehicle n at time t, and γ is sensitivity. In this case, the stimulus is expressed by the difference between the speeds of the two vehicles. Gazis [GAZ 61] expressed the sensitivity γ of the driver by the following relationship:

$$\gamma = \frac{c(v_n(t + Tp))^m}{(x_{n-1}(t) - x_n(t))^l} \tag{4.8}$$

Thus, vehicle n adjusts its speed $v_n(t)$ with respect to the distance and the difference in speeds with a delay, Tp.

Though they describe the behavior of vehicles in a microscopic environment, stimulus-response models, particularly those utilizing the Gazis model, fall far short of representing a driver's real behavior. These models do not take into account the variability of traffic flow or vehicles, which are all characterized by the same behavior.

4.2.1.4. *Psychological models*

Using equations [4.7] and [4.8], we can deduce that a driver will react to small changes in speed $(v_{n-1}(t) - v_n(t))$ even if the distance is very large. Likewise, the driver's reaction is zero if the difference between speeds is zero, even if the distance between the two vehicles is very small.

To show that the driver is limited in his/her perception of the stimulus to which s/he must react, several improvements based on perceptive psychology have been made [TOD 64]. These extensions are based on the following rules:

– when the distance that separates two vehicles is very large, the driver's reaction is no longer limited by the fluctuations in speed of the vehicle in front;

– when the distances are minimal, some combinations (speed and distance) between the vehicles do not affect the behavior of the following vehicle, since the movements are relatively small.

One of the first psychological models was proposed by Wiedemann [WIE 74], in which he makes the distinction between limited and unlimited driving. This distinction is based on the perception threshold and takes into account the laws of lane change. This psychological model has served as the basis for the development of several microscopic traffic flow models, notably another model proposed by Koppa [KOP 99] and Rothery [ROT 99], which supposes that the angular resolution of the human eye is limited.

4.2.2. *The cellular automata model*

The cellular automata model is an effective tool for describing the dynamic and complex behaviors of traffic in detail. The primary model is based on a one-dimensional vector with L cells. In general, the size of a cell is 4.5 meters [NAG 92]. The length of the cell is chosen so that the vehicle passes from one cell to the next in a single step in time. Each cell is either occupied by one vehicle or is empty. Each vehicle possesses a total speed between 0 and v_{max}, which represents the number of cells crossed at each step in time. The state of the cell is defined as equal to -1 if it is unoccupied, and to speed v if it contains a vehicle. The number of empty cells in front of a vehicle is written as Δx. The system is updated by following the stages below, applied simultaneously to all of the vehicles in the vector:

– if $v < v_{max}$ then $v = v + 1$. This rule represents a linear acceleration of the vehicle until it has attained its maximum speed;

– if $v > \Delta x$ then $v = \Delta x$.[3] This rule ensures the deceleration of the following vehicles in order to avoid collisions; and

– if $v > 0$ and $p < p_{brake}$ then $v = v - 1$. A random generator is introduced in order to slow the vehicles down. This rule models certain random driver behaviors as delayed accelerations and fluctuations in stable speed.

Thanks to these simple rules of movement and the ability to carry out parallel implementation, cellular automata are considered to be rapid simulation tools. They have been used in simulation as well as in allocation and supervision. The first single-lane route model was developed by Nagel [NAG 92] and was broadened by the same author into a multilane and multiclass model [NAG 99]. In order to make cellular automata more realistic, Wu [WU 99] directed the rules of movement toward the law of pursuit. Though still not perfect, validation work carried out on German and American highways [NAG 99, WU 99, ESS 99] showed that cellular automata perfectly reproduced the large-scale macroscopic behavior of road traffic flow.

4.3. Macroscopic models

Macroscopic models are based on an analogy with fluid dynamics. These models liken traffic flow, which is supposed to be homogeneous and one-directional, to a liquid in a conduit.

In this context, liquid flow is characterized by the following three main variables:

– outflow $q(x,t)$ expressed in the number of vehicles per unit of time;

– density $\rho(x,t)$ in the number of vehicles per unit of length; and

– speed $v(x,t)$ in units of length per unit of time.

---

3 Here, Δx corresponds not only to a distance traveled by a vehicle, but also to its speed of movement.

Using these three variables, two equations have been established to describe the evolution of traffic flow. The first equation, [4.9], expresses the law of conservation of mass:

$$\frac{\partial q(x,t)}{\partial x} + \frac{\partial \rho(x,t)}{\partial t} = 0 \qquad\qquad [4.9]$$

The second equation, [4.10], is a balance equation linking outflow, density, and average speed of flow:

$$q(x,t) = \rho(x,t)v(x,t) \qquad\qquad [4.10]$$

These two equations must be completed by a third equation in order to completely describe the evolution of traffic. This equation is used to distinguish two categories of macroscopic traffic flow models. The first equation designates first-order models, called LWR-type models, and the second equation defines second-order, or superior-order, models.

The following section provides an overview of these two categories of macroscopic models.

4.3.1. *LWR-type first-order models*

One of the first macroscopic models was proposed by Lighthill, Witham, and Richard, from whom the name LWR is derived [LIG 55, RIC 56]. This model uses the conservation equation (equation [4.9]) as well as the relationship between outflow, density and average speed (equation [4.10]). These two equations are completed by a speed equilibrium equation with respect to density, $v_{eq} = v(\rho(x,t))$.

This last equation supposes that traffic is always in equilibrium and that it evolves by passing from one state of equilibrium to another. The speed equation in the equilibrium state, called the fundamental diagram, is empirical and is used to characterize the infrastructure on which vehicles are circulating (Figure 4.1).

Greenshields [GRE 34] proposed the first analytical relationship (equation [4.11]) of a fundamental diagram:

$$v_{eq} = v_f (1 - \frac{\rho}{\rho_{max}}) \qquad\qquad [4.11]$$

where v_f is the free speed of flow and ρ_{max} is the maximum density. This relationship allows us to trace different representations of the fundamental diagram, as well as the dependence between outflow and density (Figure 4.1), between speed and density, or between speed and outflow:

– when traffic is fluid (i.e. density is close to 0), interactions between vehicles are minimal. The vehicles then drive at their maximum desired speed, which results in a limit on the speed of the stream, written as v_f;

– density is limited by a value ρ_{max} that designates the maximum number of vehicles at a complete stop that a road can contain; and

– the maximum value of outflow q_{max} designates the capacity of the section being studied.

Analysis of the fundamental diagram in Figure 4.1 shows that it is composed of two parts. The first part is typical of the fluid circulation system where, for low density values, the outflow is weak. Beyond a so-called critical density, ρ_{cr}, the density increases causing saturation of the section of road being studied. This saturation results in reduced outflow and thus reduced speed. It corresponds to the second part of the fundamental diagram, which is characteristic of a congested system. When the density attains the maximum value, the outflow and speed cancel each other out and the system is at a standstill.

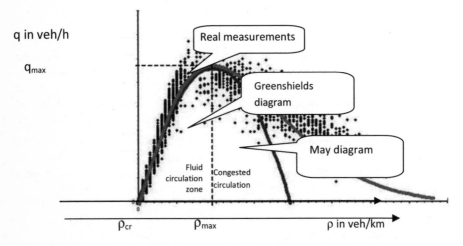

Figure 4.1. *Fundamental diagram*

The linear relationship proposed by Greenshields leads to a critical density equal to half of the maximum density, while experimental measurements show that the critical density value is generally between $0.3\rho_{max}$ and $0.2\rho_{max}$. In order to address this inconvenience, other relationships have been proposed, notably by Buisson [BUI 96] and Papageorgiou [PAP 98]:

$$v_{eq} = v_f \left(1 - \left(\frac{\rho}{\rho_{max}} \right)^l \right)^m \qquad [4.12]$$

Where ρ_{max} is the maximum density, $l, m \in \Re$ are parameters where $l > 0$, and $m \geq l$ is used to obtain different fundamental diagrams.

Other models have been proposed that allow us to more or less faithfully reproduce the observations made of different sections of road, notably May [MAY 90], who proposed another relationship:

$$v_{eq} = v_f e^{-\frac{1}{a}\left(\frac{\rho}{\rho_{cr}}\right)a} \qquad [4.13]$$

where a is a curve adjustment parameter.

In Figure 4.1, we can see that the real measurements at equilibrium are spread out, particularly in the congested zone. Models of fundamental diagrams, therefore, remain rough approximations of reality.

The solution to these equations can be found using an analytical approach or a numerical approach. When an analytical solution exists, it offers the advantage of being exact, but it is often difficult to implement. The numerical approach, on the other hand, is generally easier to find, but it is inconvenient because it only provides an approximate solution.

The analytical solution to traffic flow equations is based on the method using defined characteristics, such as lines of plane (x,t) and gradient, $\frac{dq_e(\rho)}{d\rho}$. The solution is obtained by drawing these lines in the plane (x,t) from initial conditions to form a density field. When these lines meet, a discontinuity is created, which gives rise to shock waves. The solution can be non-unique if the characteristics diverge. This is why we then have recourse to entropic solutions. These consist of only accepting shock waves for which the density upstream of the critical density is lower than that downstream. Any discontinuity, where the density upstream is greater than the critical density downstream, gives rise to a fan (for more details, we refer the reader to [GOD 90] and [ANS 90]).

There is also a third approach, called the "particulate solution" [LEC 02]. This consists of breaking down the flow into basic particles representing vehicles. These particles move towards a state of equilibrium, rather than following each other. Density is approximated at every point by the inverse of the distance that separates two vehicles that are following each other, $\rho = \dfrac{1}{d}$, where d is the distance that separates two vehicles. In the case of a section with several lanes, the relationship is expressed by $\rho_i = \dfrac{1}{d_i}$ (for each lane i). This method of solution is very effective in the treatment of certain problems, such as the assessment of road noise [LEC 02].

It is interesting to emphasize the importance of studying the solution to the LWR model in the case of the Riemann problem. This allows us to illustrate the way in which shock waves propagate, and to introduce the ideas used in the numerical solution to these equations. The Riemann problem consists of solving the LWR model in the case of specific initial conditions. At $t = 0$, we are considering a section of road for which the density is defined by:

$$\rho(x,0) = \rho_{upstream} \text{ if } x < 0; \text{ and}$$

$$\rho(x,0) = \rho_{dowstream} \text{ if } x > 0.$$

The solution to this problem shows that depending on the values of ρ_{amont} and ρ_{aval}, when $x = 0$ a fan or a shock wave can form:

if $\rho_{upstream} > \rho_{downstream}$ then a fan forms; and

if $\rho_{upstream} < \rho_{downstream}$ then a shock wave forms.

First-order models present some advantages, such as:

– reliability: they guarantee that the variables q and ρ maintain consistency at all points and at all times with the physical limits of the network (q_{max}, ρ_{max});

– existence of the analytical solution. This enables the theoretical study of flow behavior by exactly and easily calculating solutions for simple scenarios; and

– existence of expansion. This type of model has attracted the attention of several researchers [DAG 02, LEB 98, NEW 98], etc., as part of the modeling of traffic behavior in urban environments.

These models also have major inconveniences:

– they do not correctly model transitional phases; and

– they do not consider speed as a fundamental variable (which, moreover, is not defined in the discretized version of the model).

In order to remedy these insufficiencies, research [ZHA 02] has been conducted that has led to the development of another type of model that is capable of addressing the phenomena that occur outside a state of equilibrium. These models are called second-order, or superior-order, models.

4.3.2. *Superior-order or second-order models*

Second-order macroscopic models were developed in order to address the inadequacies of first-order models, and to take into account the dynamic aspects of traffic [LEC 02].

From this perspective, several authors have proposed extensions based on the dynamic flow acceleration equation defined by:

$$a = \frac{\partial v}{\partial t} + v \frac{\partial v}{\partial x} = \underbrace{\frac{v_{eq}(\rho) - v}{\tau}}_{A} + B \tag{4.14}$$

where:

– A is a term of relaxation toward the speed of equilibrium; and

– B expresses the individual behavior of vehicles. The form of this parameter allows us to distinguish the different second-order macroscopic models from one another.

If $B = -\frac{1}{\rho} c^2(\rho) \frac{\partial \rho}{\partial x}$, the general form of superior-order models is:

$$\frac{\partial \rho}{\partial t} + \frac{\partial (\rho v)}{\partial x} = 0 \tag{4.15}$$

$$\frac{\partial v}{\partial t} + v\frac{\partial v}{\partial x} = \frac{1}{\tau}(v_{eq}(\rho) - v) - \frac{1}{\rho}c^2(\rho)\frac{\partial \rho}{\partial x} \qquad [4.16]$$

The rewriting of this system of equations in a classic form leads to:

$$\frac{\partial}{\partial t}U + A(U)\frac{\partial}{\partial x}U = \begin{pmatrix} 0 \\ \dfrac{1}{\tau}(v_{eq}(\rho) - v) \end{pmatrix} \qquad [4.17]$$

where:

$$U = \begin{pmatrix} \rho \\ v \end{pmatrix} \text{ and } A(U) = \begin{pmatrix} v & \rho \\ \dfrac{c^2(\rho)}{\rho} & v \end{pmatrix} \qquad [4.18]$$

When $c^2(\rho) = -\dfrac{v'_{eq}(\rho)}{2\tau}$ (c being the characteristic velocity of the traffic), we find the first model of this type, which was proposed by Payne [PAY 71]:

$$\underbrace{\frac{\partial v}{\partial t} + v\frac{\partial v}{\partial x}}_{Acceleration} = \underbrace{\frac{1}{\tau}(v_{eq}(\rho) - v)}_{Relaxation} - \underbrace{\frac{v'_{eq}(\rho)}{2\tau}\frac{1}{\rho}\frac{\partial \rho}{\partial x}}_{Anticipation} \qquad [4.19]$$

where τ is the reaction time.

Anticipation expresses the individual behavior of drivers. In fact, each driver adapts his/her acceleration in response on the density gradient. In this way, s/he can slow down or accelerate depending on whether the zone is dense or fluid.

Though the Payne model corrects some inadequacies of the LWR model, it suffers from several inconveniences itself, such as:

– the reaction time, obtained from empirical data, can have very large values (for example one minute) to enable a physical interpretation;

– the loss of reliability during changes in the geometry of the network. Measurements taken of traffic variables, density or outflow can lead to values greater than those imposed by the characteristics of the network being studied.

Moreover, the Payne model predicts negative speeds in certain situations. This phenomenon is known as *wrong-way travel*; and

– the behavior of a driver is influenced not only by the cars in front of him/her, but also by those behind. This does not correspond to reality, since the flow of traffic is anisotropic; i.e. vehicles are only sensitive to the changes that occur in front of them. This is why the solutions to this model prove to be utopian in some cases. Daganzo has also proposed an example showing that vehicles stopped in a waiting line "draw back".

However, this last item involves not only criticisms of the Payne model; it is at the origin of a new generation of superior-order anisotropic models. These models are often written in the form of a system of hyperbolic equations that offer the advantage of having known analytical solutions. The solutions depend on the eigenvalues λ_1 and λ_2 of the matrix $A(U)$ (equation [4.20]), which represent the propagation speeds of the information.

The solution to these superior-order models (defined by equations [4.17] and [4.18]) is analogous to that of the LWR first-order models described by a system of scalar hyperbolic equations. However, the formulation of the Riemann problem leads to the study of the hyperbolic system without its second term, since its effect can be disregarded. Depending on the eigenvalues of matrix $A(U)$, the solution to the Riemann problem leads to shock waves, fans or discontinuities. We can notice from the eigenvalues of matrix $A(U)$: $\lambda_1 = v - c(\rho)$ and $\lambda_2 = v + c(\rho)$; that $\lambda_1 < v < \lambda_2$. This clearly shows that information spreads faster than vehicles in these models, and this proves to be completely unrealistic [AW 01]. The reader will find a more in-depth analysis of these criticisms in the articles by Aw and Zhang [AW 01, ZHA 00].

In this context, in the same year three pieces of research were carried out simultaneously without any of the authors citing each others' work. The matrix $A(U)$ of these three models [AW 01, ZHA 02, JII 02] has the following form:

$$A(U) = \begin{pmatrix} v & \rho \\ 0 & v + c(\rho) \end{pmatrix}$$ [4.20]

Only the coefficient $c(\rho)$ distinguishes the three models:

– Aw and Rascle: $c(\rho) = -\rho p'(\rho)$, where p is a function of ρ;

– Zhang: $c(\rho) = \rho v'_{eq}(\rho)$;

– Jiang, Wu and Zhu: $c(\rho) = -c_0$.[4]

The eigenvalues of this matrix are $\lambda_1 = v$ and $\lambda_2 = v + c(\rho)$ where $c(\rho)$ is always negative, $\lambda_1 = v$ and $\lambda_2 < v$. These models respect the anisotropy of the traffic flow. Note that the first model (Aw and Rascle) is a general form of the other models. Taking $p(\rho) = a\rho^\alpha$, we get another form of the model proposed by Aw and Rascle.

Second-order models present the advantage of addressing transitional phenomena during variations in traffic flow. By correcting the Payne model by taking into account the anisotropic character of traffic, they allow us to avoid the prediction of negative speeds and to ensure the proper propagation of information. Unlike first-order models, these models consider speed as a principal variable, which facilitates the study of vehicle kinetics.

However, second-order models have several inconveniences of their own. They do not allow us to study the transitional phases of acceleration and deceleration. Moreover, their complexity makes the analytical solution of their equations very difficult, even for simple cases of traffic modeling. In addition, the taking into account of network discontinuities (the appearance of obstacles, variations in the geometry of the network, etc.) is often misrepresented. Finally, Papageorgiou [PAP 98] confirms that second-order models do not improve on the LWR model in any way. LeRoux [LER 02] affirmed in 2002 that all attempts to improve the Payne model have been in vain, and that the problem of modeling traffic is still present today. We can therefore note the most significant inconveniences of second-order models. These are that:

– they do not allow us to study the transitional phases of deceleration and acceleration; and

– they are complicated: analytical solutions cannot be found easily, even for simple cases. Second-order models are difficult to control. They do not allow us to model network discontinuities, even though these discontinuities are numerous in urban environments. In fact, the discontinuities are due to frequent variations in the number of lanes, to the existence of obstacles, etc. Knowing that second-order models do not formalize the speed of equilibrium with respect to space and time, they are therefore incapable of taking these discontinuities into consideration.

Consequently, second-order models are more appropriate for predicting the appearance of phenomena on highways than for studying vehicle kinetics in an

---

4 c_0 is a constant that represents the speed of propagation of a disturbance [LEC 02].

urban environment (even if they are built on the dynamic equation of flow particle acceleration).

4.4. General remarks concerning macroscopic and microscopic models

4.4.1. *Links between models*

Despite the great differences that seem to separate them, traffic flow models are related. Numerous publications have shown these links between the various models:

– in their article, Klar *et al.* [KLA 98] showed that by using a simple microscopic model it is possible to determine the equations of the kinetics of gases used in the macroscopic description of flow;

– Van Aerde [WAN 94] studied the derivation of a microscopic model using discretization per particle. This was applied in the numerical solution of a second-order macroscopic model [HOC 88]. Hoogendoorn [HOO 00] used the particle discretization method to achieve a microscopic model using gas kinetics equations [LET 97];

– we saw in the previous section that most second-order macroscopic models, including the Payne model, are constructed on the basis of pursuit models. Table 4.1 gives several examples of this;

– Yserentant [YSE 97] presented a particulate method in order to obtain macroscopic model equations from a compressible fluid;

– Nagel [NAG 98] showed that it is possible to construct the fundamental diagram from cellular automata; and

– the application of the moments method [LEU 88] allows us to obtain macroscopic flow equations using a mesoscopic model.

It is interesting at this point to emphasize the works of Del Castillo [DEL 96] and Franklin [FRA 61]. Franklin developed a microscopic (stimulus-response) model taking into account macroscopic flow data, such as shock waves. Del Castillo proposed a law of pursuit; three parameters of which were obtained directly from the density-speed diagram. Shock waves propagate in the same manner in Franklin's model as they do in Del Castillo's law of pursuit.

Name of model	Method of construction
Payne [PAY 71]	$$v_n(t+\tau) = v_{eq}\left(\dfrac{1}{x_{n-1}(t) - x_n(t)}\right)$$
Zhang [ZHA 00]	$$v_n(t+\tau) = v_{eq}\left(\rho(x_n(t) + distance, t)\right)$$
Jiang [JIA 02]	$$a_n(t) = \dfrac{v_{eq}(\dfrac{1}{\Delta x}) - v_n(t)}{\tau} + \lambda(\Delta v)$$
Zhang [ZHA 02]	$$a_n(t) = \dfrac{\Delta v}{\tau(\Delta x)}$$

Table 4.1. *Construction method of macroscopic models*

4.4.2. *Domains of application of macroscopic and microscopic models*

Microscopic models are often used for an offline simulation, thus allowing us to test new infrastructures (entry/exit ramps, the elimination of a lane, etc.) or new automobile equipment (driver assistance systems), or to get an approximate idea of flow data that are difficult to obtain empirically. The application of microscopic models in the real-time regulation of flow is very limited, given the enormous calculation times such models require, and the absence of an explicit model describing the relationship between entry and exit data. Moreover, they are incapable of determining the macroscopic characteristics of flow (capacity, length of waiting line) with precision. The microscopic models that have been calibrated and validated remain rare to date [ALG 97]. In general, the calibration of microscopic models consists of reproducing the macroscopic characteristics of the flow, notably the speed–density relationship, by adjusting the parameters related to vehicles or to driver conduct.

Macroscopic models are more appropriate for the development of control laws or the simulation of road flow in a large network. METANET [KOT 99] is a road traffic flow simulator built around a macroscopic model. It is used in Paris and Amsterdam to solve traffic problems in these large metropolitan areas. Moreover, macroscopic models are well adapted to the analysis and reproduction of macroscopic flow characteristics, such as shock waves and waiting lines. Even though some work has been carried out in order to generalize macroscopic models so that they take the different categories of vehicles circulating in a multi-lane infrastructure into account, for the moment this remains very limited and is rarely applicable in practice. In addition, macroscopic representations are not adapted to the study of the microscopic behavior inherent in flow, or to the study of the effects of changes in the geometry of road infrastructure (the removal of a traffic lane, for example) on traffic. Finally, the analytical solution of macroscopic models makes them better suited to tasks such as the assessment of prediction and control of traffic flow.

4.4.3. *Movement toward hybrid models*

Using this analysis of traffic flow models as a starting point, we would like to be able to represent the flow of traffic with a level of detail adapted to the situation and to the desired objectives. With this in mind, a hybrid approach combining macroscopic and microscopic models seems to be a pertinent solution for the representation of traffic. This modeling approach, adopted more recently by transport researchers, consists of using macroscopic and microscopic models within the same application. However, one of the key points of this approach concerns the study and creation of an interface ensuring communication between the two models. The following section presents the principal hybrid models developed to date and lists their advantages and disadvantages.

4.5. Hybrid models

Work on the hybrid modeling of traffic flow is mainly oriented toward the representation of a dynamic system composed of one continuous part and one discrete part. This modeling approach takes its inspiration from studies conducted on gases. As a material, the behavior of gas can be studied at the microscopic level by representing intermolecular interactions. In this context, the study pertains to local phenomena that govern the behavior of the gas. It can also be studied at the macroscopic level with the help of the description of its overall state (a study of global phenomena) [BOU 03]. Though these descriptions are situated at different levels, the phenomena governing the behavior of a gas are closely linked. In fact, a representation at the local level can be generalized to describe a gas at the macroscopic level. This is possible thanks to the kinetic theory of gases, which is used to create macroscopic behavior equations (Navier-Stokes equations [LET 97]) from the study of interactions between molecules.

This principle of hybrid modeling has been successfully applied in several domains, such as the growth of crystals in solution [MIZ 99] and the spread of a fracture in a piece of silicon [ABR 98], as well as in the field of industrial automation [WIL 96] and liquid flow [FLE 00]. However, in the field of traffic this principle is still at the development stage, and we have not yet got a precise definition of the idea of the hybrid model. Each author brings his or her own definition and vision to this type of model. We will therefore list four types of hybrid models:[5]

– The first, proposed by Chang [CHA 85], the *MacroParticle Simulation Model*, is used to calculate the movement of traffic either from flow, or by considering a group of vehicles that adjust their speed to reach the equilibrium speed, depending on the density of traffic on the segment of road being studied.

– The second type of hybrid model was developed by Daganzo [DAG 04]. It is used to study the movement of heavy vehicles (considered to be particles) in the form of trajectories in the flow of traffic assimilated into a liquid.

– The third type of model was developed by Helbing [HEL 00] and Hennecke [HEN 00], in which individual elements of the road network (entry/exit ramps, etc.) are described at the macroscopic level, while the rest of the elements are modeled at the microscopic level. This approach is justified by the fact that it is relatively easy to describe these singular elements using a macroscopic model, since this requires the addition of only one term to the model equation, while the choice of a microscopic model requires the behavior of individual vehicles to be taken into account, which makes the description more difficult.

– The fourth type of model consists of the hybrid modeling of road traffic flow. It is described in more detail later in this section. In this category, Magne, Poshinger and Bourrel [MAG 00, POS 02, BOU 02a] have proposed models intended to solve the problems of scale inherent in the description of traffic according to two perspectives – microscopic and macroscopic. In this context, the principle consists of modeling the elements of the network that do not require too much detail at the macroscopic level, and focusing on the parts that are sensitive to sudden and intermittent changes by studying them at the microscopic level. Thus, we are able to reduce the number of vehicles addressed while ensuring a clear and detailed description of singular elements, such as intersections, filter lanes on and off the highway, etc.

Generally speaking, the main difficulty encountered in the development of this type of hybrid model involves ensuring the transmission of information between two different models of traffic representation. The principle consists of translating microscopic data characterized by vehicle position and speed variables into the terms of macroscopic data determined by parameters such as average speed, density, and outflow of road traffic.

---

5 We can also find hybrid mesoscopic-microscopic models in the literature, such as the Burghout model [BUR 04], intended for the calculation of itinerary plans with the mesoscopic model and for the simulation of flow with the microscopic model.

All of these models are distinguished from one another by the choice of models used as well as by the linking procedure. Note that the Bourrel model is considered a generalization of the other models proposed by Helbing, Magne and Poshinger, since it combines the various methods of interfacing while improving them at the same time.

4.5.1. *The Magne model (MicMac)*

The model proposed by Magne (MicMac) [MAG 00] is based on the joint use of a second-order macroscopic model called SIMERS [MES 90], which is a discretized version of the Payne model and of a microscopic (pursuit) model called SITRA-B [GAB 98].

The work by Magne *et al.* [MAG 00] emphasizes compatibility between the two models. By observing experimental flow/density data and the fundamental diagram, the authors ascertain that, whatever the model, the following constraints must be respected:

- $q = q_{max}$ *to* $\rho = \rho_{cr}$: the flow/density function attains its maximum (capacity) at density ρ_{max};

- $\dfrac{\partial q}{\partial \rho} = 0$ to $\rho = \rho_{max}$: at ρ_{max} the incline of curve $q = f(\rho)$ is zero;

- $q_\rho = 0$ to $\rho = 0$: the flow at $\rho = 0$ is zero;

- $\dfrac{\partial q}{\partial q} = v_1$ to $\rho = 0$: the incline of curve $q = f(\rho)$ is equal to the free speed at $\rho = 0$;

- $q_\rho = 0$ to $\rho = \rho_{max}$: the flow at congestion is zero.

The compatibility of the models is ensured while vehicles are stationary since all of the above constraints are respected. Generally speaking, macroscopic models satisfy all of these constraints, while most microscopic models do not.

More precisely, the microscopic model used by Magne cannot satisfy the second and fourth constraints above because for an infinitely large intervehicle distance the maximum speed tends toward infinity.

The principle of communication between the two models is based on the calculation of the parameters characterizing the macroscopic part, and the transmission of conditions to the limits of the transitional zones. These parameters are considered to be constant througout macroscopic step of time. The microscopic model, in contrast, evolves in an independent manner by using the limit conditions provided by the macroscopic model. Note that communication must be ensured:

– *In the macro-micro sense*: the macroscopic model imposes outflow and speed on the transitional zone. However, vehicles are generated from a distribution of speed (Poisson distribution) and at the times of generation (normal distribution). For the choice of lanes, a binomial distribution based on initial speed and density is used. In order to create an outflow close to that imposed by the macroscopic part, a correction is made to the distribution of generation intervals. However, the absence of space to generate a new vehicle leads to the formation of a vertical waiting line.

– *In the micro-macro sense*, the process of aggregation of parameters takes into account the average speed of the vehicles leaving the microscopic zone, as well as the outflow and density of the last microscopic cell. This information is then communicated to the macroscopic part. Nevertheless, one of the problems encountered at this level is due to the propagation of the circulation conditions of vehicles that are downstream. In fact, since the law of pursuit is only applicable in the microscopic zone, vehicles are not subject to any constraint and tend to circulate at their desired speed. In order to resolve this problem, Magne proposed the creation of a phantom vehicle representing the first vehicle leaving the transition zone. The parameters of this vehicle are determined by the conditions of circulation in the macroscopic zone (its speed is equal to the speed of flow) and are calculated at each macroscopic time step. In this way, the trajectories of the vehicles leaving the microscopic zone follow that of the phantom vehicle.

The method of validation of the hybrid model proposed by Magne consists of a comparative study with results obtained from a macroscopic model used alone.

Though the model proposed by Magne represents a certain advance in the domain of hybrid modeling, its pairing schema presents several inadequacies and generates some irregularities, mainly in a congested system. In fact, if there is insufficient space, a line of vehicles waiting to be created is formed. The next step of calculation time must then be waited for in order to be able to generate these vehicles, which causes a delay in the spread of congestion.

Magne's model also has other limitations related to the creation of vehicles in the macro–micro sense. The outflow values imposed on the microscopic part are not necessarily whole numbers. For example, for an outflow of 0.2 veh/s imposed in a macroscopic time step 8 s long, the number of vehicles generated in the microscopic part is 1.6 veh, which requires an adaptation since it is impossible to generate an incomplete vehicle at the microscopic level, which the Magne model does not address. Moreover, the stochastic generation of vehicles and the introduction of a correction at outflow in the Magne model can cause the principle of flow conservation to be broken. Finally, the absence of a procedure to correct downstream outflow values leads to the waiting line being at risk for creating unrealistic density values (greater than the maximum density).

4.5.2. *The Poschinger model*

The Poschinger model [POS 02] is based on the pairing of the *intelligent driver* pursuit model and the Payne macroscopic model. This association of two models with totally different behaviors has given rise to a heterogeneous hybrid model.

The transmission of information is done progressively, in the same manner as the Magne model. In fact, this model proposes to insert a transitional zone in order to ensure communication between the two models. In this context, the micro–macro transition is ensured by a stochastic disaggregation algorithm, while the inverse transition is done with the help of an aggregation algorithm.

The two models are synchronized in the same way as the Magne model. To ensure communication between the two worlds, the Euler method has been integrated. This is used to combine the information needed by both models at each instant, taking into consideration the last time step as a predictive piece of information that is necessary for the next time step.

The principle of the micro–macro transition is based on the generation of vehicles while taking into account the following microscopic characteristics:

– distribution of intervehicle distance;

– fluctuation of speed; and

– the law of relaxation toward speed.

Particular attention has been paid to the first characteristic. Intervehicular distance is generated in a deterministic manner by adding a random noise and a distribution of speed. In his books, the author discusses the application of two solutions that have previously been adopted to solve this problem. The first consists of using deterministic speeds by adding a virtual zone within the microscopic part, where the vehicles may eventually self-distribute. The second alternative is based on the integration of interactions (friction) between vehicles. These interactions give rise to accelerations, decelerations, passing, etc. Reaching unconvincing statistical results, the author has chosen to use the Ferrari model [FER 88] to generate the auto-correlated speeds of the cars:

$$v_i = v_{i-1} + \alpha e_i - (1-\alpha)e_{i-1}$$

where e_i are the values of a normal distribution with zero average and standard deviation σ_e. α is an average movement parameter. σ_e and α are estimated using individual vehicle data. The correlated speeds provided by this method are independent of the step-of-time. In Burghout [BUR 04] it has been shown that the level of correlation of speeds is elevated for small periods of time, but diminishes as the time period grows. This effect causes the artificial accelerations and decelerations of vehicles entering the microscopic zone.

The micro–macro interface generates strong oscillations that affect the macroscopic cells situated upstream as well as downstream. These oscillations are due to the discrete character of the outflow at the level of this interface. They have a negative effect, as they do not allow us to validate the model with any ease.

4.5.3. *The Bourrel model (HYSTRA)*

Bourrel has combined the different pairing schemas cited above and considerably improved them. The Bourrel model (HYSTRA) was developed from the pairing of a first-order LWR model (STRADA) [BUI 96] and a microscopic optimal velocity model [NEW 61] (a pursuit model based on the LWR model). The two models are synchronized, as in the case of the Magne and Poschinger models. This model also includes the ideas of the fictional vehicle and of virtual transitional cells.

In the macro–micro transition, moments of vehicle creation are calculated using the macroscopic cell exit outflow in order to obtain a uniform distribution of vehicles. The distance that separates two successive vehicle generations is therefore equal to the inverse of the outflow. When the generation time of a vehicle is obtained, it is created if, and only if, there is enough space (space $> \rho_{max}$); if not, its creation is delayed. The number of vehicles is not necessarily whole. However, Bourrel has introduced the idea of a portion of a vehicle in order to ensure the preservation of flow. The problem with this method of vehicle generation is that during congestion vehicles are generated with speeds of zero.

In the same way as in the Magne model, a fictional vehicle is created in the micro–macro transition zone in order to determine the movement characteristics of the vehicles leaving the microscopic part. The exit of vehicles depends on the vacancy in the macroscopic zone. These exits are delayed if the demand is greater than the number of spaces available. In this case, the characteristics of vehicle movement are changed in order to ensure a higher exit time.

The validation of the model consists of verifying the preservation and continuity of flow. To do this, Bourrel [BOU 03] suggested a study of the spread of congestion up- and downstream. The results were then compared to those of the STRADA macroscopic model.

The results are convincing in both the fluid and congested modes, with the exception of several oscillations that appear in the transition cell. These are due to estimates of the idea of portions of vehicles.

This model does present some limitations, however, such as:

– the use of the LWR model is not adapted to address complex phenomena that occur outside the equilibrium state (acceleration and deceleration, the spread of congestion upstream in the case of dense traffic, etc.);

– it does not take into account multilane infrastructures; and

– the homogeneous character of the model does not take into account the different types of vehicles.

Though several extensions based on stochastic considerations (distribution of desired speed, interval between vehicles) have been added to the Bourrel model, their application remains very limited due to the insufficiencies of the first-order model. In fact, since this model is deterministic by nature, the introduction of random distributions affects the compatibility of the two models brought into play in the hybrid structure and breaks the law of outflow conservation.

We will now present models that improve on the Bourrel model; namely those of Mammar, Espié and El Hmam.

4.5.4. *The Mammar model*

The hybrid model developed by Mammar [MAM 06] emerged from that proposed by Bourrel. It is based on the same pairing schema, but differs mainly in the models used. This hybrid model is based on the joint use of the second-order ARZ model (this acronym is based on the the intials of its developers Aw, Rascale [AW 01] and Zhang [ZHA 02]), and the microscopic optimal velocity model [NEW 61]. These two models were chosen so as to ensure their compatibility. In this context, the ARZ model underwent several improvements and has been used in the form of the LWR model. It is based on the idea of supply and demand.

The model is validated using two scenarios. The first is dedicated to the validation of the model at equilibrium, in order to be able to compare it to other models. The second scenario involves the study of the transmission of data in the macro–micro transition zone. Though the analytical solution to the ARZ model is very difficult to obtain, the results of the validation of the hybrid model proposed are very encouraging in the case of equilibrium and in transitional mode. However, the micro–macro transition still requires several improvements.

4.5.5. *The Espié model*

An initial feasibility study of the hybrid model was conducted within the INRETS Institute (Institut National de REcherche sur les Transports et leur Securité) by the MSIS (modélisations, simulation et simulateurs de conduite) team in 1995. The resulting model developed jointly uses the ArchiSim microscopic model and the SSMT (simulation semi-macroscopique de traffic) macroscopic model (these two models were developed by INRETS). The transmission of data is ensured by information exchange objects called "interfaces". This initial approach to hybrid modeling did not, however, take into account the idea of portions of vehicles, or synchronization problems.

Espié [ESP 06] improved this model by proposing a pairing schema ensuring the correct propagation of conditions at the limits, the preservation of flow, and the continuity of information.

Unlike the Bourrel model, the Espié model is heterogeneous; it pairs two models that do not have the same law of behavior. Nevertheless, the pairing procedure is very similar to that adopted by Bourrel. It uses the ideas of transitional zones, portions of vehicles, and the phantom vehicle.

Validation of this proposition is based on the verification of two properties of the hybrid model: preservation of flow and the correct propagation of information. The authors carried out experiments in the case of a single-lane network and a two-lane network. The results show that the Espié model preserves flow and ensures its continuity. Being heterogeneous, no validation (analytical or numerical) of the compatibility of the two models was conducted. Moreover, the same inconveniences observed in the Bourrel hybrid model have been detected here, notably those related to the procedure of discrete generation of vehicles and to the introduction of the idea of portions of vehicles. Though this model addresses multilane sections of road, there is no precision involved at this level with regard to vehicles' use of a particular lane at the entry point to the microscopic section.

4.5.6. *The El Hmam hybrid model*

The hybrid model developed by El Hmam is a heterogeneous model pairing a microscopic and a macroscopic model [ELH 05], see Figure 4.2. The microscopic model is based on the agent paradigm [FER 95]. The hybrid model that was developed has the advantage of accepting the pairing of this microscopic model with different macroscopic models taken from the literature.

The choice of representing traffic flow at the microscopic level by agents provides great freedom in calibration and thus ensures compatibility with the macroscopic model with which it will be paired.

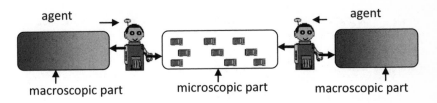

Figure 4.2. *Principle of hybridization*

Moreover, the two models are synchronized by introducing a linear relationship between the calculation steps of the microscopic and macroscopic models.

Finally, this hybrid model based on the agent paradigm constitutes the basis for a generic hybrid simulator.

4.5.6.1. *Principle of microscopic modeling based on the agent paradigm*

The quality of a microscopic model is limited by the calculation capacities that can be implemented, even more so if the laws of vehicle behavior present strong nonlinearities. In simulations, a good model is the result of a compromise between the following characteristics defined by Nagel [NAG 95]:

– resolution: the level of detail required by the simulation;

– faithfulness: the degree of realism of the model;

– size of the system;

– speed of execution of the simulation; and

– resources: time and IT material available.

Multi-agent systems allow us to address a large number of entities with complex behaviors, thus eliminating a certain number of difficulties encountered in the development of the aforementioned hybrid models.

4.5.6.2. *Architecture of the microscopic model based on the agent paradigm*

A network is composed of interconnected sections of road. Each section is made up of lanes on which vehicles drive. When several sections cross each other, they form intersections that can be directed by traffic lights or by right-of-way. To reach a destination, a vehicle moves at a variable speed between nodes (intersections) in the network, leaving from a point of origin and following its route plan toward its destination.

Figure 4.3 presents a simplified schema of a road network composed of two intersections and of sections of multilane road on which vehicles are driving. The entry and exit lanes (on and off ramps) are also represented, as well as various signaling systems intended to control traffic.

This network is itself part of a multi-agent system; the vehicles (car, bus, truck, etc.) are modeled by agents. Each of these agents evolves in an environment marked by road sections. The crossing of several environments gives rise to an intersection. At in an intersection, the management of priorities (right of way) is also ensured by an "intersection" agent. The system making up the network being studied is thus composed of a group of agents, characterized by specific behaviors and objectives.

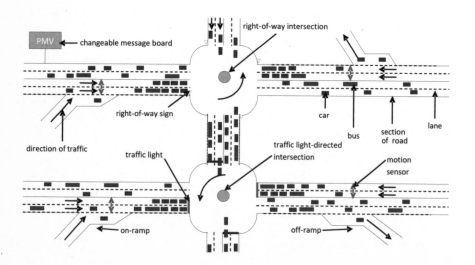

Figure 4.3. *An example of a road network*

The following section describes the basic elements of a road network, details the behavior and analyzes the functioning of the various agents.

4.5.6.2.1. Physical elements of the network

a) Sections of road

A road network is composed of a group of interconnected sections of road, characterized according to five types of functions (see Figure 4.4):

– downstream: located upstream of a macroscopic section of road;

– upstream: located downstream of a macroscopic section of road;

– origin: the entry point of a network;

– destination: the exit point of a network; and

– simple: directly connected to a microscopic section of road.

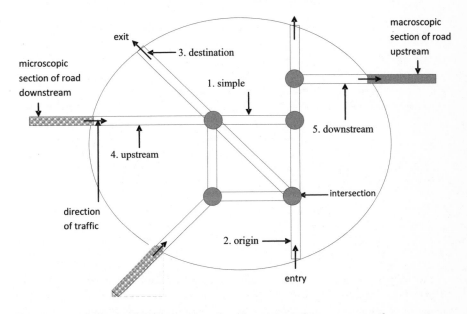

Figure 4.4. *Different types of road sections making up a network*

b) Lanes

Lanes are elements forming a section of road, and are consequently the base element from which a road network is constituted. Each lane is characterized by an identifier, a traffic direction, geographic coordinates, and the list of vehicles it contains. Other information, such as the speed authorized in the lane, the position of motion detectors, signal signs, etc., can be added to enrich the characterization of a lane depending on the objective of the simulation. Lanes are characterized by their role in the network (see Figure 4.5). Vehicles adopt relative behaviors, taking into account their environment and their location in these lanes.

c) Nodes

The intersection of two or more sections of road corresponds to a crossroads or a roundabout. A roundabout is made up of a group of lanes leading to circular lanes, while a crossroads is the intersection of a group of rectilinear lanes. The movement of vehicles at intersections is managed by a right-of-way sign or a traffic light.

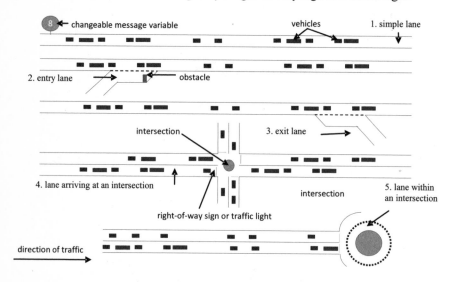

Figure 4.5. *Different types of traffic lanes*

4.5.6.2.2. Simulation agents

Two types of agents coexist within a road network: "vehicle" agents and "intersection" agents. The lifecycle of these two reactive agents is illustrated in Figure 4.6. Each agent is characterized by a limited lifespan depending on its arrival at its destination if it is a vehicle type of agent, and by the end of the simulation if it is an intersection type of agent.

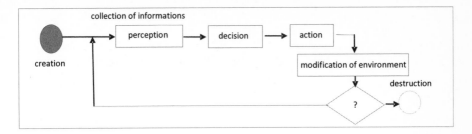

Figure 4.6. *Lifecycle of an agent*

a) Vehicle agent

A vehicle agent manages the movements of a vehicle while respecting safety regulations (safety distance, speed limit, etc.). Each vehicle agent is characterized by its maximum speed, its maximum acceleration, its itinerary, etc. The vehicle agent is autonomous. It has its own objective and its own understanding of the environment. This understanding, which is supposed to be partial, corresponds to the driver's field of vision (see Figure 4.7), and allows the agent to evolve within his immediate environment. The vehicle agent is a reactive agent [FER 95]. Its decisions are generated on the basis of its perception of the environment. Its actions are physical movements on a route. Before moving, it evaluates its environment (it detects the vehicles surrounding it and the road infrastructures). It collects all of the information pertaining to it, particularly the positions and speeds of vehicles that are close by within a radius limited by the driver's field of vision. This field of vision depends on meteorological conditions (rain), traffic (congestion), and the geometry of the road infrastructure.

During its movement, the vehicle agent adjusts its speed to attain the desired speed. It tends to accelerate if its speed is less than the desired value, depending on the space available. In the case of dense traffic, the agent's first reaction is to verify whether or not it is possible to overtake. At this stage, passing is subject to the regulations dictated by the lane-change model. Faced with the impossibility of passing, it remains on its original route, while adjusting its speed according to the car-following model.

Thus, the behavior of the vehicle agent is subject to two complementary laws; the first concerning the application of a car-following model, and the second based on the lane-change model. The following section describes the principles of these two laws.

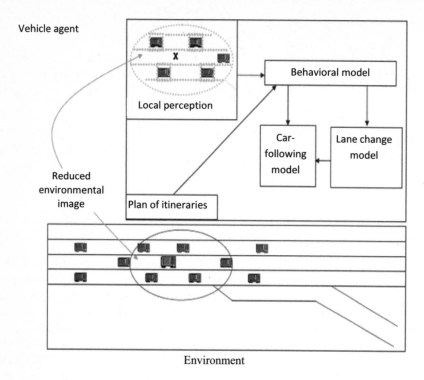

Vehicle agent

Behavioral model

Local perception

Car-following model

Lane change model

Reduced environmental image

Plan of itineraries

Environment

Figure 4.7. *Vehicle agent*

b) Laws of pursuit

The model adopted is that developed by Krauss [KRA 98]. It is based on the principle of a safe speed allowing a vehicle to remain a reasonable distance from the vehicle in front of it.

If it is respected, the safety speed enables a collision to be avoided when the downstream vehicle brakes sharply. The safety speed is calculated using the following relationship:

$$v_{safe}(t) = \tilde{v}(t) + \frac{g_t - \tilde{v}(t)\tau}{\dfrac{\tilde{v}(t)}{b} + \tau}$$

[4.21]

where:

- $\tilde{v}(t)$: the speed of the front vehicle at time t;

– g_t: the distance separating the two vehicles at time t;

– $\bar{v}(t)$: the average of the two speeds v and $\tilde{v}$ at time t;

– b: maximum deceleration of the vehicle in m = s²; and

– τ: driver's reaction time in seconds.

In addition, a vehicle's speed is limited by the speed limit imposed for the lane without passing its desired speed, v_{des}, and by its maximum acceleration. These limitations are used to calculate an intermediary speed expressed by:

$$v_{inter}(t) = \min\left\{v(t) + ah, v_{safe}(t), v_{max}, v_{des}\right\}$$ [4.22]

Knowing that a driver cannot maintain a constant speed during a given time span (due to driver imperfection), the model imposes a fluctuation in the speed. This fluctuation is expressed using a random variable η following a normal distribution in the interval [0.1], and the amplitude of the noise, ε, considered equal to the driver's reaction time. The vehicle's speed is thus expressed by the following relationship:

$$v(t+h) = \max\left\{0, v_{inter}(t) - \varepsilon a\eta\right\}$$ [4.23]

The Krauss model is a car-following model that has the advantage of being quick to execute thanks to the limited number of equations that characterize it. It also presents the particularity of being without collisions for a period of time lasting $h \leq 1$ second, $\varepsilon = \tau = 1$ second, $a = 0.2$ g, and $b = 0.6$ g where (g $= 9.81$ m/s²).

Moreover, this model is capable of perfectly reproducing the macroscopic characteristics of flow [KRA 02, KRA 04].

c) Laws of lane change

These laws constitute a group of rules that ensure the proper execution of overtaking and pulling-back maneuvers. This group of rules ensures safety during a lane change.

If a vehicle wishes to drive at a speed higher than that of the vehicle in front of it, it is prompted to overtake the car in front. This maneuver can only occur if safety conditions allow it.

Before overtaking a vehicle, the agent which models this vehicle must make sure that a certain number of conditions are fulfilled, so that it cannot hit, or be hit by, another vehicle. This certainty is achieved with the help of information collected during the perception of its environment.

d) Intersection agent

An intersection agent manages access to intersections. Depending on the type of intersection (right-of-way or light traffic), it takes on behavior that allows it to ensure the safety of vehicles, notably by estimating the future position of the vehicles after each step of the calculation.

4.5.6.3. *Hybrid model validation procedure*

A hybrid section of road has been subjected to two tests. The first consists of applying an increased traffic flow, and the second a reduction of this traffic flow at the entry point to the section of road.

The results are compared to those obtained from the same test applied to a section of road that was completely simulated using a macroscopic model (see Figure 4.8). They show the perfect compatibility of the models, which explains the interest in this modeling approach.

4.5.7. *Comparison of the hybrid models presented and general remarks*

Table 4.2 shows the principal elements used to compare the hybrid models presented above.

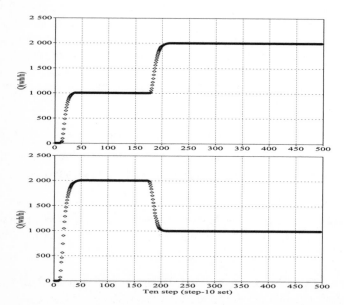

Figure 4.8. *Results of tests during an increase in traffic flow*

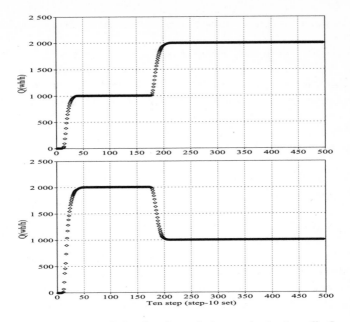

Figure 4.8. (continued) *Results of tests during a reduction in traffic flow*

Name of model	Microscopic model	Macroscopic model	Pairing procedure and type of infrastructure
Magne (2000)	SITRA-B+	SIMRES	Heterogeneous and multi-lane
Poschinger (2002)	Intelligent driver model	Payne	Heterogeneous and multi-lane
Bourrel (2003)	Optimal velocity	LWR	Homogeneous and multi-lane
El Hmam (2004)	Optimal velocity	LWR, ARZ and Payne	Heterogeneous, generic, and multi-lane
Espié (2006)	ARCHISM	MSIS	Heterogeneous and multi-lane
Mammar (2006)	Optimal velocity	ARZ	Homogeneous and multi-lane

Table 4.2. *Elements of comparison of the hybrid models that have been presented*

The study of hybrid models leads us to eventually draw several conclusions:

– hybrid models are mainly differentiated by:

- the flow models used within the same structure. In this context, when the two models are generated using the same law of behavior, we refer to a homogeneous hybrid model; if not, the model is heterogeneous,

- pairing procedure, and

- the type of network being studied, which can be formed of multilane or single-lane sections of road;

– the compatibility of the two representations within hybrid models is often difficult or even impossible to prove. Compatability is generally obtained by deriving the microscopic model from the macroscopic equation applied solely to the law of pursuit. Given that microscopic representations integrate other behavioral laws besides the law of pursuit (such as the lane-change law, etc.), it is difficult to prove whether the two models are equivalent or not, particularly in the congested mode;

– hybrid models do not truly satisfy the constraints that a hybrid model must satisfy, and they are generally difficult to implement due to their complexity. In fact, the Magne and Poschinger models introduce undesirable effects into the propagation of information, particularly the fluctuations detected at the exit points of sections of road. The Mammar and Espié models have adopted the same pairing procedure as used in the Bourrel model, improving it by the application of second-order macroscopic representations. They retain the same flaws as the second-order model, however, notably the idea of portions of vehicles, which cause fluctuations and can affect the preservation of flow;

– all of the work done on hybrid models emphasizes the aggregation and disaggregation of data and the compatibility of two representations, without focusing on real applications; and

– hybrid models remain underdeveloped, and are rarely used in the development of control laws.

In the following section, we will examine the major principles adopted for the regulation of road traffic.

4.6. Different strategies for controlling road traffic flow systems

4.6.1. *Regulation of access: definition and history*

Excess demand for access is a major cause of congestion. The regulation of road flow on high-traffic routes is most often carried out by controlling the outflow of vehicles entering a highway using a slip or rapid lane (ramp meter). This outflow control is used to keep demand at a level below the capacity of the highway downstream of the ramp, beyond which there is congestion, and consequently to avoid a capacity drop. Moreover, the regulation of access is also used to control vehicle insertion times, which allows us to reduce conflicts and traffic backlog and consequently to improve the safety of users.

Regulation of access principally addresses the problems related to recurring congestion. It has no effect – and is therefore not implemented – during periods of average or low traffic, particularly at night.

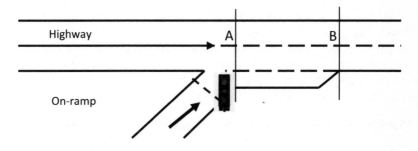

Figure 4.9. *A highway with an on-ramp*

Access can be regulated:

– locally in a fast lane (local control or localized regulation), see Figure 4.9; or

– globally on an axis with several access points (coordinated control or axis regulation).

Regulation of access is not a new traffic management technique. The initial access regulation systems appeared in the United States, with the first experiments occurring in Detroit. The first regulated access point was installed in Chicago in a fast lane in 1963. It was based on the use of a police officer whose role was to allow only a single vehicle at a time to pass, according to a predetermined outflow. This experiment was followed by others, notably in Los Angeles in 1968 and then in Minneapolis in 1970.

The Minneapolis site (Minnesota, United States) is one of the best-known access-regulation systems in the world; it includes nearly 433 regulated access points over 500 km. The access control principle functions with the help of traffic lights, either in an isolated manner using fixed traffic-light plans, or connected to a centralized system that controls the regulation parameters.

This American access regulation has been widely shown to be effective in increasing the average speed of vehicles, increasing outflow, and improving safety, with a significant drop in accident rates at peak times.

In France, the first tests occurred in 1967. They were conducted on the A13 highway. The first five truely regulated access points were installed in 1975, on highway A1[6]. As part of the "Ile-de-France mornings" operation in 1976, a system functioning during the peak hours in the morning and on Sunday evening was installed on the A1, A3 and A6 highways. It was based on regulation via fixed-cycle traffic lights and had 40 access points[7].

In the UK in 1986, an access regulation system was installed on the M6 (the Midlands) highway and progressively expanded to six isolated access points in 1989. Currently, only the cities of Birmingham and Southampton are equipped with access regulation[8]. In Southampton, on the M3 and M27 highways, six two-lane access points are regulated, either via the demand–capacity system or by other control systems (telematics and road security).

Today, numerous other sites have implemented access regulation systems:

– in the Netherlands, on the A10 West highway near Amsterdam;

– in Glasgow, Scotland;

– in Essen, Germany; and

– in Louvain, Belgium;

Many other sites are being studied in Italy, the UK, Switzerland, and Spain. In Canada, such regulatory systems have been installed in Montreal, Ottawa and Toronto.

---

6 www.certu.fr.
7 http://lara.inist.fr/bitstream/handle/2332/975/CERTU-97-18.PDF?sequence=2.
8 www.highways.gov.uk/knowledge/documents/Ramp_Metering_Summary_Report.pdf.

4.6.2. *Access regulation methods (metering systems)*

We can find various methods used to implement access regulation in the literature. Among these methods, we can distinguish two levels of regulation: static and dynamic.

4.6.2.1. *Static regulation*

This type of regulation acts on the number of waiting lines by:

– modifying the access route to reduce its capacity; and

– managing access by channeling vehicles entering in a single line using a ground marker (see Figure 4.10). This access management reduces the ramp outflow and consequently reduces the number of conflicts between cars entering the highway. It also has a very low implementation cost.

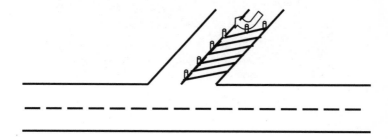

Figure 4.10. *Marking of an access point*

4.6.2.2. *Dynamic regulation*

Dynamic regulation consists of dividing up the number of vehicles entering the highway into smaller groups. It assumes the implementation of traffic lights or barriers on the on-ramps (see the Fourvière tunnel in Lyon shown in Figure 4.11), where the access points are closed for a span of time varying from five to 10 minutes; this closure is communicated to users via changeable message boards. Barrier regulation is effective but sudden and difficult to adjust, and can irritate drivers.

In the following section, we will examine only those access regulation strategies that use traffic lights. In this case, the flow of vehicles authorized to access the fast lane from an on-ramp is converted into a cycle of traffic lights. The access flow is adapted to variations in traffic. These regulation strategies usually use historical measurements, real-time data, and estimations or predictions of demand. Most traffic-light regulation strategies (see Figure 4.12) allow us to ensure the flow of vehicles from ramps in two ways:

– via flow through barriers, which allows "batches of vehicles" to enter during each cycle; and

– via "drop-by-drop" flow, which limits entry to a single vehicle per cycle.

Figure 4.11. *The Fourvière tunnel, Lyon*

Figure 4.12. *Drop-by-drop flow on the Mt. Wellington on-ramp*

Traffic-light access regulation strategies can be grouped into two main categories: fixed-cycle regulation strategies and adaptive strategies.

4.6.2.3. *Fixed-cycle access regulation strategies*

Preset operation is the simplest form of access regulation and is used in France and the United States. This approach to regulation was first suggested in [WAT 65], followed by other strategies such as that proposed by Schwartz [SCH 77]. These regulation strategies are also called fixed-cycle strategies; they use fixed-duration green lights, and the number of vehicles admitted per cycle is constant. They are based on simple static models. The reader can find an overview of these control strategies in [PAP 02].

This type of strategy, based on constant historic demands, does not take into account fluctuations of traffic in real time, unlike adaptive strategies that are based on road motion detectors and provide real-time information about the presence or absence of vehicles at given places and times. The calculation of the cycle is always carried out in advance, using historical measurements of ramp and highway demand. Demand is not constant and may vary depending on the day of the week or in the case of events that are not necessarily predictable.

The use of historical data can lead to on-ramp flows that are not suitable to the current situation. The absence of real-time measurements on the state of traffic can cause the highway to be underused or overloaded (congested). The advantage presented by this type of strategy, however, is its very simple material configuration.

4.6.2.4. *Adaptive access regulation strategies*

Adaptive control strategies offer real-time calculation methods of admissible flow using one or more parameters characteristic of the state of traffic: rates of occupation, outflow, and speed. These are variables measured using sensors placed on the road surface, on the active part of the highway and on the access ramp. The ramp outflow thus calculated is then converted into a traffic-light cycle. These strategies are intended to keep highway traffic conditions close to a desired behavior, based on real-time measurements [PAP 04].

There are local access regulation strategies and coordinated access regulation strategies. The former consist of regulating isolated access points and are based on approximate measurements for each ramp, in order to calculate the corresponding individual access outflows. The latter manage several access points in a portion of highway and use the available measurements for this entire portion.

In the following section, we will examine adaptive strategies.

4.6.3. *Adaptive local access regulation strategies (responsive ramp metering control strategy)*

These are local regulation techniques that consider access points in a manner isolated from one another. The access outflow in these strategies is based on real-time measurements near the ramp. The goal is to keep traffic conditions on the section of ramp close to a desired behavior. The appropriate access outflow is calculated by analyzing the occupation or flow via sensors on the ramp and the main section.

These systems are costly to install and maintain, but they are able to regulate unusual and unforeseen changes in traffic, and generally give good results. The material configuration is similar to that of fixed-cycle strategies, with the addition of sensors on the main section near the ramp.

The main criticism of these algorithms is that they adjust access outflows after the appearance of congestion. The two regulation strategies, the demand-capacity strategy and the occupancy strategy [MAS 75], are part of this type of access regulation and are popular in the United States.

Another closed-loop access regulation strategy (*Asservissement LINéaire d'Entrée Autoroutière*, or Linear Highway Entry Control, known as ALINEA) was proposed by [PAP 91]. It is based on classic feedback concepts and is popular in Europe.

Results have shown the effectiveness of ALINEA compared to other regulation strategies, as well as to uncontrolled environments [PAP 98].

According to the INRETS report [HAJ 88], an access point marketing evaluation report, this strategy improves insertion, thus reducing the time spent in congestion by 41%. The method has since been implemented in Paris on the ring road.

Most access regulations pertain to the regulation of access to a ramp toward a highway, but there are also adaptive on-highway access regulation strategies. On-highway control is a local control action that is applicable where the parts of two highways merge.

On-highway control can be considered to be a form of local access regulation. The main difference lies in access outflow. Compared to classic access regulation, the access outflow of on-highway control is larger (depending on the number of lanes in the highway).

In the following, we will explore the best-known adaptive regulation strategies. Since the intention is to keep the state of traffic downstream of the ramp close to a desired behavior, the desired optimum may be a maximum outflow (demand-capacity algorithm) or an occupation rate.

4.6.3.1. *The demand-capacity strategy*

The demand-capacity strategy [MAS 75] was introduced with the first implementations of local adaptive (reactive) access regulations.

This strategy determines, locally and in real time, the access outflow $r(k)$ (number of vehicles authorized to enter during period k) using entry–exit capacity data, based on the following relationship:

$$r(k) = \begin{cases} q_{cap} - q_{in}(k-1), & \text{if } o_{out}(k) \le o_{cr} \\ r_{min}, & \text{else} \end{cases} \qquad [4.24]$$

where:

– q_{cap} is the highway capacity measured downstream of the ramp, which is a value predetermined using the fundamental diagram;

– outflow $q_{in}(k-1)$ is the measured flow during the period $k-1$ in real time by magnetic loops (or other sensors) upstream of the ramp;

– $o_{out}(k)$ is the occupation measured downstream of the ramp, while

– o_{cr} is the critical occupation for which traffic flow is maximal.

This strategy allows us to add a flow $r(k)$ to the entry flow upstream $q_{in}(k-1)$ in order to attain the capacity q_{cap} of the highway downstream of the ramp (see Figure 4.13).

This adaptive strategy requires two measurement stations; one upstream of the access point to calculate outflow q_{in}, and the other downstream to determine the occupation rate o_{out}. Its advantage is that it takes into account real-time variations in traffic, while its disadvantage is that it functions in an open loop.

The INRETS demand–capacity strategy is a variant of the standard demand–capacity strategy wherein another sensor is installed at the access point (the convergence point) in the fast lane in order to take into consideration the state of congestion at this point. It was tested on the Paris ring road in 1988.

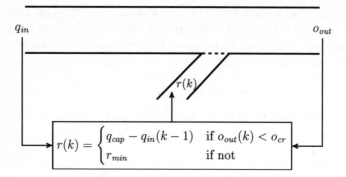

Figure 4.13. *Standard demand–capacity strategy*

4.6.3.2. *Occupancy strategy*

The second category of local regulation is the occupancy strategy [MAS 75]. This strategy is used in the United States (Chicago, Los Angeles, etc.) and is based on the same principal as the standard demand–capacity strategy defining ramp outflow $r(k)$ as the additional outflow upstream measured in order to obtain the highway capacity downstream. However, in this case, the authorized ramp outflow $r(k)$ is based on the measurement of the occupancy upstream of the ramp.

This strategy is economical and only requires a single sensor upstream of the ramp for the measurement of the occupation rate. It is known for its low installation cost and simplicity of implementation, but since the sensor is located upstream of the access point, this strategy often reacts too late to the appearance of congestion downstream of the access point.

4.6.3.3. *Wotton-Jeffreys strategy*

Other access regulation strategies have been developed; for example, the British Wotton–Jeffreys (W&J) strategy, which operates in real time. In this strategy, the downstream capacity changes depending on the state of traffic. The operating principle of this strategy is the same as it is for the others: the measurement of the upstream outflow (Q_{am}) is completed by the ramp outflow $r(k)$ in order to obtain capacity (Q_{max}) downstream. It is governed by the following rules:

– if $Qr + Q_{am} > Q_{max}$ then the ramp traffic light changes to red; and

– if $Qr + Q_{am} < Q_{max}$ then the ramp traffic light changes to green.

This strategy requires three measurement stations placed respectively on the ramp, upstream and downstream of the road section in order to determine capacity.

Wotton and Jeffreys developed software to determine this capacity in real time using the measurement of outflow (Q_{av}) and speed (V_{av}).

This strategy has two advantages: its reactivity, and the optimization of the number of vehicles entering the road. However, it is very difficult to calibrate, and requires the installation of a large number of sensors.

4.6.3.4. *Rijkswaterstaat strategy*

The Dutch Rijkswaterstaat strategy uses the same principle as the standard demand–capacity strategy. It is used in the Netherlands. Congestion is detected using speed measurements upstream and downstream of the access point (flow is supposed to be in congestion if traffic speed is lower than 35 km/h).

It is used in Amsterdam in the "vehicle-by-vehicle" filtering mode. It has the advantage of easy calibration and only requires two sensors, but it remains an open-loop control.

4.6.3.5. *Predictive local access regulation algorithms: the ALINEA strategy*

This type of algorithm uses the closed-loop control principle to locally determine the access outflow and to try to anticipate operational problems. ALINEA [PAP 91] is used to determine the appropriate access outflow using real-time traffic measurements downstream of the ramp.

ALINEA is the first local access regulation strategy based on a simple application of the classic feedback control theory. Tested in France, the Netherlands, and the UK, it has given very good results when compared to several other strategies [PAP 98].

The ALINEA algorithm obeys the principles of first-order control systems; its objective is to keep occupation downstream of the ramp on the highway equal to a value o_d defined in advance, called the set-point or desired value in order to guarantee an absence of congestion. This is preferably – but not necessarily – inferior to the critical value (o_{cr}).

The number of vehicles $r(k)$ (in veh./h) authorized to enter the highway during each period of time k is based on the following relationship:

$$r(k) = r(k-1) + K_R(o_d - o_{out}(k))$$
[4.25]

The ALINEA strategy is activated at each interval of control time, with a length between 10 and 60 seconds. ALINEA is based on the principle of a discrete integral regulator [PAP 03]; entry $r(k)$ is obtained by integrating the control error $(o_d - o_{out}(k))$ where:

– $r(k)$ is the number of vehicles (in veh./h) authorized to enter during the interval of time $[kT, (k+1)T]$ and is used to calculate the ramp flow $r(k+1)$, and T is a defined interval of control time, usually between 10 seconds and one minute;

– o_d is the desired occupation chosen by the user. It is assumed to be known, and can be changed at any time [KOT 04]. It is often equal to critical occupation (which corresponds to a downstream flow close to capacity q_{cap});

– $O_{out}(k)$ is the average occupation measured (in Per cent) downstream of the ramp during the preceding interval of control time $[(k-1)T, kT]$. The measurement o_{out} of occupation used by ALINEA must be taken a few hundred meters downstream of the most probable site of congestion; and

– $K_R > 0$ is the regulator gain determined heuristically at the site (its value is homogeneous to a flow).

Experience shows that the results of regulation using ALINEA are not greatly affected by the choice of parameter K_R [HAS 02, KOT 04]. The value $K_R = 70$ veh./h is chosen by most authors.

Bellemans [BEL 06] presents the results of simulations using the ALINEA strategy on the E17 Ghent–Antwerp highway in Belgium. It is noted that fluctuations (in speed, flow, density, and access outflow) are larger and can become more dangerous when the regulator gain K_R increases. Therefore, the smaller this gain, the greater the delay in traffic light control with regard to the appearance of congestion; the more important it is; and the more reactive the the control is, causing instabilities.

By definition, vehicle outflow $r(k)$ is often included in the interval $[r_{min}, r_{max}]$. Imposing r_{min} prevents the total closure of the ramp, which allows us to limit vehicle waiting time in the line on the ramp during regulation during high traffic demand. Imposing r_{max} limits the outflow $r(k)$, which must not exceed the capacity of the on-ramp.

The flow $r(k)$ calculated by ALINEA is truncated, and is used as $r(k-1)$ in the following period of time, in order to avoid the wind-up effect of the integral regulator.

ALINEA optimizes the occupation rate of the sensor, and not the outflow, as in the capacity–demand strategy, which allows us to determine real traffic conditions. The principal reason for this is that a state of fluid traffic and a state of congested traffic both correspond to a flow value (see the fundamental diagram - Figure 4.1).

Moreover, the occupation o_d that is chosen as is often close to the critical occupation o_{cr}. In addition, in comparison to the capacity q_{cap} used by the demand–capacity strategy, critical occupation is less sensitive to changes in environmental conditions (weather, for example), or to the composition of traffic (such as the presence of trucks) [KEE 86].

ALINEA requires a single sensor on the principal road surface in order to measure the occupancy, $o_{out}(k)$, downstream of the on-ramp. The placement of this sensor must be such that recurring congestion is visible in the measurements. ALINEA operates in a closed loop and reacts to the differences $(o_d - o_{out}(k))$, which allows us to avoid congestion and stabilizes traffic flow at a higher level [PAP 02]. However, its parameters are difficult to set, particularly the gain parameter K_R. Inadequate setting increases the risk of fluctuations.

Papageorgiou [PAP 97] has presented the main characteristics of ALINEA, as well as the results of the first implementation of the strategy on a single on-ramp in Briançon (France), or in the case of several on-ramps (METALINE: not yet implemented), on the Paris ring road and the A10 West Highway in Amsterdam (the Coentunnel on-ramp).

ALINEA has been compared to other control strategies, including the demand–capacity control strategy, the occupancy strategy, the W&J strategy, and the Rijkswaterstaat strategy. The results show that ALINEA provides the best outcome.

4.6.3.6. *Comparison of the ALINEA strategy with the demand–capacity and occupancy strategy strategies*

The demand–capacity and occupancy strategy strategies are based on measurements of flow and occupation on the principal section of road upstream of the ramp, while ALINEA is a closed-loop regulator based on occupation measurements downstream of the ramp.

The demand–capacity strategy reacts to heavy occupations o_{out} once a threshold value o_{cr} has been attained, while ALINEA reacts to small differences $(o_d - o_{out}(k))$. It can thus avoid the appearance of congestion while stabilizing the traffic flow to a considerable degree.

Recent applications of ALINEA have shown certain problems and needs that are not resolved by ALINEA or by the other access regulation strategies, such as:

– the use of upstream measurements (rather than downstream ones);

– the use of measurements based on flow (rather than occupation);

– a real-time adjustment of the desired values in order to maximize flow in the downstream fast lane; and

– an effective regulation of the waiting line in order to avoid the spread of congestion in the secondary network.

Smaragdis [SMA 04] proposes an extension of ALINEA called the AD-ALINEA (adaptive ALINEA) strategy. It contains an algorithm to estimate critical occupation using real-time measurements of $q_{out}(k-1)$ and $o_{out}(k-1)$ downstream of the ramp. This procedure is useful in the case where there is difficulty estimating critical occupation, or when this occupation changes in real time due to changes in environmental conditions or the composition of traffic (trucks, buses, etc.).

The strategy AD-ALINEA needs downstream real-time measurements to estimate q_{out} and o_{out}. In cases where such measurements are not available, another strategy, UP-ALINEA (which stands for Upstream-ALINEA) is suggested. In this strategy, a method for estimating q_{out} and o_{out} from upstream measurements is proposed [SMA 03].

In [YIB 06], the ALINEA (integral regulator) strategy was modified into a proportional–integral strategy in order to resolve the case of narrowing located downstream of the on-ramp. The results showed that ALINEA was less effective in this case, while its expansion into a proportional–integral regulator brought satisfying improvements.

In a book by Bellemans [BEL 06], the ALINEA strategy is applied to the E-17 Ghent–Antwerp highway in Belgium, and is compared to optimal predictive control using simulation techniques. The results show that ALINEA causes a gain in total time spent and is able to limit waiting lines to values close to the maximum limit. This limit of waiting lines means that fluctuations appear in the access outflow, traffic density and average speed on the section of road to which the ramp is connected. In Bellemans's work, predictive control of access leads to higher performances (low total time spent) compared to the ALINEA strategy. Moreover, no fluctuations appeared; the access outflows of predictive control were smooth, as were densities, average speed, and flow. Thus, limitations on waiting lines in access lanes were better respected.

All access regulation strategies measure an access outflow to avoid or reduce congestion; this outflow causes a limitation in the number of vehicles accessing the fast lane. This limitation causes an increase in the waiting line in terms of access. The increase in the waiting line can be detected by sensors placed upstream on the ramp.

If the waiting line becomes longer than the ramp's capacity to hold vehicles, it can stretch to the surface network, so it is important to limit the length of this line. The access regulation strategies mentioned below do not take into consideration the length of the waiting line in their control algorithms. Once the maximum limit of the waiting line has been reached, the action of the regulator can be canceled to allow a larger number of cars to access the fast lane and reduce the number of vehicles waiting. These constraints are valid for any regulation strategy.

The performance of an access system depends largely on the access flow and the control strategy, while the access flow depends on the objective of the regulation system. If the system is planned to eliminate or reduce congestion on the principal section of road, the access flow is based on the demand in the principal section upstream of the ramp, the capacity downstream, and the demand on the ramp. If the combination of flow upstream of the ramp and the flow on the ramp exceed the capacity of the highway, access outflows are activated to reduce ramp flow so that the downstream capacity is not exceeded.

4.6.4. *Adaptive strategies for coordinated access regulation (multivariable regulator strategies)*

In the case of a fast line with several critical access points, local strategies (demand–capacity strategy, INRETS demand–capacity strategy, W&J, ALINEA, etc.) do not lead to the optimum sought. In this case, access point regulation must be applied globally on all ramps in order to obtain maximum efficiency. This is called coordinated regulation.

Coordinated strategies have the same objectives as local strategies: they attempt to keep traffic conditions close to the desired values. They are intended to minimize the total time spent by the group of vehicles on the highway and at the access points. In contrast, unlike local strategies that optimize the state of traffic locally and only take into account the traffic conditions at the access points, coordinated strategies take into consideration not only all the available measurements taken at all access points, but also those taken between these points [PAP 02]. This allows for an overall optimization of the highway's capacity.

Additionally, a coordinated strategy is able to act at the moment there is congestion caused by an accident. When congestion forms, it spreads upstream. Access control can only react from the moment when the congestion reaches the measurement station. With its measurement stations between access points, a coordinated strategy detects the occurrence of an incident sooner than this.

Finally, the implementation of coordinated actions allows for the distribution of waiting time over various access points. Without coordination, only the vehicles coming from the access point situated just before the congestion will be able help the traffic to flow more steadily; control of the access point makes them wait so that access points upstream are not affected by the congestion.

The regulation of the coordination of access points can be carried out using synchronized local strategies (pseudo-coordination or synchronization). Local strategies can be fixed-cycle strategies or adaptive strategies. For example, in Amsterdam one coordinated strategy consists of linking the start of the Rijkswaterstaat strategy (with the aid of an operator) to an access point regulating other access points that are downstream of it.

There are also synchronized local ALINEA strategies that have been tested on the A6 highway in France. The synchronization here is different to that of Rijkswaterstaat, as it is automatic. The zones of influence must be determined in order to define which upstream access points need to be activated. The disadvantage here is that coordination only occurs at the access points. There is no taking into account of situations between access points.

Coordinated regulation techniques are more complicated; these seek to optimize a multitude of highway on-ramps. They are based on various control approaches, such as multivariable control strategies [PAP 90, DIA 94] or optimum control strategies [PAP 82, CHE 97, ZHA 99, KOT 02, KOT 04, GOM 06]. The system has more precise information. So, the calculation of the time when vehicles enter onto the highway from the on-ramp is more concise. This is better in order to prevent congestion from forming or to avoid aggravating it in the case of a non-recurring event (such as an accident). However, this assumes a link to an automatic incident detection system.

4.6.4.1. *The METALINE strategy*

The METALINE multivariable regulator strategy [PAP 90, DOA 94] devised by INRETS is a coordinated feedback control strategy developed as part of the EUROCOR project and based on the linear quadratic optimization theory. It was tested by using the METANET model on the Paris ring road and the A10-West highway in Amsterdam.

For all simulation tests carried out on the A10-West highway, the METANET macroscopic traffic model is used as a modeling and simulation tool. The simulation results are summarized according to evaluation indices: total trajectory time, total waiting time at point of origin, total time spent, total consumption of fuel, and maximum length of waiting lines at the points of origin.

The objective of this strategy is to maximize exit flow (so as to minimize the time spent in the network being studied) in a coordinated manner simultaneously controlling the flows of m on-ramps with respect to the occupation rates measured in real time for a group of n axis stations (where $n > m$). The principle consists of keeping occupation downstream of controlled ramps in the neighborhood of certain values. This strategy requires a flow traffic model from which a linear quadratic integral control law is obtained. The METALINE strategy can be seen as a generalization and expansion of ALINEA [KOT 04].

4.6.4.2. *Comparison of ALINEA and METALINE*

A comparison of local and global control strategies leads to the conclusion that local strategies are easier to design and implement [PAP 97].

Simulation tests and results regarding the effectiveness of the ALINEA and METALINE control strategies have led to the following conclusions [PAP 98, PAP 90]:

– faced with recurring congestion, METALINE does no better than the ALINEA strategy when applied locally at each ramp; and

– faced with non-recurring congestion, METALINE gives better results than ALINEA, thanks to the large number of measurements.

This can be explained by the fact that non-recurring congestion (due to a traffic incident, such as an accident) can arise anywhere on the axis before spreading upstream. The ALINEA strategy can only react when congestion reaches the measurement station placed on the ramps. METALINE, on the other hand, takes into account measurements taken between access ramps; it therefore detects the formation of a non-recurring congestion event sooner than ALINEA. Recurring congestion (due to an overly large flow demand) forms on the ramps; therefore, ALINEA and METALINE detect the congestion from the moment of its formation.

4.6.5. *Implementation of regulation via traffic lights*

Access point control consists of limiting the outflow between the on-ramp and the main route using traffic lights. Most access control strategies do not determine how the lights should change. In fact, from among the access controls that we have presented, only the W&J strategy consists of defining the color of the light according to traffic conditions. The other strategies calculate the outflow of vehicles authorized to leave the ramp. It is thus a matter of converting this outflow into traffic-light cycles. The relationship that exists between the outflow and the traffic-light cycle is shown by the following relationship:

$$g/c = r/Qsat$$

[4.26]

where:

  – c: total cycle time;

  – g: duration of the green light phase;

  – r: ramp outflow calculated by the strategy in vehicles per second; and

  – $Qsat$: outflow of ramp saturation in vehicles per second, corresponding to the ramp's flow capacity.

Using the outflow calculated by the access control, relationship [4.26] gives only the g/c ratio. It remains to determine the values of g and c. The filtering method is used to obtain them.

The "drop-by-drop" method limits insertion to one vehicle per cycle; the duration of the green light is constant and corresponds exactly to the time of crossing the fast lane by a single vehicle (around four seconds). In this filtering mode, the time of the cycle (and consequently the duration of the red-light phase) varies depending on the flow r calculated by the access control.

In the barrier filtering mode, vehicles are inserted at each cycle. In this case, the duration of the cycle c is fixed (generally at around 40 seconds) and the duration during which the traffic light stays green varies. However, to avoid the complete closure of the access point the duration of the green light cannot drop below a minimum value, g_{min}.

All access control strategies can function in either the drop-by-drop mode or the barrier mode. The usefulness of the drop-by-drop mode lies in ensuring better insertion of vehicles compared to barrier flow. Its disadvantage is the limitation of the maximum outflow authorized to leave the ramp; it cannot exceed 900 veh./h in the case of an average cycle of four seconds.

4.6.6. Evaluation of access control (effects of access regulation)

Access regulation is a direct traffic management tool that is most frequently used and most effective at controlling and improving highway traffic. Various positive effects have been observed if access point control is properly installed. With regard to the effects on congestion, we have [PAP 04]:

  – an increased outflow at the exit of the section of the network being studied;

– a reduction in the total time spent by all vehicles in the network (this time includes the time spent traveling in the network as well as the time spent waiting at access points);

– an increase in average speed; and

– an effective reaction in the number of incidents.

There are also other positive effects, such as the delay in the appearance of congestion and the increased rapidity of the return to fluidity (as shown by experiments on the A10 West highway). Traffic jams last for shorter periods of time when the system is regulated, and they cover a smaller distance in the fast lane. Results of studies conducted at INRETS show that the regulation of access points produces beneficial effects not only on ring road traffic, but also on that of the Boulevards des Maréchaux in Paris with regard to the average circulation speed of vehicles.

In addition, control has a positive impact on safety. This is explained by the fact that access control improves vehicle insertion [MAC 98], as well as by the fact that reduced congestion causes a reduction in the number of accidents.

Access point regulation is implemented in urban areas where surface network problems can appear, so negative effects can also be observed, such as:

– increased waiting time at access points; and

– the transfer of traffic onto a secondary network due to the length of waiting lines.

The regulation of access leads to additional waiting time on access ramps (waiting line management). In these conditions, and when the waiting time becomes too long, users tend to modify their itinerary (traffic transfer). Waiting lines on ramps tend to grow longer and to generate traffic jams in neighboring lanes. This is why access regulation systems also include devices to measure waiting lines. When the waiting line reaches a certain limit, access regulation is temporarily canceled and the system is left to operate freely.

Since surface roads cannot support a large traffic transfer from a saturated highway, the sole objective of fluidity in the fast lane is insufficient. Control strategies must therefore integrate measurements of the state of traffic on roads that are attached as well as information for users regarding traffic predictions.

4.7. Conclusion

Without being exhaustive, this chapter presents as complete an overview as possible of the modeling and control approaches of the most frequently implemented road traffic flow systems. This presentation could be expanded to include the modeling of pedestrian flow, a domain that has obvious connections to the one presented here. Moreover, recent work has shown that more complicated control techniques are being implemented in numerous research laboratories all over the world than those presented here. These have not been addressed; however, the bibliography below will allow the reader to expand his or her knowledge of this subject. Less informed readers have been provided with an overview of the basic elements developed in the past as a foundation on which to build their knowledge.

Many development perspectives exist, particularly in the domain of control algorithm studies. The modeling of traffic flow systems is certainly not perfect, and still requires many improvements. Models are far from perfect and from faithfully representing the real behavior of these systems, which must more accurately integrate aspects related to human behavior. This area of study also has connections to other domains that were not mentioned above, such as the estimation of vehicle travel time, the study of itinerary strategy, vehicle routing, etc.

Most studies are based on simulation techniques. This also assumes the development of more realistic traffic flow simulators, particularly in the case of the studying large road networks integrating both urban and interurban zones. Hybrid models should soon be able to allow for the proper conducting of such studies.

4.8. Bibliography

[ABR 98] ABRAHAM F.F., BROUGHTON J.Q., BERNSTEIN N. *et al.*, "Spanning the length scales in dynamic simulation", *Computers in Physics*, vol. 12, no. 6, pp. 38-546, 1998.

[ALG 97] ALGERS S., BERNAUER E., BOERO M., BREHERET L., DI TARANTO C., DOUGHERTY M., FOX K., GABARD J.F., "Review of micro-simulation models", *SMARTEST Project. Deliverable D3*, Institute for Transport Studies, University of Leeds, United Kingdom, 1997, available at: www.its.leeds.ac.uk/projects/smartest/deliv3.html.

[ANS 90] ANSORGE R., "What does the entropy condition mean in traffic flow theory?", *Transportation Research Part B*, vol. 24, no. 2, pp. 133-143, 1990.

[AWA 01] AW A., RASCLE M., "Resurrection of "second order" models of traffic flow", *Journal of Applied Mathematics*, vol. 60, no. 3, pp. 916-938, 2001.

[BAN 95] BANDO M., HASEBE K., NAKAYAMA A. *et al.*, "Dynamical model of traffic congestion and numerical simulation ", *Physical Review E*, vol. 51, pp. 1035-1042, 1995.

[BEL 06] BELLEMANS T., DE SCHUTTER B., DE MOOR B., "Model predictive control for ramp metering of motorway traffic: A case study", *Control Engineering Practice*, vol. 14, no. 7, pp. 757-767, 2006.

[BOU 02] BOURREL E., HENN V., "Mixing micro and macro representations of traffic flow: a first theoretical step", *Proceedings of the 9th Meeting of the Euro Working Group on Transportation*, pp. 610-613, 2002.

[BOU 03] BOURREL E., LESORT J.P., "Mixing micro and macro representations of traffic flow: a Hybrid Model based on the LWR theory", *82nd Annual Meeting of the Transportation Research Board*, January 12-16, 2003.

[BRA 76] BRANSTON D., "Models of single lane time headway distributions", *Transportation Science*, vol. 10, pp. 125-148, 1976.

[BUC 68] BUCKLEY D.J., "A semi-poisson model of traffic flow", *Transporation Science*, vol. 2, pp. 107-132, 1968.

[BUS 96] BUISSON C., LEBACQUE J.P., LESORT J.B., "STRADA, a discretized macroscopic model of vehicular traffic flow in complex networks based on the Godunov scheme", *CESA'96 IMACS Multiconference. Computational Engineering in Systems Applications*, pp.976-981, Lille, France, July 9-12, 1996.

[BUR 04] BURGHOUT W., Hybrid microscopic-mesoscopic traffic simulation, PhD thesis, Royal Institute of Technology, Stockholm, Sweden, 2004.

[CER] Certu: www.certu.fr.

[CHA 58] CHANDLER R.E., HERMAN R., MONTROLL E.W., "Traffic dynamics: Studies in car following", *Operations Research*, vol. 6, pp. 165-184, 1958.

[CHA 85] CHANG G.L., MAHMASSANI H.S., HEMAN R., "Macroparticle traffic simulation model to investigate peak-period commuter decision dynamics", *Transportation Research Records*, vol. 1005, pp. 107-121, 1985.

[CHE 97] CHEN O.J., HOTZ A.F., BEN-AKIVA M.E., "Development and evaluation of a dynamic metering control model", *Proceedings of Eighth IFAC/IFIP/IFORS Symposium on Transportation Systems*, pp. 1162-1168, Chania, Greece, 1997.

[DAG 95] DAGANZO C.F., "Requiem for second-order fluid approximations of traffic flow", *Transportation Research part B*, vol. 29, pp. 79-93, 1995.

[DAG 02] DAGANZO C.F., "A behavioural theory of multi-lane traffic flow. Part I: Long homogeneous freeway sections", *Transportation Research part B*, vol. 36, pp. 131-158, 2002.

[DEL 96] DEL CASTILLO J.M., "A car following model based on the Lighthill-Whitham theory", *Transportation and Traffic Theory*, Elservier, pp. 517-38, 1996.

[DIA 94] DIAKAKI C., PAPAGEORGIOU M., Design and Simulation Test of Coordinated Ramp Metering Control (METALINE) for A10 West in Amsterdam, Internal report 1994-2, Dynamic Systems and Simulation Laboratory, Technical University of Crete, Chania, Greece, 1994.

[ELH 05] EL HMAM M.S., JOLLY D., ABOUAISSA H., BENASSER A., "Modélisation hybride du flux de trafic", *Méthodologies ET Heuristiques pour l'Optimisation des Systèmes Industriels*, pp. 193-198, MOHSI, Hammamet, Tunisia, 2005.

[ESP 06] ESPIÉ S., GATTUSO D., GALANTE F., "Hybrid traffic model coupling macro and behavioral microsimulation", *85th Annual Meeting of Transportation Research Board*, January 22-26, Washington D.C., 2006.

[ESS 99] ESSER J., NEUBERT L., WAHLE J., SCHRECKENBERG M., "Microscopic online simulations of urban traffic", *Proceedings of the 14th International Symposium of Transportation and Traffic Theory*, pp. 517-534, 1999.

[FER 95] FERBER J., *Les Systèmes Multi-agents, vers une Intelligence Collective*, InterEditions, Paris, 1995.

[FER 88] FERRARI P., "The reliability of the motorway transport system", *Transportation Research*, vol. 22b, pp. 291, 1988.

[FLE 00] FLEKKØY E.G., WARNER G., FEDER J., "Hybrid model for combined particle and continum dynamics", *Europhysics Letters*, vol. 52, no. 3, pp. 271-276, 2000.

[FOR 58] FORBES T.W., ZAGORSKI H.J., HOLSHOUSER E.L., DETERLINE W.A., "Measurement of driver reactions to tunnel conditions measurement of driver", *Highway Research Board, Proceedings*, vol. 37, pp. 345-357, 1958.

[FRA 61] FRANKLIN R.E., "The structure of a traffic shock wave", *Civ. Eng. Pulb. Wks. Rev*, vol. 56, pp. 1186-1188, 1961.

[GAB 98] GABARD F., BREHERET L., "THE SITRA-B+ microscopic traffic simulation model. Examples of use and future developements", *INFORMS meeting*, Montreal, Canada, 1998.

[GAZ 61] GAZIS D.C., HERMAN R., ROTHERY R.W., "Nonlinear follow the leader models of traffic", *Operations Research*, vol. 9, pp. 545-567, 1961.

[GOD 90] GODLEWESKI E., RAVIART P.A., *Hyperbolic Systems of Conservation Laws*, Ellipse, Paris, 1990.

[GOM 06] GOMES G., HOROWITZ R., "Optimal freeway ramp metering using asymmetric cell transmission model", *Transportation Research part C, Emerging Technologies*, vol, 14, no. 4, pp. 244-262, 2006.

[GRE 34] GREENSHIELDS B.D., "A study of traffic capacity", *Proceedings of the Highway Research Board*, vol. 14, pp. 48-477, 1934.

[HAJ 88] HAJ SALEM H., BLOSSEVILLE J.M., DAVEE M.M., PAPAGEORGIOU M., Alinea un Outil de Régulation d'Accès Isolé sur Autoroute, INRETS Report, no. 80, INRETS, October 1988.

[HAS 02] HASAN M., JHA M., BEN-AKIVA M., "Evaluation of ramp control algorithms using microscopic traffic simulation", *Transportation Research C*, vol. 10, pp. 229-256, 2002.

[HEL 97] HELBING D., *Verkehrsdynamik neue Physikalische Modellierings-konzepte*, Springer-Verlag, Berlin, 1997.

[HEL 00] HELBING D., HENNECKE A., SHVETSOV V. *et al.*, "Micro and Macrosimulation freeway traffic", *Mathematical and Computer Modelling*, vol. 35, no. 5-6, pp. 517-547, 2000.

[HEN 00] HENNECKE A., TREIBER M., HELBING D., "Macroscopic simulation of open systems and micro-macro link", in HELBING D., HERRMANN H.J., SCHRECKENBERG M., WOLF D.E., *Traffic and Granular Flow '99: Social, Traffic, and Granular Dynamics*, pp. 383-388, Springer, Berlin, 2000.

[HOC 88] HOCKNEY R.W., EASTWOOD J.W., *Computer Simulations using Particles*, Adam Higler, Bristol, 1988.

[HOO 98] HOOGENDOORN S.P., BOVY P.H.L., "A new estimation technique for vehicle-type specific headway distributions", *Transportation Research Record*, vol. 1, no. 1646, pp. 18-28, 1998.

[HOO 99] HOOGENDOORN S.P., Multiclass continuum modelling of multiclass traffic flow, PhD thesis, Delft University Press, 1999.

[HOO 00] HOOGENDOORN S.P., BOVY P.H.L., "Modelling multiple user-class traffic flow", *Transportation Research B*, vol. 34, no. 2, pp. 123-146, 2000.

[HOO 01] HOOGENDOORN S.P., BOVY P.H.L., "State-of-the art of vehiculart flow modelling", *Journal of Systems and Control Engineering, Special Issue on Road Traffic Modelling and Control*, vol. 215, no. 4, pp. 283-304, 2001.

[JEP 98] JEPSEN M., "On the speed-flow relationships in road traffic: A model of driver Behaviour", *Proceedings of the Third International Symposium on Highway Capacity*, pp. 297-319, 1998.

[JIA 02] JIANG R., WU Q.S., ZHU Z.J., "A new continuum model for traffic flow and numerical tests", *Transportation Research Part B*, vol. 36, pp. 405-419, 2002.

[KEE 86] KEEN K.G., SCHOFIELD M.J., HAY G.C., "Ramp metering access control on M6 motorway", *Proceedings of 2nd IEE International Conference on Road Traffic Control*, pp. 39-42, London, United Kingdom, 1986.

[KLA 98] KLAR A., WEGNER P., "A hierarchy of models for multilane vehicular traffic I and II: Modelling", *SIAM Journal of Applied Mathematics*, vol. 59, no. 3, pp. 983-1001, 1998.

[KOP 99] KOPPA R.J., "Human factors", chapter 3 in N.H. GARTNER, C.J. MESSER AND A.K. RATHI (eds.), *Traffic Flow Theory, Transportation Reseach Bord Monograph*, pp.3.1-3.32, Washington, DC, 1999.

[KOT 99] KOTSIALOS A., PAPAGEORGIOU M., MESSMER A., "Optimal co-ordinated and integrated motorway network traffic control", *Proceedings of the 14th International Symposium of Transportation and Traffic Theory*, pp. 621-644, 1999.

[KOT 01] KOTSIALOS A., PAPAGEORGIOU M., "Efficiency versus fairness in network-wide ramp metering", *Proceedings 4th IEEE Conference on Intelligent Transportation Systems*, pp. 1190-1195, 2001.

[KOT 02] KOTSIALOS A. *et al.*, "Coordinated and integrated control of motorway networks via nonlinear optimal control", *Transportation research Part C*, vol. 10, no. 1, pp. 65-84, 2002.

[KOT 04] KOTSIALOS A., PAPAGEORGIOU M., "Motorway network traffic control systems", *European Journal of Operational Research*, vol. 152, no. 2, pp. 321-333, 2004

[KRA 02] KRAJZEWICZ D., HERTKORN G., RÖSSEL C., WAGNER P., "An example of microscopic car models validation using the open source traffic simulation SUMO", *14th European Simulation Symposium And Exhibition*, vol. 1, pp. 318-322, October 23-26, 2002.

[KRA 04] KRAJZEWICZ D., *Using the Road Traffic Simulation "SUMO" for Educational Purposes*, German Aerospace Centre, 2004.

[KRA 98] KRAUSS S., "Microscopic Modelling of Traffic Flow: Investigation of Collision Free Vehicle Dynamics", *Computer and Information Science*, 1998.

[LAV 05] LAVAL J.A., DAGANZO C.F., "Multi-lane hybrid traffic flow model: a theory on the impacts of lane-changing maneuvers", *The 84th Transportation Research Board's Annual Meeting*, Washington, DC, United States, 2005.

[LEB 98] LEBACQUE J.P., LESORT J.B., GIORGI F., "Introducing buses in first order traffic flow models", *Transportation Research Records*, vol. 1644, pp. 70-79, 1998.

[LEC 02] LECLERCQ L., Modélisation dynamique du trafic et applications à l'estimation du bruit routier, civil engineering thesis, INSA Lyon, Villeurbanne, 2002.

[LER 02] LEROUX A.Y., *Sur la Modélisation du Trafic Routier au Niveau des Carrefours*, Ecole d'Automne de Modélisation Mathématique du Trafic Automobile, Paris, November 28-30, 2002, available at: www-gm3.univ-mrs.fr/~leroux/publications/ay.le_roux.html.

[LEU 88] LEUTZBACH W., *An Introduction to the Theory of Traffic Flow*, Springer-Verlag, Berlin, 1988.

[LET 97] LE TALLEC P., MALLINGER F., "Coupling Boltzmann and Navier-Stockes equations by half fluxes", *Journal of Computational Physics*, vol. 136, pp. 51-67, 1997.

[LIE 02] LIEBERMAN E., RATHI A.K., Update and extension of the Transportation Research Board Special Report: Traffic Simulation, vol. 165, pp.10.1-10.25, Chief of State Programs at National Highway Institute of Traffic Flow Theory, 2002.

[LIG 55] LIGHTHILL M.J., WHITHAM G.B., "On kinematic waves II. A theory of traffic flow in long crowded roads", *Proceedings of the Royal Society, A*, vol. 229, pp. 317-345, 1955.

[MAG 00] MAGNE L., RABUT S., GABARD J.F., "Towards an hybrid macro-micro traffic flow simulation model", *Proceedings of the INFORMS Salt Lake City String 2000 Conference*, Salt Lake City, United States, 2000.

[MAM 06] MAMMAR S., LEBACQUE J.P., HAJ-SALEM H., "Hybrid model based on second-order traffic mode", *85th Annual Meeting of Transportation Research Board, 1(06-2160)*, Washington, DC, United States, January, 22-26 2006.

[MAS 75] MASHER D.P., ROSS D.W., WONG P.J., TUAN P.L., ZEIDLER H.M., PERACEK S., Guidelines for Design and Operating of Ramp Control Systems, Stanford Research Institute Report NCHRP 3-22, SRI Project 3340, SRI, Menid Park, California, 1975.

[MAY 90] MAY A.D., *Traffic Flow Fundamentals*, Prentice-Hall, Englewood Cliffs, 1990.

[MCL 98] MCLEAN T., BRADER C., HANGLEITER S., TSAVACHIDIS M., DAMAS C., MAXWELL B., BARBER P., "Urban integrated traffic control evaluation results", *Deliverable 8.3, Eur. Transport Telematics Project TABASCO*, Transport Telematic Office, Brussels, 1998.

[MES 90] MESSMER A., PAPAGEORGIO M., "METANET: A macroscopic Simulation Program for Motorway Networks", *Traffic Engineering and Control*, vol. 31, pp. 466-470, 1990.

[MIZ 99] MIZUSKI H., KAWAZOE Y., "Simulation of crystal growth in solution by hybrid modelling", *Material Transaction JIM*, vol. 40, no. 11, pp. 1337-1341, 1999.

[NAG 92] Nagel K., Schreckenberg M., "A cellular automaton model for freeway traffic", *Journal of Physics France*, vol. 2, pp. 2221-2229, 1992.

[NAG 95] NAGEL K., High-speed microsimulations of traffic flow, PhD Thesis, Faculty of Mathematisch Naturwissenschaftlichen, University of Cologne, 1995.

[NAG 98] NAGEL K., "From particle hopping models to traffic flow theory", *Transportation Research Record*, vol. 1644, pp. 1-9, 1998.

[NAG 99] NAGEL K., Simon P., Rickert M., Esser J., "Iterated transportation simulation for Dallas and Portland", BRILON W., HUBER F., SCHECKENBERG M., WALLENTOWITZ H. (eds), *Traffic and Mobility' Simulation, Economics, Environment*, pp. 95-100, Springer-Verlag, Berlin, 1999.

[NEW 61] NEWELL G.F., "Non linear effects in the dynamics of car-following", *Operations Research*, vol.9, pp. 209-229, 1961.

[NEW 98] NEWELL G.F., "A moving bottleneck", *Transportation Research part B*, vol. 23, pp. 531-537, 1998.

[PAP 82] PAPAGEORGIOU M., MAYR R., "Optimal decomposition methods applied to motorway traffic control", *International Journal of Control*, vol. 35, no. 2, pp. 269-280, 1982.

[PAP 90] PAPAGEORGIOU M., BLOSSEVILLE J.M., HAJ-SALEM H., "Modeling and real-time control of traffic flow on the southern part of Boulevard Périphérique in Paris, Part II: Coordinated on-ramp metering", *Transportation Research A: General*, vol. 24, no. 5, pp. 361-370, 1990.

[PAP 91] PAPAGEORGIOU M., HAJ SALEM H., BLOSSEVILLE J.M., "ALINEA: A local feedback control law for on-ramp metering", *Transportation Research Record*, vol. 1320, pp. 58-64, 1991.

[PAP 97] PAPAGEORGIOU M., HAJ SALEM H., MIDDELHAM F., "ALINEA local ramp metering: Summary of field results", *Transportation Research Record*, vol. 1603, pp. 90-98, 1997.

[PAP 98] PAPAGEORGIOU M., "Some remarks on macroscopic traffic flow modelling", *Transportation Research part A*, vol. 32, no. 5, pp. 323-329, 1998.

[PAP 02] PAPAGEORGIOU M., KOTSIALOS A., "Freeway ramp metering: an overview", *IEEE Transactions on Intelligent Transportation Systems*, vol. 3, no. 4, pp. 271-281, 2002.

[PAP 03] PAPAGEORGIOU M., DIAKAKI C., DINOPOULOU V., KOTSIALOS A., YIBING W., "Review of road traffic control strategies", *Proceedings of the IEEE*, vol. 91, no. 12, pp. 2043-2067, 2003.

[PAP 04] PAPAGEORGIOU M., *Overview of Road Traffic Strategies*, IFAC DECOM-TT Automatic System for Building the Infrastructure in Developing Countries, October 2004.

[PAV 75] PAVERI-FONTANA S.L., "On Boltzmann-like treatments for traffic flow: a critical review of the basic model and an alternative proposal for dilute traffic analysis", *Transportation Research B*, vol. 9, pp. 225-235, 1975.

[PAY 71] PAYNE H.J., "Models of freeway traffic and control", *Mathematical Models of Public Systems*, vol. 1, pp. 51-61, 1971.

[PIP 53] PIPES L.A., "An operational analysis of traffic dynamics", *Journal of Applied Physics*, vol. 24, no. 1, pp. 274-287, 1953.

[POS 02] POSCHINGER A., KATES R., KELLER H., "Coupling of concurrent macroscopic and microscopic traffic flow models using hybrid stochastic and deterministic disaggregation", in TAYLOR M.A.P. (eds), *Transportation and traffic Theory for the 21st century: Proceedings of the 15th International Symposium on Transportation and Traffic Theory*, Pergamon, Oxford, 2002.

[PRI 61] PRIGOGINE I., "A Boltzmann-like approach to the statistical theory of traffic flow", in HERMAND R. (ed.), *Proceedings of the 1st International Symposium on the Theory of Traffic Flow*, pp. 158-164, 1961.

[PRI 71] PRIGOGINE I., HERMAN R., *Kinetic Theory of Vehicular Traffic*, Elsevier, New York, 1971.

[RIC 56] RICHARDS P.I., "Shockwaves on the highway", *Operations Research*, vol. 4, pp. 42-51, 1956.

[ROT 99] ROTHERY R.W., "Car following models", Chapter 4 in GARTNER N.H., MESSER C.J. and RATHI A.K. (eds), *Traffic flow Theory, Transportation Reseach Bord Monograph*, Washington DC, pp.4.1-4.42,1999.

[SCH 77] SCHWARTZ S.C., TAN H.H., "Integrated control of freeway entrance ramps by threshold regulation", *Proceedings of the IEEE Conference on Decision and Control*, pp. 984-986, 1977.

[SMA 03] SMARAGDIS E., PAPAGEORGIOU M., "A series of new local ramp metering strategies", *82nd Annual Meeting of the Transportation Research Board*, Paper No. 03-3171, Washington DC, United States, 2003.

[SMA 04] SMARAGDIS E., PAPAGEORGIOU M., KOSMATOPOULOS E., "A flow-maximizing adaptive local ramp metering strategy", *Transportation Research Part B: Methodological*, vol. 38, no. 3, pp. 251-270, 2004.

[TOD 64] TODOSIEV E.P., BARBOSA L.C., "A proposed model for the driver-vehicle system", *Traffic Engineering*, vol. 34, pp. 17-20, 1964.

[WAT 65] WATTLEWORTH J.A., "Peak-period analysis and control of a freeway system", *Highway Research Record*, vol. 157, pp. 1-21, 1965.

[WIE 74] WIEDEMANN R., Simulation des Straßenverkehrsflußes, Technical Report, Institute for Traffic Engineering, University of Karlsrühe, Germany, 1974.

[WIL 96] WILLIAMS E.J., AHITOV I., "Integrated use of macro and micro models within a simulation study", *Proceedings of the AutoFact Conference*, pp. 169-179, Dearborn, MI, United States, November 12-14, 1996.

[WUN 99] WU N., BRILON W., "Cellular automata for highway traffic flow simulation", *Proceedings 14th International Symposium on Transportation and Traffic Theory* (Abbreviated presentations), pp. 1-18, 1999.

[YIB 06] YIBING W., PAPAGEORGIOU M., "Local ramp metering in the case of distant downstream bottlenecks", *Intelligent Transportation Systems Conference, ITSC '06*. IEEE, pp. 426-431, 2006.

[YSE 97] YSERENTANT H., "A new class of particle methods", *Numerical Mathematics*, vol. 76, pp. 87-109, 1997.

[ZHA 99] ZHANG M., RECKER W., "On optimal freeway ramp control policies for congested traffic corridors", *Transportation Reseach Part B*, vol. 33, no. 6, pp. 417-436, 1999.

[ZHA 00] ZHANG H.M., "Structural properties of solutions arising from a nonequilibrium traffic flow theory", *Transportation Research Part B*, vol. 34, no. 7, pp. 583-603, 2000.

[ZHA 02] ZHANG H.M., "A non-equilibrium traffic model devoid of gas-like behaviour", *Transportation Research Part B*, vol. 36, no. 3, pp. 275-290, 2002.

Chapter 5

Criteria and Methods for Interactive System Evaluation: Application to a Regulation Post in the Transport Domain

5.1. Introduction

The evaluation of interactive systems and, more particularly, their human–machine interface (HMI), has been a recurring problem for the past 30 years. The evolution of interaction methods between user and machine, as well as the needs and specificities inherent in the evolution of information and communication sciences and technologies, systematically necessitates new criteria and methods for the evaluation of human–machine interactions. It has been shown that many users today have problems working with interactive systems, and that their needs are poorly analyzed, poorly perceived, insufficiently evaluated or not evaluated at all, and thus these systems do not always respond correctly to user needs.

In order to improve the quality of human–machine interactions, numerous studies have been conducted to evaluate interactive systems from several angles and perspectives. In this chapter, we will look most closely at Trabelsi and Tran [TRA 06, TRA 09] in order to present, in a representative but non-exhaustive manner, the most frequently cited, studied and/or currently used types of evaluation methods. Before beginning this presentation, we will first illustrate the principle of evaluation and the categories chosen for presentation.

Chapter written by Houcine Ezzedine, Abdelwaheb Trabelsi, Chi Dung Tran and Christophe Kolski.

We will then present a range of evaluation methods. These methods are divided into three main categories:

– methods based on the observation of real users and a collection of interaction data;

– methods based on the involvement of experts (in human–machine interaction, cognitive psychology, or software ergonomics); and

– so-called analytical methods.

In each category, the most representative evaluation methods, or those that have served as the basis for other methods, are described.

We will examine automated (or semi-automated) evaluation methods used to help evaluators in some of their activities; for example, the automatization of the capture and analysis of events related to human–machine interaction. The first version of an environment to assist the evaluation of interactive systems based on an agent-based architecture will be described in the next section of this chapter.

Finally, in the last section, we will look at a case study of the evaluation of an interactive system intended for a dispatching office in the transport domain.

5.2. Principles and criteria of evaluation

5.2.1. *Principle of evaluation*

In order to define evaluation, we turn to the definition proposed by Senach [SEN 90], who states that "every evaluation consists of comparing one model of the object being evaluated to a reference model and then drawing conclusions".

The principle of this definition is shown in Figure 5.1. During evaluation, the "observed" model is compared to a reference model. This model must be representative of the adequacy of the interface evaluated with respect to specific needs defined by the designer. The result of this comparison between the observed model and the reference model defines the level of adequacy of the interface with respect to the needs already specified, and is thus used to determine the changes and improvements to be made to the HMI.

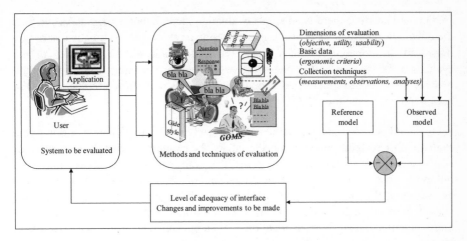

Figure 5.1. *Basic principle of evaluation inspired by*
Senach [SEN 90] and Grislin [GRI 95]

When the approach is user-centered [NOR 86], we cannot discuss evaluation without speaking of *usability* and *utility*. These two properties are normally examined in the evaluation of HMIs [SEN 90, NEI 93, BAS 01, BAC 05, MOH 05]. Researchers in this domain generally define utility and usability as follows:

– *Utility*: determines whether the interface responds to the needs of the user; in other words, if the application allows the user to achieve his or her work objectives. Utility includes the idea of system performance, functional capacity, and quality of technical assistance offered [SEN 90, NEI 92].

– *Usability*: this concept dates from the early 1980s [EAS 84]. Asking himself the question "what do we have to know about users in order to construct a quality interface?", Robert [ROB 03] specifies that the factors responsible for the usability of HMIs are numerous[1]: these include compatibility, consistency, visual clarity, flexibility, control, informational feedback, online assistance, error management, etc. (see also the criteria defined in [RAV 89, NIE 92] and [BAS 93]).

There are many evaluation methods; each method prioritizes one or more attributes of usability through the measurement of various variables – duration of execution of a task; error rate; number of assistance uses; etc. – or through the opinions or attitudes of users [ROB 03].

---

1 A broad definition of these factors can be found in [NEI 93, GRI 95]. An overview of usability evaluation methods can also be found at: www.usabilityhome.com.

On the face of it, there is no single evaluation method that is more effective than the others. In reality, the quality of the results of an evaluation technique is strongly linked to the context[2] within which it is applied and to the objective of the evaluation. For example, it is not effective to use user questionnaires to determine between two design options and choose the one that will allow a reduction in the duration of task execution [FAR 97].

It should be noted that researchers are currently paying particular attention to the evaluation of Web interfaces, but it should also be emphasized that the evaluation of HMIs dedicated to interactive systems that can be categorized as traditional (allowing access to a group of functions and/or services) is different from the evaluation of Web interfaces [IVO 01a], while still being related to the necessity for human–machine interactions. Indeed, so-called 'traditional' interactive systems are more functional than Web applications. In more concrete terms, the user of an interactive system accomplishes tasks sequentially or in parallel, such as, for example, the initiation of a calculation, the writing and sending of a document, the printing of a report, the study of different pieces of information, etc. Web applications (or most of them, at any rate), offer relatively limited functionalities, such as the selection of a link or the filling out of a form; their principal role is to provide information. On this subject, in a study involving 130 methods for evaluating interactive systems and websites, Ivory [IVO 01a] specifies that only 29 methods can be applied to websites as well as to more traditional interactive systems. Readers interested in website evaluation[3] will find complete studies of interest on this topic in [MAR 05, BEI 04]. We, however, will focus on the evaluation of interactive systems that are considered traditional, and are intended for a target audience (unlike Web interfaces, which are often accessible to the public at large).

There are many standard evaluation methods. In order to present them properly, it is necessary to classify them. In the following section, we will present several classifications that are among the best known in the literature.

5.2.2. *Classifications of evaluation methods*

The problem of classifying evaluation methods is one of size. According to Bastien [BAS 02], classification should allow us to describe existing methods of

---

2 Interested readers will find a complete study of the idea of context in human–machine interaction in [REY 05].

3 The following websites address website evaluation: www.ergoweb.ca/; www.auditweb.net; and www.cyberbee.com/guides.html.

evaluation in a thorough and adequate manner in order to facilitate selection according to criteria such as:

– *the objectives of the evaluation*: is it a diagnosis; that is, is it intended for the detection of design errors in order to provide design alternatives, or for a evaluation that will be used to determine how well adapted the interactive system is for the tasks for which it was designed, or even for an evaluation of its compliance with norms?

– *the source of evaluation data*: what are the user results? The characteristics of the interface? Interaction? etc.; and

– *the time of evaluation*: what determines the state, form and representation of the interactive system being evaluated. For example, this may be a specification, a mock-up, a prototype, etc.

We can see that several themes for the categorization of evaluation methods are possible. Our objective here is not to criticize or analyze existing classifications in order to propose a new one[4], but to illustrate well-known classifications in the literature in order to describe the standard evaluation methods later, while categorizing them according their global evaluation approach.

Several approaches have been proposed for the classification of interactive system evalution methods:

– *The Senach classification* [SEN 90], which is an important source of inspiration for us. It distinguishes evaluation methods according to behavioral data (empirical methods) or interface data (analytical methods):

- empirical evaluations consist of gathering data related to user behavior during use of the system. This type of evaluation requires the existence of a real system (mock-up, prototype, or final system) and the presence of users,

- analytical evaluations evaluate the design of the system and not its use. Interfaces are studied according to a group of referents in order to check whether they possess certain qualities and to detect problems that they may pose. These referents may be formal or loose,

– *The Whitefield classification* [WHI 91] groups evaluation methods according to the real or representation of a user and a system. In this way, four possible evaluation approaches are obtained:

---

4 The reader wishing to find a nearly exhaustive study of the classification of evaluation methods may refer to volume 13 (1998) of the *Human-Computer Interaction* journal or to several theses, such as those of Farenc [FAR 97] and Mariage [MAR 05].

- analytical methods (representation of a user and a system): these use a representation of the user and the system to predict the performances that the user can execute. A typical representation is a task model [DIA 04],

- specialist reports (real system, representation of a user): these do not use real users, but they do use the presence of a real system for evaluation. Ergonomic guides can be useful in this case,

- user reports (real user, representation of a system): these are generally used when the real system is not available. In this case, users are asked to judge certain general design aspects of the system. For example, the questionnaire technique may be used,

- observation methods (real user and system): as their name indicates, these consist of observing the user interacting with the system in order to determine the errors and flaws of the latter.

This classification possesses convergence points with the one proposed by Bastien [BAS 01], see below;

– *The Holyer classification* [HOL 93] introduces categorization according to the discipline that serves as the basis for the methods planned. The basic idea behind this classification is to separate evaluation methods according to their "philosophy of origin". Four types of methods may be distinguished here:

- methods based on cognitive psychology, which try to identify the cognitive process of the user when interacting with the system,

- methods based on social psychology, which are principally based on questionnaires and interviews,

- methods based on social sciences, which consist of the observation of a user by one or more experts; for example, these include approaches that are considered empirical, and

- approaches based on engineering, which group evaluation methods based on the experience of one or more specialists.

– *The Balbo classification* [BAL 94] groups evaluation methods according to several parameters. The dimensions involved in this classification are:

- the required knowledge characterized by the cognitive cost of accessing the method and descriptions that represent information on the subject of the evaluation that are necessary to the evaluation process (user model, task model, external specifications, etc.),

- the material resources that correspond to all of the physical means implemented for the evaluation, such as supports for data capture, the subject of the evaluation, and the abstraction level of the data captured,

- the situational factors that describe the context of the evaluation according to five dimensions: the stage in the development process during which the evaluation is taking place; the site of evaluation; the type of application characterized with respect to the task; the typology of the interfaces (graphic interface with direct manipulation, multimodal interface, etc.), as well as the budgetary parameters and the evaluation schedule,

- the human means; that is, the group of individuals involved in the evaluation process: their number and source,

- the results obtained are characterized by the level of abstraction and the type of information obtained from the evaluation.

– *The Farenc classification* [FAR 97] separates evaluation approaches according to three central elements of human–machine interaction; specifically the user, task and system:

- user: a method of evaluation can be applied by taking into account one or more users representative of the final users, or without taking users into account. In the latter case, the evaluation method is used whatever the user, and is thus valid for *N* users,

- task: in the same vein, certain evaluation methods are applicable for a single task that must be specified in the evaluation framework. Other methods are applicable whatever the number of tasks, and

- system: another dimension pertaining to the choice of evaluation method is the nature of the method's results. These results can relate to the system, the interface, or both.

– *The Bastien classification* [BAS 02] separates evaluation approaches into two main categories:

- methods requiring the direct participation of users, which is essentially based on the presence of the user. This category combines two approaches: user reports and user observation [WHI 91], and

- methods applicable to characteristics of the interface, which is distinguished from the preceding methods by the absence of direct interaction between the user and the system. In this category, both users and their tasks are represented.

– *The Grislin classification* [GRI 96] groups evaluation methods into three main approaches:

- approaches centered on the opinions and/or activities of users,

- approaches considered to be expert, centered on the judgment of experts in human–machine communication or on the use of evaluation grids or questionnaires listing the qualities of a good HMI, and

- approaches considered as analytical, centered on the modeling of an HMI and/or human–machine interaction. These most often consist of evaluation using objective metrics based on a descriptive model of human tasks or a description of page-screens.

We will retain this last classification (in a simplified version) in Figure 5.2, since in most existing classifications it explicitly or implicitly contains the three approaches proposed by Grislin [GRI 96]. The complete classification is available in [GRI 95] and surveys 40 methods (see also [KOL 97]). A more recent classification oriented toward multimedia applications is available in [HUA 08].

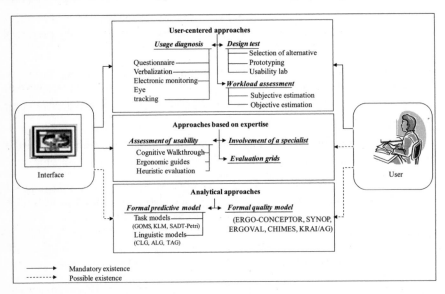

Figure 5.2. *Essentials of the classification of methods and techniques of evaluation [GRI 96]*

However, as is emphasized in [GRI 95, ABE 01, BAS 01], it is unrealistic to consider these groupings independently of one another. Indeed, transversal relationships between methods are often very useful. For example, during the analysis of reference situations with users, it is often useful to proceed with modeling tasks for the sake of specification, but it is also possible to reuse this model when the interactive system is completed, in order to compare it with a model of real user activities [ABE 98].

Remember that our objective in this chapter is not to make an exhaustive survey of existing evaluation methods, since there are several documents available that address this subject; rather, it is to present the most representative evaluation methods. This is the objective of the next section.

5.3. Methods, techniques and tools for the evaluation of interactive systems

This section presents an overview of the most frequently cited evaluation methods. These methods are grouped into three main categories according to the principle described in the previous section (see Figure 5.2):

– methods based on techniques of observing real users and gathering interaction data;

– methods based on the involvement of experts in human–machine interaction, cognitive psychology or software ergonomics; and

– analytical methods based on formal predictive models integrating knowledge about the task and about formal – that is, quality-related – grammars or models.

In each category, we will describe the most representative method or methods, or those that have served as the basis for other methods. For each method, the following points will now be briefly defined[5]:

– *objective*: the objective of an evaluation method is generally to test the purpose and/or usability of the system being evaluated; however, each method focuses on a particular dimension or interpretation of these two factors;

– *principle and description*: the principle as well as the use of the method are described in this section; and

– *advantages and disadvantages*: here, the main advantages and disadvantages of the method that may be encountered during use are described.

---

5 The domain of HMI evaluation is extremely vast. For a more in-depth look at these methods, some of which are very rich, the interested reader is advised to consult the references cited. There are good summaries available as well; see, for example, [WIL 96, WIL 05, STA 05] or [BAC 05]. Very interesting summary chapters can be found in the human–computer interaction handbooks by Helander [HEL 88, HEL 97] and Jacko [JAC 02] (or more recent publications).

5.3.1. *User-centered approaches*

These approaches are based on ways of observing the real user (final user) and gathering interaction data (questionnaire, interview, verbalization, tracking eye movement, estimation of workload, etc.) in order to analyze the traces of user activity. These approaches allow us to detect the real problems encountered by the user when s/he executes his/her task with the system. The results have to do with the interface and the system, but as Farenc [FAR 97] emphasizes, they do not offer the means to correct errors.

Among these user-centered approaches, we can cite the empirical approaches for diagnosing usage (which can be used when the HMI is totally or partly complete), approaches centered on the assessment of workload, and approaches based on design tests (conducted throughout the development cycle of the HMI).

5.3.1.1. *Usage diagnosis*

This approach is only possible if the HMI is operational and ready to be presented to the final users (exceptions for interfaces that are in a very advanced stage of development can be made) or is already widely used. This approach is very useful since user experience already exists. The evaluation is based mainly on the collection of information. Among the numerous empirical methods that exist, the best known are: questionnaires, interviews, electronic monitoring, and tracking of eye movement. We will now examine these four methods.

5.3.1.1.1. Usage questionnaire

This technique's objective is to collect, using structured documents, a set of user assessments, opinions and attitudes after the user has interacted with the system. Questionnaires are especially helpful in determining the satisfaction of or problems experienced by the user, which are difficult or impossible to measure by means other than a questionnaire [NIE 93]. There are questionnaires in the literature specially designed for HMI (see, for example, a survey in [HUA 08]).

It involves questioning the user about information needs, interface inconsistencies, and strong or weak points noted during use of the system, and possibly about suggestions of ways to correct them [BAC 05]. The questionnaire may address aspects related to the functioning of the system and/or the ergonomics of the interface. A questionnaire is made up of a series of questions. It must be well written, with well-defined options in order to avoid vagueness, redundancy and useless data [KOV 04]. Each question must respond in part to the problem being addressed, and must not provide in itself an overall response. For example, to evaluate the ergonomic aspect of the interface, several questions may be asked in order to gather the user's opinion on this aspect. An overly general question such as "do you think that the ergonomics of the interface are well done?" should be avoided. More targeted questions, such as "what do you think of the colors used?" or "are the menu components easily identifiable?" should be prioritized, with, for example, a response in the form of a scale.

Different types of questions can be found in a questionnaire that is used to evaluate a particular aspect of the system, or quite simply to obtain the user's opinion:

– *Open questions*: these allow the user to express him/herself freely, using his/her own language. They help us to understand an opinion or gather general information about the system. An open question might be something such as, "what is your favorite aspect of the interface?" or "what are the main problems you encountered when using the system?" These questions are not recommended when a specifically determined aspect of the system is being evaluated; in this case, closed questions are preferable.

– *Closed questions*: unlike open questions, these offer a group of predetermined responses. These questions are based on multiple choice questions. The evaluator may limit the user to a single response, or allow him/her the possibility of making several choices. However, the development of the list of choices must be thoroughly researched so that the user will be able to find a response that s/he agrees with. If this is not the case, the user risks responding in a random fashion or not responding at all. A closed question can also give the user the possibility of expressing him/herself. These are called semi-closed questions. Figure 5.3a shows an example of a semi-closed multiple-choice question; in this example, the user can fill in his/her own answer if s/he does not find one that s/he agrees with.

– *Scalar questions*: these allow the user to express his/her opinion using a predetermined scale. This scale can have only two values (binary scale: True/False or Yes/No) or several values (multiple scale: up to five, seven, even 10 values). In [BAC 05], scalar questions on a multiple scale are grouped into three categories:

- Likert scale: the user is questioned about his/her agreement or disagreement with a statement (Figure 5.3c),

- ranking scale: the user is asked to rank the answers to a question in order of importance (Figure 5.3b), and

- semantic differential scale: the user is asked to judge the system according to two lists of antonyms. For example (easy, useful, pleasant, fast) and (difficult, useless, unpleasant, slow).

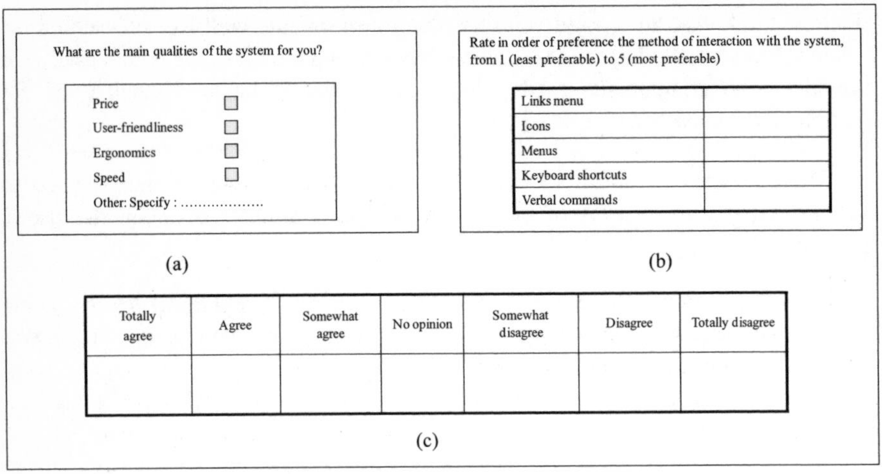

What are the main qualities of the system for you?	
Price	☐
User-friendliness	☐
Ergonomics	☐
Speed	☐
Other: Specify :	

Rate in order of preference the method of interaction with the system, from 1 (least preferable) to 5 (most preferable)

Links menu	
Icons	
Menus	
Keyboard shortcuts	
Verbal commands	

(a)   (b)

Totally agree	Agree	Somewhat agree	No opinion	Somewhat disagree	Disagree	Totally disagree

(c)

Figure 5.3. *Sample questionnaire: a) multiple choice with the last question being open; b) ranking scale; and c) Likert scale*

This technique has the advantage of being economical and usable in most situations [RUS 86]. It allows the user to work at his/her leisure, even if this is liable, according to [ROO 83], to cause a bias in the answers because s/he is not always in a position to remember the difficulties encountered during the various work situations.

Though this technique seems to be easy to implement, the development of a reliable questionnaire – one that will result in the collection of truly useful information for evaluation – is not always easy. According to Baccino [BAC 05], recurring problems that are encountered when building questionnaires are:

– the use of emotionally charged, overly imprecise, or overly ambiguous terms. For example, a question addressed to American computer science students as "what is your first language?" received answers such as C++, JAVA, etc., while the authors of the questionnaire were expecting responses such as English, French, etc.; and

– the possibility of suggesting the desired response or causing discomfort when the subject believes s/he is being evaluated on his/her response. For example, a question such as "do you have a good memory?" can intimidate the user, who will tend to give an erroneous response.

5.3.1.1.2. Interview

The objective of an interview is to get an initial overview of the problems of utility and usability of the system being evaluated. It gives the evaluator knowledge about the difficulties of the system, improvements to be planned, and the user's level of satisfaction.

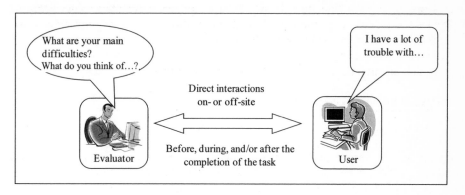

Figure 5.4. *Direct interaction via an interview between the user and the evaluator*

The interview consists of asking questions on representative subjects in order to get a quick overview of problems related to utility and usability encountered by users during their interaction with the proposed system (see Figure 5.4). It is broadly based on techniques used in social psychology [HOL 93]. The effectiveness of an interview depends on its preparation and the skills of the evaluator guiding it. Indeed, the evaluator must plan and prepare in advance the central questions to ask the user.

5.3.1.1.3. Electronic monitoring

Electronic monitoring is intended to gather automatically objective data (user actions and their repercussions on the system) in real work situations. The data collected are subsequently analyzed (manually or automatically) [BAS 02, MAR 05, EZZ 05a]. Information is gathered discreetly and transparently for the evaluator. The objective data gathered through human–machine interactions can then be analyzed and displayed in a summarized form to the evaluator, facilitating his analysis of the usage problems.

Besides being able to collect objective data on human–machine interactions, the advantage of electronic monitoring is its transparency with regard to the user. In fact, during the evaluation, the user is theoretically not disturbed at any time by the presence of the monitor, and therefore behaves in a way that can be considered normal.

The disadvantage of electronic monitoring lies in the processing of the quantity of information recorded, and in the level of granularity of the analysis [BAS 02]. The evaluator may find himself facing an enormous collection of data requiring hours or even days to go through. In addition, if the electronic monitoring does not include an aid for the evaluator for the interpretation of data (in the form of graphs, recommendations, etc.), the data collected may be inadequately used, or require several hours in order to draw conclusions that are useful for evaluation.

We will return to this method in section 5.4.

5.3.1.1.4. Eye tracking

Ocular movement analysis, or tracking of eye movements, enables us to know where a person is looking. The ocular movements of users can be monitored thanks to an acquisition device called an eye tracker, in order to determine indices such as the length of time a person looks at an area of the HMI, the identification of HMI interest zones, and/or successive sequences of observation, which are then correlated with HMI actions and reactions [ABE 90, SIM 93, EZZ 97, PIV 06, CGA 01]. A good summary of this method and its potential uses is available in [DUC 03].

The ocular movement technique consists of recording the trajectories and ocular pauses generated during reading, a search for information, or the inspection of a HMI. It has been shown that in the execution of industrial procedures using graphic tools (and particularly supervision), people depend heavily on the visual perception of information. In this case, the absolute direction of a person's gaze becomes a usable element in parallel with other means of analyzing the activity of a human operator in front of a screen or a group of informational supports [ABE 90]. The recordings of ocular movements can be replayed in groups and commented on with (and by) users.

Figure 5.5 gives an example of an ocular movement capture device. This device is composed mainly of a transmitter that generates a magnetic field; the helmet receiver connected to it, and a processing unit. The center of the transmitter constitutes the source of the referential in which the operator proceeds. The position and orientation of the receiver with respect to the transmitter are calculated from the characteristics of the magnetic field and the tensions measured at the boundaries of the coils constituting the receiver [SIM 93]. This figure is simply illustrative, since several types of acquisition and processing technologies have been proposed in recent years, and they continue to evolve.

Interested readers will find more detail about this technique by referring, for example, to the work carried out by the LAMIH laboratory: it was started there, particularly in situations of analysis of control and supervision activities (in the aerial and railroad domains, for example) [ABE 90, ABE 01, SIM 93, EZZ 97,

EZZ 02]. More recently, it has been used in numerous projects related to evaluation in automobile driving situations [LOS 03, LOS 08, GIR 09]. There are numerous documents in the literature centering on HMI; see, for example, [RAY 98, CHA 01, MUL 01, BAC 05, BOJ 05].

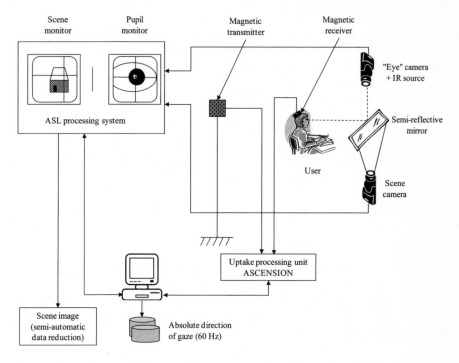

Figure 5.5. *Principle of evaluation via acquisition and analysis of ocular movements: the ASL-ASCENSION system [SIM 93]*

The advantage of this technique is that, after data reduction, it allows a refined study of the manner in which users search for and locate useful information depending on various situations of system function (normal mode, damaged mode) and to identify lacuna related to HMIs during certain crisis situations [KOL 97]. Note that pieces of equipment for capturing ocular movement have been developed that allow the user greater freedom. The user is no longer obliged to wear a helmet, which can disturb him/her during the evaluation process. As an example, the device used by Chalon [CHA 04] includes two adjustable infrared transmitters and an infrared camera that can be directed toward the user's eye.

A disadvantage of this technique lies in the limitation of the field of vision with most devices. The reduction of results is generally a painstaking task, and requires a great deal of time, especially if it is not assisted by the appropriate software.

5.3.1.2. *Estimation of workload*

Based on the approximation of the cognitive workload of the user, the estimation of workload is used to measure the level of difficulty related to the use of the HMI. It allows us to make a qualitative and/or quantitative estimation of the activity level of the user executing a task. This is a whole domain of research in itself [WIE 79, WIE 83, MIL 88, SIM 93, BAY 02, CIR 07, GAW 08].

The estimation of the workload has direct repercussions on the content of graphic views, as well as on the manner of presenting information to the user. A number of disciplines contribute to the evaluation of workload: physiology, psychology, ergonomics, engineering sciences, etc. Note that the methods of estimating workload can be:

– subjective [COO 69, WIE 83], consisting of asking the user to estimate his/her workload using subjective scales. There are several questionnaires dedicated to this subject (see, for example, [STA 05]);

– objective [SPE 96], using measured physical or physiological parameters to estimate workload. Among the objective methods for estimating workload are temporal approaches that define workload as the relationship between the time necessary for a human operator to carry out a task and the time s/he actually has to carry it out [MIL 88].

The advantage of this method is that it can be used *a priori*, when the interactive system is in the mock-up or prototype stage, and *a posteriori* when it is available and can be put in the hands of users, or is already widely used. Moreover, the results obtained using this method can reveal sensitive points in the graphic tools used by human operators in a control room, and subsequently lead to ergonomic developments in these tools [KOL 97]. The major disadvantage of these methods is that they provide only an estimation of workload. For more precise measurements, several methods must be combined, possibly necessitating the participation of specialists and experts in the domains of psychology or physiology.

5.3.1.3. *Design tests*

Design test methods are intended to evaluate and validate an interactive system or a HMI according to an iterative cycle throughout the development process, with representative users if possible.

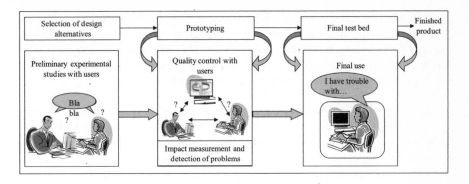

Figure 5.6. *Three complementary approaches for design tests*
(Drawn from [SEN 90, GRI 95])

Inspired by the Spiral[6] model [BOE 88], design test methods consist of gathering data using tests that give rise to modifications to be made to the system being evaluated. These modifications lead to a new version that will also be tested, and so on until the final system is obtained (see Figure 5.6).

According to Senach [SEN 90], this sequential organization remains theoretical, given that in reality – due to constraints related to time, budget, development, etc. – approaches are often less structured and tests are not systematic.

Design tests combine three complementary approaches:

– *The selection of design alternatives*: this is done when there are no obvious choice criteria among several possibilities; the gathering of empirical data must allow us to rank the solutions envisioned. This method is generally executed upstream of prototyping [SEN 90].

– *Prototyping*: this is used for the early evaluation of certain specific aspects of the interface with users. The objective of this technique is to minimize the development costs of the interface while ensuring the progressive optimization of its quality depending on the frame of mind introduced by the Spiral model. Two principal criteria are considered: general ergonomic criteria, such as those cited in [BAS 93, VAN 94], and application-specific criteria (quality, safety, environment, etc.). Various techniques and tools in this subject are described in [BEA 02];

---

6 The Spiral model was introduced by Boehm [BOE 88]. It consists of an iterative process wherein each spiral cycle develops four activities: the identification of the objectives of the phase, alternatives to obtain these objectives and their constraints; analysis and resolution of risks; development and verification of the objective of the phase; and planning of the next phase.

– *Usability labs*: this is usable once the interface has been implemented. It allows us to control the quality of the final product by measuring the overall usability of the system. Objective and subjective data are collected from subjects who are able to take the software in hand and/or use it, thanks to specially developed evaluation stations, called usability labs (eye tracker, camera, microphone, etc.).

These methods are well known in software engineering and human–machine interaction and offer several advantages. The alternative selection method ensures the ranking of the envisioned solutions. Prototyping allows us to compare design choices to the reality of the terrain and thus to catch problems early. The usability labs allows the user to test the final system, and thus to detect new problems (or problems that have persisted since the selection of design alternatives).

Design test methods also have limits. For example, the selection of design alternatives has been criticized for having often been instigated outside of the real context of the task, its limitations, and its environment. Prototyping does not allow us to test all functions in detail when it is "low fidelity"; on the other hand, it limits the maneuvering margin in terms of correction when it is "high fidelity". The important thing is to find the right environment depending on the system being developed [BAC 05]. The usability labs allow an exploratory and global approach in many cases, and cannot be referred to as a true method [GRI 95].

5.3.1.4. *Conclusions about user-centered approaches and their place in the development cycle*

User-centered approaches are generally only applicable if the development of the interface is quite advanced. They are based on the idea that the best way to detect a system's problems is to observe a real user interacting with the interface while carrying out a real task. In this vein, Karat [KAR 88] confirms that in most cases user tests allow us to detect design errors that the most sharp-eyed developers miss. As Farenc [FAR 97] points out, the results and data necessary for the application of these methods are not reusable. For each system, each user (or type of user), and each task, the method must be implemented all over again from the beginning. It seems to us that a proper capitalization strategy would be beneficial here.

The development of a product rarely starts from nothing, and is generally intended to improve an existing situation that is computerized or manual. In this case, all of these evaluation techniques can be imagined *a priori*, beginning with the stages of analysis and specification, and an evaluation may be conducted in order to learn about strong and weak points in the reference site(s). They are also more often than not used *a posteriori*; that is, after the implementation, testing and operation phases, when the HMI is concrete, in order to evaluate and improve it [GRI 96].

The major advantage of these methods is that they take into account the reality of the use of the system with a real task and a real user. This aspect ensures results that are more trustworthy than those provided by any so-called "theoretical" methods (expert-based methods, analytical methods) [SEN 90, BAL 94, FAR 97, BAS 02], some of which will be examined later in this chapter.

When the interface does not exist, or when data and measurements pertaining to human–machine interaction cannot be recorded, evaluation may be done using expert-based approaches.

5.3.2. Expert-based approaches

Evaluations conducted by an ergonomics expert or a specialist in human–machine communication help to provide a judgment on the ergonomic quality of an interface and to compare the attributes and characteristics of an HMI to ergonomic recommendations or norms, in order to detect design errors and propose improvements.

Expert-based approaches are used when data pertaining to interface interaction cannot be recorded, is unavailable, or when the interface does not yet exist. They can be combined with other user-centered approaches. Among the many expert-based evaluation methods that extist, there are specialist intervention, inspection methods (including the cognitive walkthrough method, guidelines, and heuristic evaluation) and evaluation grids. These methods are presented below.

5.3.2.1. Specialist intervention

The objective of this method is to assess the ergonomic quality of the interface by a specialist in human–machine communication and to propose improvements.

This method undoubtedly provides the best results; however, it remains underused. Specialist intervention evaluation consists of carrying out an expert evaluation of an interface and determining all of the problems liable to be encountered during the use of the interface. The involvement of different specialists for the expert evaluation of an interface shows that each one focuses on specific aspects of the interface, and bases his/her evaluation on his/her own approach [HAM 84, NIE 90]. Consequently, the ideal strategy is to bring in several specialists (psychologists, knowledge engineers, graphic designers, etc.), and to compare and synthesize all of these areas of expertise in order to determine the improvements to be made to an interactive system (see Figure 5.7).

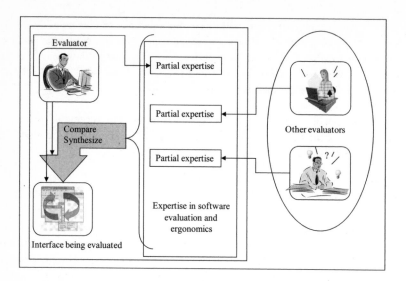

Figure 5.7. *Principle of expert intervention*

The advantage of this method is that it costs little [BAS 02] and is easy to implement for a rapid diagnosis of design errors [NEN 99]. The disadvantage is that the involvement of a single specialist in human factors, even an experienced one, results in the identification of an average of half of the potential problems of an interface [POL 91], and budgetary or organizational reasons may render the use of several evaluators impossible.

5.3.2.2. *Usability inspection methods*

Usability inspection methods combine a group of approaches that rely on the judgment of evaluators, whether they are experts in usability or not [NIE 94]. All of these methods generally target the detection of aspects of interfaces that may cause difficulties of use or weigh down users' work.

Inspection methods[7] are numerous and do not all share the same objective. They are distinguished from one another by the way in which evaluator judgments are derived, and by the evaluation criteria on which these judgments are based. According to Bastien and Abed [BAS 01, ABE 01], the most documented methods, and the ones that have been subjected to tests and comparisons, are:

– *The cognitive walkthrough method*: this method is used to evaluate the ease of learning a system and to predict problems that the user may encounter [POL 92,

---

7 References for usability inspection methods are available at: http://mentalmodels. mitre.org/ cog_eng/ce_references_III.htm

JAC 00]. By putting him/herself in the place of a user exploring the interface by carrying out predetermined tasks, the evaluator determines the problems liable to be encountered by the user at each stage of the execution of a task. The interface must then be modified and the necessary improvements made (described in reports written by the evaluator). In reality, there are various versions and numerous extensions of this method [MAH 09b].

– *Compliance with recommendations and ergonomic dimensions* (ergonomic guidelines): the evaluation of this consists of assessing the compliance of elements of the interface with the rules listed in various documents, generally taking the form of a compendium. Examples of this are style guides, ergonomic guides, [SMI 86, BAS 93, VAN 94] and norms [ISO 96, AFN 03]. Note that compendia have been more specifically suggested for particular domains, for example multimedia and the Internet [BAS 98, VAN 98]; see also [NOG 08].

– *Heuristic evaluation*: this consists mainly of the carrying out of a review of the interface by one or more evaluators [NIE 94]. Its objective is to survey usability problems related to the interface. Using a list of heuristic criteria based on experiments in the domain of evaluation based on usability, and taking into account the context of use, experts (evaluators) group together the problems encountered in terms of these heuristics. Indications are then given of the criticality of the problems encountered.

The cognitive walkthrough method has been widely used, first with relatively simple tasks for interactive systems [POL 92] and more recently for the evaluation of websites; see the *cognitive walkthrough for the web* method) [BLA 02]. Attempts to automate this method have been made [REI 91]. Note that, for complex tasks, the cognitive walkthrough method may prove unwieldy to use. This method has also been the subject of numerous studies since its first appearance [MAH 09a].

The major inconvenience of guidelines lies generally in their large size (they can contain thousands of rules), which can make their use tedious and complicated. According to Bastien [BAS 01], when these guides are studied there is a noticeable lack of uniformity in the presentation of the recommendations, which makes the search for a specific rule extremely difficult. For this reason, it is important to try to standardize them in assistance systems (this point will be explored in section 5.4).

Heuristic evaluation has already been used many times and has proven itself. As an example, Nielsen and Garzotto [NEI 94, GAR 97] rely on heuristic evaluation in proposing low-cost usability evaluations. The disadvantage of this method is that it is difficult to reproduce the context of use. Experts cannot predict the user's actions, which can sometimes be unexpected. They can note results intended to cover the majority of cases, but not specific cases.

5.3.2.3. *Evaluation grids*

Evaluation grids are used to evaluate an interface according to a group of ergonomic criteria. When using evaluation grids, the evaluator describes the interface systematically according to a scale generally including three to five points, or sometimes 10. An evaluation grid includes a group of questions to which the evaluator, reviewing the interface, must respond. The response to these questions is generally made via boxes to be checked or grades to be given to each ergonomic aspect being studied. A checklist evaluation method was introduced by Ravden [RAV 89] (see Figure 5.8) and has been very widely used in the industrial and academic sectors; it can be used by designers, human factor specialists, and even final system users.

N°	Answer the questions below by putting an X in the corresponding column					
	Questions	Always	Often	Sometimes	Never	Don't know
In terms of <u>consistency</u>						
1	Are the colors used consistently?	X				
2	Are the abbreviations, codes, and other information used consistently?		X			
3	Are the graphic representations, symbols, icons, and other pictoral information used consistently?	X				
4	Does the cursor appear in the same initial position for similar displays?					X
.	...					
In terms of <u>clarity</u> and <u>cleanness</u>						
12	Are the stages that the interface may go through during the execution of a task easy to understand?	X				
13	Does the user always know where he is?		X			
14	Are the operations in each part of the interface easy to understand?			X		
.	...					
	Do you wish to add any further comments?	Bla bla bla…				

Figure 5.8. *Sample of an evaluation grid (drawn from [RAV 89])*

This is considered to be an effective method, since if the evaluator has a group of grids [SCA 86, RAV 89] as well as ergonomic criteria guidelines [NIE 93, VAN 94] there is less risk of forgetting important criteria during the evaluation. Though this method is a satisfactory means of obtaining consistent responses, [SEN 90] points out that its limits are obvious, given that it does not allow us to identify the user's business organization, and no information is provided on the structure of work procedures.

5.3.2.4. *Conclusions on expert-based approaches and their place in the development cycle*

Above, we have presented several expert-based evaluation approaches. These approaches can be used whether or not there is a system to be evaluated. As Grislin [GRI 95] specifies, the involvement of a specialist is only feasible once the interface is completed, while evaluation grids and usability inspection methods can be used simultaneously with the design process.

The advantage of these evaluations is that they can be done fairly rapidly; they cost relatively little; and they can be done fairly early on in the design process [NIE 94]. Studies carried out on the activity of experts in evaluation situations, however, show that individual performances are highly variable in terms of the number and type of errors detected and the evaluation strategies adopted [POL 91, BAS 01].

5.3.3. *Analytical approaches*

These approaches, also called model-based approaches [GRI 96], are based on formal models of HMI and/or interaction, as well as the progressive implementation of objective metrics. These models are used to predict, by means of specifications, certain aspects related to human–machine interaction, such as the ranking of tasks, user action pathways, time required to complete a task, etc. Metrics are implemented to measure certain aspects associated with the quality of interaction (consistency, compatibility with the user's mental image, screen quality, etc.) in an objective manner. The use of these abstract representations allows for predictions related to performance, which cannot be made with an empirical approach, since there is not yet any experience with the use of the interactive system [SEN 90, GRI 95].

To illustrate these approaches, we will return to the Senach classification [SEN 90], which consists of distinguishing between two categories of models: formal predictive models and interface quality models. These two models are presented below.

5.3.3.1. *Formal predictive models*

Formal predictive models use the hypothesis that certain user performances can be predicted, and thus considered, during the design and evaluation phase of the interface. We distinguish two types of models that can be used in support of the evaluation: task models and linguistic models.

5.3.3.1.1. Use of task models as evaluation supports

The objective of these models is to analyze and represent user activity in the form of a structure of tasks [DIA 89, DIA 04]. In this way, they provide a support for the predictive evaluation of the performance by proposing a measurable description of the user's behavior and performances.

Task models consist of the breaking down of tasks, usually into a hierarchy, into primary units in order to analyze and represent the user's cognitive activity. Without providing an exhaustive list[8], the best known task models are:

– *GOMS* (*Goals, Operators, Methods, and Selector*) *model*: GOMS [CAR 83] describes the cognitive activity of a user (expert) engaged in carrying out a routine task without error. It can be broken down into *Goals* organized in a hierarchy; an operator corresponding to primary actions (*Operators*); *Methods* or procedures for attaining an objective; and *Selection rules* for choosing methods when several solutions can be used to reach the same goal. Note that the CPM-GOMS model [JOH 96] proposes an extension of GOMS in the form of a calculation of the route necessary to complete a task; it describes user tasks via a representation in the form of a network.

– *Keystroke-Level Model* (KLM): this is mainly used to predict the execution time of user tasks [CAR 83]. A task is analyzed in terms of its task-units, for example seize, move, erase, etc. The execution time of each task-unit is estimated by adding the execution times of the basic operators that compose it. This model contains six types of basic operators, and for each of these operators, an execution time is estimated:

- K: press a button,

- P: indicate an area of the screen with a mouse,

- H: direct the hand toward a device,

- D: draw a line segment,

- M: prepare mentally to carry out an action, and

- R: response time of the system during which the user is waiting.

– *SADT-Petri method*: developed by Abed [ABE 90] for LAMIH, this method uses analysis and modeling tools (SADT) [IGL 89] for the functional breakdown of the system and the static modeling of tasks, and Petri nets [DAV 92] to describe the

8 It would, for example, have been possible to add DIANE [BAR 88] and its extension DIANE+ [TAR 93], HTA [SHE 93], MAD [SCA 89], CTT [PAT 00], etc. It would also have been possible to cite numerous works in HMI using Petri nets (see for example [PAL 97, MOU 02, KON 03, BER 08].

dynamic component of tasks. This method has developed toward *Task Oriented Object Design* (TOOD) by introducing an objective-oriented description of tasks [MAH 97]. Tabary [TAB 01] and Abed [ABE 01], have introduced the *Model Based user interface Design* or MBD approach[9] to TOOD methodology in order to facilitate the modeling of highly interactive applications.

Each method or model has its advantages and disadvantages. The GOMS model is used to predict and simulate the behavior of an expert operator, but it assumes that this expert will not make any errors, which is a major limitation of this model. The KLM model has the benefit of being easily understandable by designers, but its implementation quickly poses numerous problems [COU 90]. Moreover, it does not allow the prediction of the effectiveness of the operator when complex tasks are carried out. The SADT-Petri method has the advantage of being able to use Petri Nets for the comparison of the model of the task to be carried out (theoretical task model) and the task observed (task actually executed) in order to return to the interface specification.

5.3.3.1.2. Use of linguistic models as evaluation supports

These models attempt to produce both an explicit representation of the interface structure, and the actions liable to be carried out by the final users of the HMI, by means of grammar.

These models can be used to describe interaction tasks between the user and the interface, mainly for the purpose of evaluating the language of commands and its consistency [GRI 96]. The following models are representative of this:

– *Command Language Grammar (CLG) model* [MOR 81]: this is a grammatical structure that is used to represent a system by four levels of abstraction: the task, semantic, syntactic, and interaction levels. According to Moran, the CLG model can contribute to a predictive evaluation of the ease of use of an interface and to pinpoint, the evaluation decisions that will be essential for the user [COU 90].

– *Action Language Grammar (ALG) model* [REI 84]: this consists of constructing a model of actions taken by the user in the form of production rules. These rules are: TO complete an action, and DO these operations. During the evaluation, the ALG model is used:

- to identify design choices liable to cause errors in use and thus to return to specifications, and

- to compare alternatives of comparison according to an ease of use criterion.

---

9 The MBD approaches refer to an explicit, largely declarative description, and capture the semantics of the application and all of the knowledge necessary for the specification of both the appearance and behavior of the interaction [SZE 96, TAB 01].

– *Task Action Grammar (TAG model* [PAY 89]: TAG is a formal grammar used to describe a group of tasks and actions in the form of rules, and to ensure the correspondence of task semantics to action sequences. The use of TAG has several limitations; in particular, it considers only primary tasks, and does not model interactive systems. To remedy this type of problem, Tauber [TAU 90] introduced an extension of TAG, *Extended Task-Action Grammar* (ETAG), and provided a conceptual model of the interactive system [DEH 01].

The main disadvantage of the CLG model is that it does not allow the evaluation of a finished product developed with another model; it would be necessary to translate the interface into CLG in order to analyze it. Even though the ALG model is of interest for the construction of a model of actions taken by the user, it does not take into account that tasks that are easy to describe can be difficult to execute [SEN 90]. TAG helps to judge the structure of tasks described with the aid of a language, but this is limited to simple tasks; i.e. to the description of specific functions of the device. It should be noted that there is no relating of various simple tasks to higher-level tasks. However, to evaluate the ergonomic qualities of an interface, it is necessary to observe information that is visualized based on the description of conceptual interface models [EZZ 02].

5.3.3.2. *Formal (quality) HMI models*

Formal interface quality models are complementary to formal predictive models. They are used to identify the measurable properties of the HMI, according to formalized usability criteria, which may have an effect on the user performance, notably by limiting difficulties of use. These approaches are based on the idea that certain ergonomic problems related to interface use can be avoided *a priori*. However, they must be integrated into an overall evaluation approach according to a group of interconnected criteria meant to manage consistency with regard to different operational contexts [GRI 05]. Senach's classification distinguishes two approaches [SEN 90]:

– a cognitive interface quality approach that takes into account the cognitive processing of information; in other words, the quality of the interface depends on its compatibility with the mental representations developed by its users; and

– an optimal system quality approach: this approach does not consider the semantic aspects, and evaluates the interface according to criteria that are usually quantitative and related to the presentation of information.

Each method or model has its advantages and disadvantages. The GOMS model is used to predict and simulate the behavior of an expert operator, but it assumes that this expert will not make any errors, which represents a major limitation of this model. The KLM model has the benefit that designers can easily understand it, but its implementation quickly poses numerous problems [COU 90]. Moreover, it does not allow the prediction of the effectiveness of the operator when complex tasks are carried out. The SADT-Petri method has the advantage of being able to use Petri nets for comparison of the model of the task to be carried out (theoretical task model) and the task observed (task actually executed) in order to return to the interface specification.

Formal quality models are also very useful, since they clearly underlie the proposition of relevant software aids, in particular automated and semi-automated aids. These can be separated into two categories:

– *Automated display evaluation systems*: these consist of using computed tools capable of automatically taking ergonomic measurements on page-screens, most often independently of the context of use. For the evaluation of interactive systems, these approaches try to avoid ergonomic problems related to the use of the interface before their appearance, by being integrated into the design approach. This category contains knowledge-based systems that have been proposed since the 1980s (see for example [KOL 91]); and are still being suggested, especially in the Internet sector [BER 04]. For the sake of clarity and the structure of this chapter, we will go into more detail later about these approaches, as well as their advantages and disadvantages relating to the automatic evaluation of HMIs.

– *Automated display generation systems*: these target the automatic generation of the HMI or the generation of HMI specifications. Their objective is to produce displays respecting *a priori* basic ergonomic guidelines. The MBD research trend belongs to this category, and is also consistent with the *Model Driven Architecture* approach proposed by the *Object Management Group* (OMG).

5.3.3.3. *Conclusions about analytical approaches and their place in the development cycle*

The predictive models listed above, based on task models or linguistic models, describe human–machine interaction aimed at predictive evaluation, particularly performance-based evaluation, since they offer a measurable description of user behavior. The model obtained is then used for ergonomic evaluation by analyzing the representation of probable user activities during the execution of their tasks. As Kolski [KOL 97] points out, it is often forgotten that such models can also be used once the interface is completed to model user activities and compare it with the model created pertaining to the tasks envisioned by designers, in order to observe the consequences in terms of developing HMIs and/or user training programs.

Formal (quality) HMI models are usually those at the research prototype stage, even if they have been validated in concrete cases. Such systems should eventually be integrated into graphic development environments. Note, however, that for the evaluation of websites, some automatic evaluation or evaluation assistance tools already exist [BEI 04, MAR 05].

5.3.4. *Synthesis of evaluation methods, techniques and tools*

A wide variety of methods exist that contribute to the evaluation of HMIs. These stem more or less directly from various domains, such as software engineering, ergonomics, psychology, knowledge acquisition, or human automation. They contribute in a general manner to the vast and multidisciplinary domain of human–machine interaction.

We have presented some existing classifications of evaluation methods and techniques dedicated to interactive systems, and particularly to HMIs. A classification has been chosen in order to present an overview of existing evaluation methods and techniques:

– user-centered approaches consist of collecting data representative of interaction using measurements or observations taken from the use of the interface by users who are representative of the final population. Evaluation must be carried out in a context that is as close to reality as possible;

– expert-based approaches are used when data pertaining to human–machine interactions cannot be recorded, are not available, or when the interface does not exist; and

– analytical approaches centered on the modeling of the interface and/or human–machine interaction are used when the interface is non-existent, when the user is unavailable, and/or when it is possible to proceed with a partially or totally automated evaluation. In this case, the use of abstract representations yields predictions pertaining to performance that cannot be established with an empirical approach, since there is not yet enough experience with the use of the interactive system [SEN 90].

The common point of all evaluation methods and techniques remains the problem of choosing the most appropriate method for evaluating a given system. It is true that the choice of a method depends partly on the method's capacity to fulfill evaluation criteria, and partly on contextual factors that are the limitations facing evaluators, such as available budget, type of application, available time, etc. Moreover, during the evaluation, the methods and techniques used and the data collected are generally numerous and sometimes require a considerable amount of processing time in order to draw conclusions about the quality of the interface, especially during the evaluation of a complex system. In this case, the evaluator may feel disoriented if no assistance is given to him/her, and make poor choices in terms of evaluation.

A number of responses to these problems are currently available in the form of evaluation aid systems, with various types of assistance being possible. The next section will address these aids.

5.4. Toward automated or semi-automated evaluation assistance tools

For the past 30 years, a number of software tools have been proposed to aid in the evaluation of interactive systems. A first category can be designated based on [BAS 02, IVO 01a]:

– tools used to help the evaluator make decisions concerning the choice of evaluation methods or techniques. For example, the ADHESION system (Aid with Human Decision-Making for the Evaluation of Interactive Systems and their evaluatiON) [NEN 99a, NEN 99b]; the Denley [DEN 97] evaluation assistance tool, etc.;

– tools for the organization of evaluation, such as *Fast Audit based on Cognitive Ergonomics* (FACE) [HUL 96], which is aimed at helping the evaluator target the evaluation situation, choose the evaluation technique to apply, and present the results. Mahatody's works [MAH 09] are of this type, while focusing on the operation of variants and evolutions in the cognitive walkthrough method;

– some tools correspond to software versions of methods exploiting initially only paper documents, see for instance the software version of the cognitive walkthrough method [REI 91];

– some tools use ergonomic guidelines [VAN 99] to aid in determining whether the interface is in violation of these guidelines; and

– tools used to gather data during interaction between the user and the interactive system in order to assist the evaluation. This is then possibly combined with tools used to carry out an analysis.

These tools provide a varying level of automation of the evaluation. According to Ivory [IVO 01a, IVO 01b], the automatization of evaluation brings several advantages:

– it reduces the cost and time of evaluation because tools automate certain evaluation activities, such as data capture and the analysis of the data or criticisms captured;

– it facilitates the detection of errors. Possible interface-assistance activities can in fact be specified with task models such as *ConcurTaskTrees* (CTT) [PAT 97].

Tools can automatically detect errors or inconsistencies depending on this specification;

– it reduces the need to use evaluation experts, since the automation of evaluation activities such as capture, analysis, and criticism is a primary aid to designers who, very often, have little knowledge or experience in evaluation; and

– it increases the coverage of aspects evaluated. It is not always possible to independently evaluate each aspect of the interface due to time constraints, limited resources, or high costs. Thanks to tools, the number of aspects evaluated can be increased[10].

Automation is not a substitution for manual evaluation techniques, but serves as a complement to them. The various techniques are intended to reveal additional problems. For example, subjective measurements such as user satisfaction are difficult to predict using automated methods [IVO 01b].

Among the types of evaluation assistance tools cited above, we are particularly interested in the last two; that is, tools using ergonomic guidelines, and electronic monitoring that captures data during interaction between the user and the interactive system in order to assist in the evaluation. We will present representative examples in the following two sections.

5.4.1. *Tools utilizing ergonomic guidelines*

Today, ergonomic guidelines are used as an important source in the detection of problems with the user interface of an interactive system in order to improve it. The term "guideline" encompasses possible abstract or concrete recommendations that are used for the design (by designers) and evaluation of interactive systems (by usability experts) in order to design more effective and user-friendly interfaces [GRA 00a, GRA 00b]. According to Vanderdonckt [VAN 94], an ergonomic guideline constitutes a principle of design and/or evaluation to be observed in order to obtain and/or guarantee an ergonomic HMI. Vanderdonckt [VAN 94] also distinguished five types of recommendations: design standards, recommendation articles, recommendation guides, style guides, and ergonomic design algorithms. Guidelines may correspond to general recommendations that are independent of domain, as in [SCA 86, SMI 86], etc. They can also be grouped into style guides specific to a system, an environment, or a particular organization, as in [APP 92,

---

10 Interested user can consult [IVO 01a] or [IVO 01b] for more details about these advantages.

HP 88, IBM 93, MIC 95, OSF 93], etc. Currently, there are numerous sources describing economic guidelines:

– international standards, such as ISO 9241, ISO/IEC 9126, etc.;

– national standards such as HFES (in the United States), AFNOR (France), CBN (Belgium), BSI (United Kingdom), etc.;

– summary documents reviewing ergonomic criteria such as [SCA 86, SMI 86, VAN 94], etc.;

– standards issued by companies such as Apple [APP 92], IBM [IBM 93], Microsoft [MIC 95], etc.

During the design of a HMI, ergonomic guidelines are intended to ensure compliance with one or more ergonomic criteria [VAN 94]. Each criterion constitutes a recognized dimension on the path leading to the development of an effective, sophisticated interface that is more user-friendly and less inclined to error [SCA 86]. As an example, eight general criteria can be identified and retained [BAS 93, VAN 94]: guidance, dialog control, error management, consistency, workload, adaptability, compatibility, and significance of codes and names. Vanderdonckt [VAN 94] has developed a guideline tree that includes 12 divisions (data capture, data display, dialog, graphics, means of interaction, styles of interaction, user guidance, messages, online assistance, documentation, evaluation, and implementation) into which each guideline falls.

Ergonomic guidelines are often documented in reference manuals. To use guidelines, these documents must be consulted. The use of this type of guidelines reveals several disadvantages. Grammenos [GRA 00b] has noted some limitations on this subject, as well as with regard to the content of these rules (though the value and importance of these guidelines is indisputable):

– difficulty with rule management: for example, it may be difficult to select a subgroup of rules, or to combine rules from different manuals;

– difficulty updating (addition of new rules, elimination of existing rules);

– difficulty modifying the content of existing rules;

– paper manuals are difficult to distribute;

– these manuals are difficult to "skim". A search may require a great deal of time; and

– rules are often independent of the context; therefore, they must be interpreted, perhaps in-depth, in order to be used correctly. Designers and developers are not always familiar with the languages and styles used to express these rules.

These disadvantages have led to the development of a type of tool that is considered to use ergonomic rules. Among the numerous tools and methodologies of this type proposed in the literature, we will note the following:

– In the system proposed by Parush [PAR 00], each rule is stored in a database using a specific structure composed of three levels: 1) section (example: Dialog Boxes Layout); 2) subsection; and 3) title. There are also additional parts: recommendation, additional notes, image file, etc. The user can enter rules into the database using the construction module. This provides the user with an interface s/he can use to add rules, new rules (as well as information concerning these rules) and to modify existing rules in the database. The reading module provides the user with an interface allowing him/her to:

  - skim the rules according to the hierarchical structure of the system, or

  - query the database in order to recover a specific subgroup of rules according to the needs of the evaluator, based on information pertaining to the rules (name of section, subsection, title, etc.).

– Sherlock [GRA 00a, GRA 00b] is a guideline management system. It is an integrated environment used to access rules, reuse past experiences, and facilitate automated, semi-automated or manual inspection from the perspective of usability. An evaluation conducted using Sherlock must utilize a predetermined textual description of the HMI and appear in a report detailing problems of usability: reason, recommended actions, level of seriousness, theoretical basis and examples, solutions implemented in the past, etc. Figure 5.9 illustrates the overall structure of Sherlock (the client–server architecture). The Sherlock client module and the Sherlock server module can reside in the same machine or different machines; they connect to each other through the Internet or the company's intranet network.

– The methodology of the DESTINE project (*Design and Evaluation STudio for INtent-based Ergonomic websites*) is aimed at evaluating Web pages individually (at the page level) through the static analysis of its code, utilizing the guideline review technique. With regard to the extended version of this solution presented in [JAS 01], the authors claim that it can be used to evaluate the quality of a site (at the site level); in this case, all of the pages of a site must be collected and evaluated. The methodology of the DESTINE project, as presented by [BEI 04], is illustrated in

Figure 5.10; it divides the entire evaluation process into two stages: rule structuring and evauation. In stage 1 (specifying the formal rules), rules must be selected that come from various available sources. This selection is done manually for new rules, since access to the rules can occur in different ways (articles, books, websites, etc.). Then these rules must be transformed (they are usually initially expressed in natural language) into structures that the evaluation tool can understand and process. These structures are stored in XML form, respecting the syntax of a rule-definition language called GDL. The evaluator can select individual rules concerning certain ergonomic aspects (accessibility, user satisfaction, usability, etc.) depending on the objective of the evaluation. In stage 2 (website evaluation), the Web pages being evaluated are first downloaded and analyzed in order to capture usability data pertaining to instances of HTML and CSS components (the analysis is conducted individually on each downloaded page). Then, the evaluation engine applies evaluation logic (already defined in stage 1) to the instances of HTML or CSS components captured in order to detect compliance with or violation of the rules. The results are presented in the form of a detailed evaluation report. This methodology is associated with several tools (a knowledge management tool, a GDL editor, an ergonomic quality evaluator for websites, an ergonomic repair tool for websites posing usability problems, etc.).

– In the WebTango project, Ivory [IVO 01a] proposed an automated website evaluation methodology as well as the associated tools. The author's proposal is based on two criticisms: 1) the approaches of existing guideline reviews cover only a small fraction of the aspects of usability, according to [BRA 00]; 2) few of the rules for Web design and the existing guideline review approaches are validated on the basis of empirical calculations. Consequently, the author proposes a new methodology based on empirical calculations related to 141 measurements at the page level, and 16 measurements at the site level. These measurements concern several aspects of Web interfaces, such as consistency, use of colors, page text, speed of download, etc. These measurements and the categorizations (carried out by experts) of a large number of high-ranking websites are used by this methodology to determine statistical models of highly-rated Web interfaces called profiles. These models are then used for the automated analysis of Web pages and sites in a manner similar to the guideline review method. The author considers this methodology a synthesis of measurement techniques in the domain of performance evaluation and of guideline review techniques in the domain of usability evaluation. An overview of this methodology is shown in Figure 5.11.

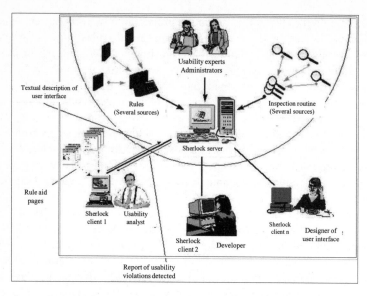

Figure 5.9. *Architecture of Sherlock [GRA 00a, GRA 00b]*

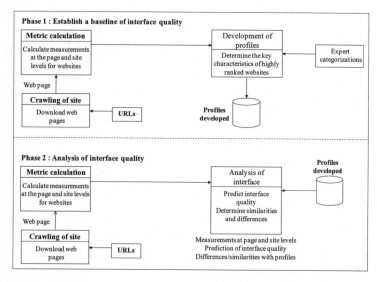

Figure 5.10. *Initial version (corresponding to the initial version of GDL) of the methodology of the DESTINE project [BEI 04][11]*

---

11 *To crawl a site*: download Web pages from this site and store them locally.

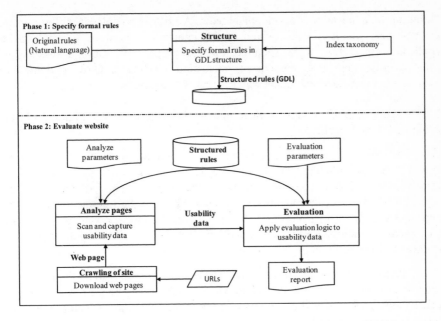

Figure 5.11. *Methodology of analysis of the WebTango project [IVO 01b]*

5.4.2. *Tools for the collection of interaction data to support the evaluation*

Tools in this category are also called "electronic monitors". They are tools that automatically capture objective data during interaction between the user and the interactive system in a real work situation. The data captured are analyzed afterward either manually or automatically [BAS 02, EZZ 97, EZZ 05, MAR 05]. Several differences should be noted between electronic monitors and some similar tools:

– An electronic monitor is different from a so-called monitoring tool. The latter monitors or captures data without offering any subsequent analysis. An electronic monitor is used to capture and record data and it can also offer a more or less in-depth analysis of the data captured [MAR 05].

– An electric monitor is also different from quality feedback agents (QFAs), which are software tools used to capture data pertaining to the history of an application if that application malfunctions. A QFA simply captures technical data (for example, the version of the operating system, type of processor, type of screen, registries, functions used just before the failure of the application, etc.) from the moment when the application had a problem. These data are sent to the development team to help them understand the problem and the reason for the application's failure, and improve the future version of the application. A QFA can also allow the user to send a report of what s/he was doing with the application at the time of the failure to the application's development team. A QFA is completely different from an electronic monitor, which captures the interactions between a user and an application in a real work situation for the purpose of subsequent analysis. Consequently, for the evaluation of interactive systems, a QFA is limited in comparison to an electronic monitor [TRA 08a, TRA 08b].

The theoretical function of an electronic monitor is illustrated in Figure 5.12. It is composed of three stages:

– The monitor captures data generated by the interaction between a user and a system in a work situation (for example, the actions of users and their repercussions on the system, such as pressing a button on the keyboard, clicking the mouse, the selection of an object in a menu, a click on a button in the interface window, the appearance of a warning message, the opening or closing of a window, etc.). This data capture is done discreetly and openly so that the user of the application is not disturbed by the function of the monitor.

– The data captured are stored in a database and then analyzed by the monitor in order to help the evaluator in his/her activities. Analyses can be the result of various calculations, such as statistics, and they can be provided to the evaluator in different forms (diagrams, text, tables, etc.).

– Thanks to the recordings obtained, the evaluator can reconstruct models of the user's activity and the reactions of the HMI. These models are called observed models, and they can be compared to models of tasks to be carried out that are previously specified by the designer [EZZ 97]. The result of these comparisons can be useful to the designer in the improvement of the interactive system. Interview and questionnaire techniques can be used in order to better understand the activities and motivations of users when using the application.

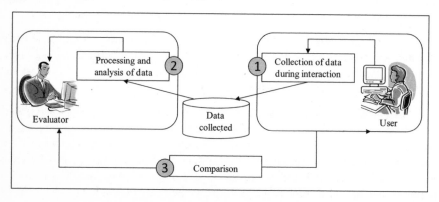

Figure 5.12. *Global functioning of electronic monitoring [EZZ 97]*

The strong point of the electronic monitor is its openness to the user; the user's work is not disturbed during his/her activities. The weak points of the electronic monitor lie in the processing of the data captured and stored, and also in the level of granularity of the analysis [BAS 02]. The quantity of this data can be enormous, and analysis can take hours or even days. Consequently, the monitor must provide data analysis to facilitate the evaluator's work. Otherwise, the data captured and stored can require more time in order to draw conclusions that are useful to the designer for the purposes of improvement.

It is important to emphasize that this method only directly captures objective data. It cannot directly capture subjective information, such as the preferences and opinion, etc., of the user [IVO 01b]. Moreover, real users must be involved in order to apply this method of evaluation; it is therefore costly, but reliable, if we consult the user's perspective [LEC 98].

We will now briefly describe several representative electronic monitors that have appeared in the past 10 years. This is not an exhaustive list, and some monitors were developed by the same team[12]:

– the USINE (*USer INterface Evaluator*) method [LEC 98] was proposed for the evaluation of *Window, Icons, Menus, Pointing device* (WIMP)-type interfaces. It is used in the analysis of the physical actions of the user on the interface (press or release of mouse buttons, pressing on keyboard keys, clicking on an area, seizure of text in a text box, etc.) from information stored in "log" text files, using a CTT model [PAT 97] previously specified with the help of an editor. With CTT, a task is described hierarchically from a high level of abstraction to a low level (corresponding to physical action), with sub-tasks being connected by temporal relationships (sequence, parallelism, choice, etc.). "Log" files are text files that store the physical actions of the user on the interface. The table of prerequisites specifies activation conditions between tasks. Using this method, the author must install additional software (JDK, QC/Replay) on the client's machine in order to record these user actions during a session. Figure 5.13 illustrates this method. The evaluation results are of several types:

- accomplished, failed, or never performed tasks,

- violation of time limits,

- pointless actions,

- numerical and temporal information pertaining to tasks and errors,

---

12 Interested readers may consult [HIL 00] to learn about older tools. USINE, RemUSINE, WebRemUSINE, Multimodal WebRemUSINE, and Multidevice WebRemUSINE (presented below) were developed by the same team. All of them use the CTT task model and empirical data concerning the physical actions of the user on the interface for evaluation.

- time taken for each task,

- times when errors are committed,

- patterns of tasks (sequences of completed tasks that appear several times),

- etc.

Results are displayed in the form of text or graphics; the evaluator then uses them to interpret problems and suggest improvements.

– Paterno *et al.* [PAT 99, PAT 00] have proposed the *Remote USer INterface Evaluator* (RemUSINE) method for the evaluation of WIMP-type interfaces. Its functioning is similar to USINE while including the possibility of remote evaluation. It is aimed at evaluating interactive applications that can be used by several users and situated in different places. The analysis of the actions in log files may be done for an individual session or a group of sessions in order to determine whether a problem is often encountered by several users, or if it is limited to specific users in a particular circumstance.

– Operating in a similar manner to USINE and RemUSINE, the *Web REMote USer INterface Evaluator* (WebRemUSINE) method [PAG 02, PAG 03] is intended for the evaluation of Web interfaces. It also uses the CTT model and log files (storing the events that are produced in the Web navigator) for its evaluation. Figure 5.14 illustrates this method. In the method, three types of events are recorded in log files: 1) events generated by user interactions with the Web navigator – these events correspond to interaction tasks in the CTT task model; 2) interior Web navigator events (page loading, the sending of a form, etc.) – these correspond to system tasks (also called automatic tasks) in the CTT task model; and 3) events related to a change in the user's target task (possible tasks are visible and can be selected from a list for the purpose of evaluation). This method can detect problems similar to those detected with RemUSINE and USINE, such as results concerning the execution of tasks (success or failure), errors committed (two types of errors), as well as pertinent statistical information. It can also detect other problems related to Web pages as well as offering the associated statistical information:

- pages visited and access numbers, as well as the average number of users accessing each page,

- page visit patterns (sequences of pages visited that appear multiple times) during navigation and their frequency,

- time taken to visit or download each page, and

- average time taken to visit or download a page.

– An extension of WebRemUSINE, the *Multimodal WebRemUSINE* method [PAT 06] is aimed at evaluating Web interfaces using the CTT model and integrating data from several sources, such as the log files storing events that have occurred in the Web navigator, video (via webcam), and an eye-tracker so that the evaluator will have access to the most complete information possible for the interpretation, analysis and evaluation of the Web interface being studied. The webcam and eye-tracker are assumed to be available in the client environment to capture both video data and data concerning the ocular movements of the user. Figure 5.15 illustrates this method.

– MESIA (Electronic Monitor dedicated to the Evaluation of Agent-Oriented Interactive Systems) [EZZ 03, TRA 06] is meant to be used in the evaluation of interactive systems based on a structure made up of interface agents [EZZ 05b]. In its initial version, its principle is to connect each of the *n* interface agents to an evaluation agent (also called a monitoring agent). Figure 5.16 gives an illustration of a case study involving six interface agents. Each monitoring agent provides a page-screen for the evaluator, allowing him/her to visualize the group of actions related to the corresponding interface agent. In order to make the monitor more generically applicable, it has been extensively revised and added to the EISEval environment described in the next section.

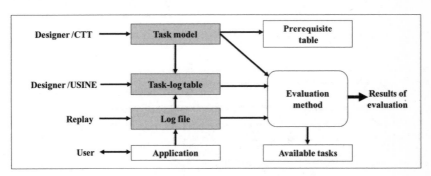

Figure 5.13. *USINE evaluation method using the CTT task model, translated from [LEC 98]*

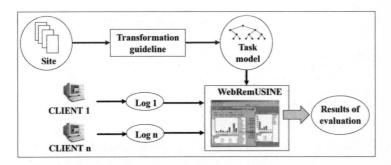

Figure 5.14. *WebRemUSINE evaluation method, translated from [PAG 02, PAG 03]*

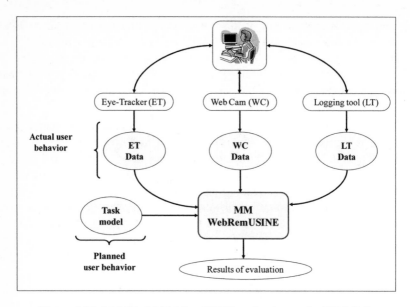

Figure 5.15. *MultiModal WebRemUSINE evaluation method [PAT 06]*

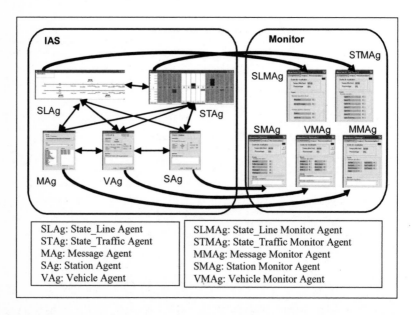

Figure 5.16. *Basic principle of pairing between a MESIA monitor and the system being evaluated – association of each monitoring agent with each system interface [TRA 06]*

5.5. Proposal of a generic and configurable environment to aid in the evaluation of agent-based interactive systems: EISEval

In this section, the limitations of traditional monitors are presented. Then we will successively describe the principles that the EISEval (*Environment for Interactive System Evaluation*) environment must respect, the abstract levels of events considered in it, and the formal description of the agent-based structure of interactive systems. Finally, the modular structure and each module of EISEval will be discussed and illustrated with examples. This section is based on [TRA 09].

5.5.1. *Motivation*

We have proposed and developed an evaluation environment that extends the capabilities offered by traditional monitors and by MESIA. Indeed, the motivation of the proposal of the EISEval evaluation environment takes its source of limitations from the MESIA monitor (discussed above), but also from that of traditional monitors:

– several monitors have been proposed, but they do not take into account the particularities related to agent-based structures of interactive systems for evaluation;

– the majority of traditional monitors are focused on the user interface of the interactive system. They do not greatly facilitate the evaluation of non-functional system properties, such as response time, reliability, etc. However, these properties are very important in evaluating the proper functioning of a system; and

– traditional monitors often capture events generated by the user interface or events relating to interaction devices, and are used for low-level analyses of these data; for example, the search for an interaction sequence, statistical calculations or the visualization of these results. Traditional monitors are often limited to this stage. The evaluator must interpret these analysis results him/herself in order to draw useful conclusions and suggest the necessary improvements to the designer.

In conclusion, the EISEval evaluation environment proposed must respect a group of principles in order to remedy these flaws and disadvantages. The principles involved are described below.

5.5.2. *Principles of the proposed EISEval evaluation environment*

Six principles are targeted:

– The proposed environment, for the purposes of evaluation, must take into account the particularities of the agent-based structure of interactive systems. The inclusion of these particularities has several theoretical benefits. The evaluator must more thoroughly understand the problems of the interactive system being evaluated; s/he must be able to respond faster to questions such as: what are the (agent) services that have malfunctioned multiple times (by failing or by taking a long time, etc.)? What are the interactions (between interacting services) that have taken a long time? What are the interface agents that have often or rarely interacted with the user? What are the application agents that have been often or rarely called on to contribute? What are the agents that have had problems with regard to their services or interfaces etc.? Using the answers to these types of questions, it becomes easier for the evaluator to determine the improvements that must be made so they can be communicated to the designer.

– The proposed environment must capture all system interactions: between the user and the interface agents (in the form of EVIU (user–interface events) and EVDI (interaction device events) and between the agents themselves (in the form of services) for the purposes of analysis. Note that traditional monitors often only capture interactions between the user and the interactive part of the system.

– The proposed environment must go further than traditional monitors. It must help the evaluator to interpret the results of the analysis of data captured. As specified above, this interpretation must help with the evaluation of various aspects of an agent-based interactive system: evaluation of the user interface of the system; evaluation of some non-functional system properties; response time; reliability; etc; as well as the evaluation of some user properties (ability to use the system; habits; preferences; etc.) and the comparison of different users' performances.

– The environment proposed must be generic; i.e. it must be independent of interactive systems. To achieve this, it is necessary to have a formal description of the agent-based structure of interactive systems available.

– The environment proposed must be configurable; i.e. it must be able to be configured in order to help in the evaluation of different interactive systems.

– The environment proposed must be able to distinguish the abstract levels of events.

We will now present the EISEval environment that was proposed and developed.

5.5.3. *Structure of the environment proposed*

Figure 5.17 shows the structure of the EISEval evaluation environment proposed. This is a modular structure. This environment has already been introduced in [TRA 07], and has been described in detail in [TRA 08a, TRA 08b]. It is composed of seven modules that do not communicate directly with each other. Thus, the developer can modify one of them without affecting the others:

– *Module 1* is responsible for capturing events that occur in the agent-based interactive system being evaluated. These captured events might be: EVDIs at the lowest abstract level, and or EVIUs that occur on interface agents and/or services executed by mid-level agents.

– *Module 2* recovers mid-level events (services, EVIUs) captured by module 1 so that the evaluator can connect them to the corresponding tasks at the highest abstract level. The associations created correspond to the tasks that the user has completed during his/her time using the interactive system.

– *Module 3* recovers the data covered by module 1 (EVIUs, EVDIs, services) and the data from observed tasks created by module 2 for analysis (statistics, calculations of measurements, etc.). Then, it displays the results of analysis in forms the user can understand. These analysis results can be interpreted by the evaluator using module 6 to critique the system and suggest the necessary improvements to the designer.

– *Modules 4 and 5* allow the evaluator to generate Petri nets and compare them. *Module 4* uses mid-level events (services, EVIUs) captured and recorded in the databases by module 1, the BSA (agent specification database), and the database of tasks observed in order to generate the Petri nets (called the observed Petri net or the real Petri net) for tasks. Each Petri net generated describes the real actions of the user (in the form of EVIUs) and the real actions of the system (in the form of the services executed by agents) to accomplish a task. These Petri nets are stored in a database of observed tasks. The database of tasks to be completed (theoretical task database) that is created by the designer contains Petri nets that describe the processes of activities s/he has planned to execute tasks. The Petri nets generated are described using *Petri Net Markup Language*;

– The objective of *module 6* is to help the evaluator in the global evaluation task. For now, this model provides the evaluator with the indications necessary for the interpretation of the analysis results. This interpretation is used to evaluate three aspects of the system (user interface, some non-functional properties of the system, and some properties pertaining to the user);

– *Module 7* helps the evaluator to configure the environment in order to be able to evaluate different interactive systems. The evaluator must sieze a batch of information pertaining to the interactive system being evaluated; for example, general information, information pertaining to the tasks that can be executed using this system (planned tasks, theoretical tasks, or tasks to be executed), and the BSA (agents, services, EVIU).

To illustrate the activities of these seven modules, we have used the data from an experiment implementing the EISEval environment to evaluate an information assistance system (IAS). This experiment shows the advantages and problems of the

IAS and suggests necessary improvements. It is also used to test the proposed EISEval environment. It is presented below.

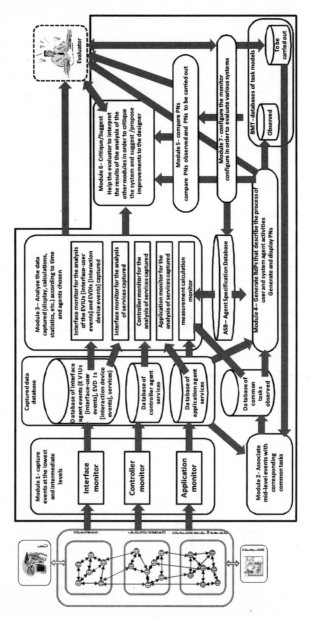

Figure 5.17. *Structure of the EISEval evaluation environment*

5.6. Context of operation of the proposed evaluation environment

5.6.1. *SART project*

The objective of the SART project was to design and create a system that helps controllers in the control room to better accomplish their tasks in both the normal and damaged modes of function of the transport network. It must allow for the minimization of waiting time for travelers, in damaged mode, in centers of exchange, and also to ensure as possible the continuity of movement in multi-modal networks (as far as possible). It is thus a matter of improving the quality of the services rendered to travelers and of keeping travelers informed [HAY 01].

According to [FAY 03], regulation is the process of real-time adequation of the working plans of different modes of transport in real operating conditions. The regulation of traffic is an overall regulation of the collective transport network. The SART project's system of assistance in the regulation of the transport network is composed of three subsystems, as shown in Figure 5.18:

– *Operating Assistance System (OAS)*: this system is used for the real-time monitoring of the operation of an urban transport network; it is constantly evolving thanks to technological advances in the domains of communication and information processing. The OAS can process very large quantities of information, but despite its very important assistance, sometimes controllers are not able to take into account the large amount of information carried by this system in their decision-making in the event of a disturbance [SAR 07]. In the context of the experiment that will be presented in the next section, the OAS is composed of a public ground transport network traffic simulator developed with Quest (*QUeue Event Simulation Tool*), a low-profile event simulation tool created by DELMIA[13]. This simulator automatically determines the placement of vehicles and the various disturbances in the network in real time.

– *Decision-making Assistance System (DAS)*: this system is a software solution used to help human controllers make decisions and provide solutions to complex problems. When the DAS receives a disturbance from the OAS, it is responsible for analyzing this disturbance and providing controllers with possible solutions for regulation. The controllers can choose the solution that seems most appropriate to them (according to their experience), or they can decide not to choose any of the solutions offered.

– *IAS*: this is an interactive system that was designed to help controllers supervise the public ground transport network. It shows controllers information

---

13 www.delmia.com.

about the current state of traffic and allows them to send necessary information or commands to the drivers of vehicles, as well as to travelers in stations and vehicles. During the experimental process, the evaluation environment was used to evaluate this system. We will now present this system before going into detail about the experiment, as well as its results.

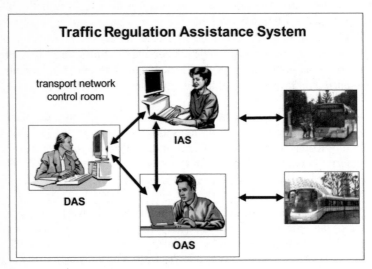

Figure 5.18. *Three subsystems of the traffic regulation assistance system (SART Project)*

5.6.2. *The IAS agent-based interactive system*

The agent-based interactive system being evaluated, called IAS, is a prototype intended for control-room staff. This IAS system is made up of six interface agents (state of traffic, state of a line, station, vehicle, message, and global view). We will present an overview of this system below. Interested readers may consult [EZZ 03, TRA 04, TRA 06] for more detail.

5.6.2.1. *State of traffic interface agent*

This agent is used by controllers to find out the current state of vehicle circulation (delayed or ahead of time) in a visual and general manner. Monitoring is done in real time. Figure 5.18 depicts this agent.

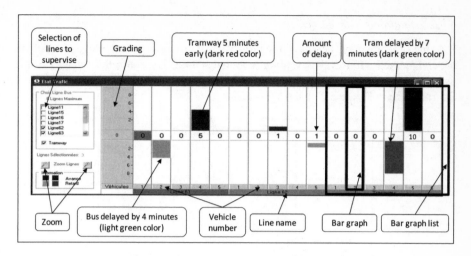

Figure 5.19. *IAS State of a traffic interface agent [TRA 06]*

5.6.2.2. *State of a line interface agent*

Figure 5.20 shows this agent. The agent displays any given transport line. It allows the controller to choose a line to supervise. This agent is made up of several elements, such as the stations or vehicles of the line displayed. The controller can open any line by clicking on the representation of this line in the state of traffic interface agent.

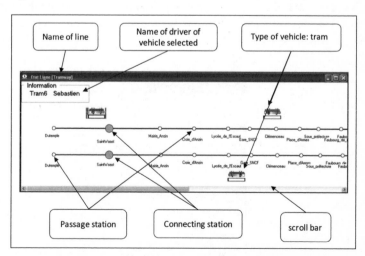

Figure 5.20. *IAS State of a line interface agent [TRA 06]*

5.6.2.3. *Station interface agent*

This agent displays details of the properties of any station, and allows controllers to send messages to travelers waiting in/at that station. The controller can access this agent by clicking on the representation of this station in the associated state of line interface agent. Figure 5.21 shows this agent.

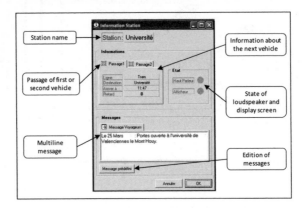

Figure 5.21. *IAS Station interface agent [TRA 06]*

5.6.2.4. *Vehicle interface agent*

Similarly, this agent displays detailed information about the properties of any vehicle. It allows controllers to send a message to the travelers inside this vehicle or to its driver. The controller can access this agent by clicking on the representation of the vehicle in the associated state of line interface agent. Figure 5.22 shows this agent.

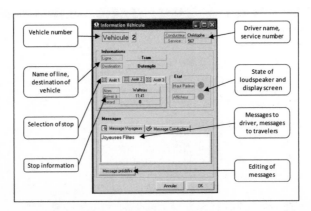

Figure 5.22. *IAS Vehicle interface agent [TRA 06]*

5.6.2.5. *Global view interface agent*

This agent currently provides the controller with an overall view of the traffic in the network, as Figure 5.23 shows. In its current version, this agent does not yet possess interactive functions.

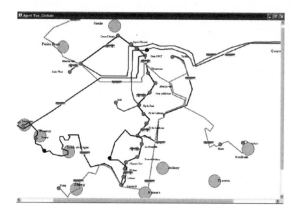

Figure 5.23. *IAS global view interface agent [TRA 06]*

5.6.2.6. *Message interface agent*

This agent provides controllers with a summary view of messages to send to vehicles or stations. It allows controllers to send a message to one or more vehicles or stations on one or more different lines. This agent also provides a list of available messages; the controller can access this list by using a pop-up menu on the interface agent. Figure 5.24 shows this agent.

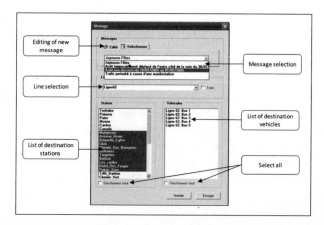

Figure 5.24. *IAS message interface agent [TRA 06]*

5.6.3. *Application of the proposed EISEval environment to evaluate IAS*

5.6.3.1. *Preparation of evaluation*

An experiment has been carried out in our laboratory with 10 individuals. They are accustomed to the use of computer software in general, but they are not experienced users of control software.

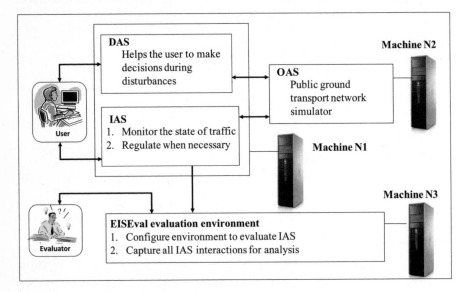

Figure 5.25. *Configuration of experiment*

The preparation includes two stages:

– *Deployment of modules*: initially four modules are deployed: IAS, DAS, OAS and the EISEval proposed evaluation environment, on different machines. Figure 5.25 shows the configuration of the experiment. IAS and DAS have been installed on the first machine. It is on this machine that the individuals (taking the role of controller) interact with these two modules. The OAS simulator has been installed on a second machine (remember that the OAS simulates the traffic on the public transport network). The EISEval environment has been installed on a third machine for the purpose of assisting the evaluator in evaluating the IAS and suggesting improvements to the IAS's designer based on these criticisms. All of these systems communicate with one another via a socket mechanism[14].

---

14 *Socket*: logical communication between two systems connected to the Internet (from the definition of the Internet Lexicon, www.apiguide.net/08aide/lexique.htm).

– *Configuration and launch of modules*: this stage is composed of two activities:

- configuration of the EISEval environment: after having installed these four modules on the three machines, the EISEval environment has been configured to evaluate the IAS. The evaluator seizes a batch of information pertaining to the IAS by using module 7 of the environment; and

- launch of modules: the modules must be launched before any individual participating in the experiment begins his/her tasks.

5.6.3.2. Experiment scenario

During the experiment, information concerning the positions of vehicles during their movements is sent in real time to the IAS by the OAS simulator. The subjects must execute nine regulation and notification tasks. Table 5.1 describes these tasks.

Tasks	Description of tasks (if no response from the IAS, the task needs to be redone)
T1	Send a message to the "Gare SNCF" station on the tramway line: "Next tramway stop in station 2 minutes"
T2	Send these two messages to vehicle N3 of the tram line: "Stop for 2 minutes at the Gare SNCF" for its driver and "We will stop for 2 minutes at the Gare SNCF" for its passengers
T3	Send a message to the "St Wast" station on line 15: "Next stop for bus 15 3 minutes in station"
T4	Send these two messages to vehicle N4 of line 15: "Stop for 3 minutes at St Wast" for the driver and "We will stop for 3 minutes at St Wast" for its passengers
T5	Send a message to the "Vaillant" station of line 16: "Next stop for bus 16 3 minutes in station"
T6	Send these two messages to vehicle N5 of line 16: "Stop for 3 minutes at Vaillant station" for the driver and "We will stop for 3 minutes at Vaillant station" for its passengers
T7	Send a message to the three stations "Canada", "Ardenne", and "Concorde" of line 62: "This stop is closed tomorrow and the day after tomorrow due to works"
T8	Send a message to all stations on all lines: "Risk of disruption on Monday of next week"
T9	Send a message to all vehicles on all lines: "Happy Holidays"

Table 5.1. *The nine regulation and notification tasks to be implemented*

The first six tasks are relatively easy to perform; the three latter tasks are fairly complex. All of the tasks involve sending messages to stations and/or vehicles. In case of disruption (delay, vehicle breakdown), the OAS sends these disruptions to the IAS and the DAS. Table 5.2 describes the process the subjects must complete in case of disruptions. After having finished a task or addressed a disruption, individuals must await the return of the IAS.

Information about disruption received from OAS	Process to be carried out in case of disruption (if no response from the IAS, the task is to be redone)
X minute delay of a vehicle (X minutes less than or equal to 7 minutes)	1. Close the delay warning window 2. Use the IAS to spend the following two messages to this vehicle: - "X minutes behind schedule, please accelerate" to the driver - "Attention, speeding up to compensate for delay" to passengers
X minute delay of a vehicle (X minutes greater than or equal to 7 minutes)	1. Close the delay warning window 2. Use the IAS to spend the following two messages to this vehicle: - "You are X minutes behind schedule" to the driver - "Attention, X minutes behind schedule" to the passengers 3. Send the following message to the next station for this vehicle: "X minutes behind schedule", then apply the control solution suggested by the DAS[15]
Breakdown of a vehicle	1. Close the breakdown warning window 2. Send the following two messages to this vehicle: - "The breakdown service will arrive in 10 minutes" to the driver - "This bus has broken down. Thank you for your understanding" to the passengers

Table 5.2. *Processes to be executed to react to information about disruption received by the IAS from the OAS*

---

15 Readers may consult [SID 06] to learn about the DAS, which offers control solutions for vehicle delays.

If there is no reply message from the IAS, the subjects must carry out this task or process again. The evaluation environment captures data during the experiment and then analyzes them. These analysis results must help the evaluator to detect problems related to the IAS system and to its users, and to propose improvements to the IAS designer. These evaluation results will be presented later.

After the capture and storage of data by module 1, the evaluator can use the environment to evaluate the IAS using the approach described in the following section.

5.6.3.3. *Approach for the evaluation of an interactive system using EISEval*

Module 6 of the evaluation environment provides the evaluator with the indications necessary to carry out her/his tasks (see Figure 5.26). The evaluator uses the evaluation criteria provided by module 6 (these criteria are associated with the analysis results provided by modules 3, 4 and 5 of the evaluation environment) to critique the interactive system and suggest improvements to the designer. These evaluation criteria can be general or specific.

In this case of IAS evaluation, the evaluator has added two evaluation criteria specific to the IAS to the list of criteria from module 6.

5.6.3.4. *Results of evaluation of the IAS based on module 6 criteria*

In this section, the results of the evaluation of the IAS based on the module 6 criteria are given in detail. From among all of the criteria evaluated, we will present two criteria as examples.

5.6.3.4.1. Readability criterion

The readability criterion concerns the lexical characteristics of the presentation of information on the screen, which can hinder or facilitate the reading of this information (luminosity of characters, contrast of characters, size of letters, space between words, line spacing, space between paragraphs, length of lines, etc.).

Performance is increased when the presentation of information on the screen takes into account the cognitive and perceptive characteristics of users. Good readability facilitates reading of the information presented. For example, dark letters on a light background are easier to read than the inverse; text presented in capitals and small letters is read more quickly than text presented in capital letters only [BAS 93].

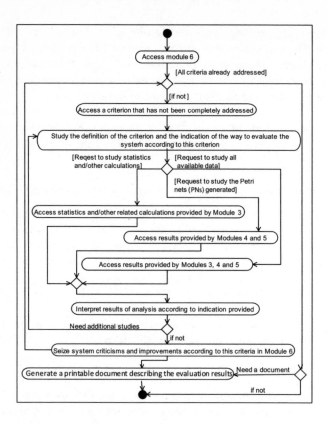

Figure 5.26. *Approach to the evaluation of an interactive system using the EISEval environment*

a) Interpretation of analysis results for an evaluation according to this criterion;

The evaluator can use the results of the analysis of the evaluation environment to partially evaluate the system according to this criterion:

– if the frequency of appearance of user-interface events (EVIU) allowing the user to see the interface more clearly (such as zoom in, zoom out, change of view size or window size, etc.) is high, then the evaluator may conclude that the readability of the system interface is not good;

– the evaluator can also use Petri nets generated by module 4 and the result of the analysis of user-interface events (EVIU) from module 3 to evaluate this criterion. These generated Petri nets reconstruct the process of the user's real activities and those of the system to carry out tasks. Through these processes, the evaluator can detect the EVIUs corresponding to the presentation of information. If the time interval between the appearance of an EVIU corresponding to the display of a window and the appearance of another EVIU corresponding to the following user action in this window is long, then the evaluator can interpret that the user may have spent a large amount of time in this window before implementing the next action. In this case, the evaluator may ask the question "Why did the user take such a long time to start the next action?", and may think that poor readability is one possible reason. Then another method of evaluation, for example a questionnaire or a verbalization, may be used in addition in order to understand the reason, and to gain a more complete and exact evaluation with regard to this criterion.

b) Critiques and improvements suggested by the evaluator based on this criterion

In the experiment with the 10 individuals, using the analysis result from module 3 of the environment (Figure 5.27 shows part of the screen capture on this subject), the evaluator may note that the EVIUs zoom in and zoom out were never implemented. Consequently, we may suppose that the IAS system interface is easily readable, and that the subject has no difficulty in reading information on it. To develop this criterion, additional studies will be necessary.

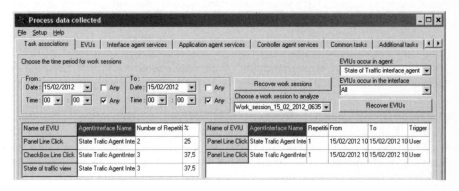

Figure 5.27. *Partial screen capture of the results of the analysis of EVIUs from module 3*

5.6.3.4.2. Criterion: protection against errors

The "protection against errors" criterion concerns the means implemented to detect and anticipate data entry errors or command or action errors with harmful consequences. It is preferable to detect errors during seizure rather than during validation; this avoids disturbances in planning [BAS 93]. According to these authors, there is a difference between "protection against errors" and "prompting": several ways of offering protection against errors are possible. We can, for example, implement an automatic entry verification mechanism. At the moment of entry validation, an error message appears if the entry format does not comply with what is expected. This is a case of the "protection against errors" criterion. Another option consists of providing information that tells users what type of data is expected, or the way in which to format entries; this is the "prompting" criterion. These two mechanisms may also coexist [BAS 93].

a) Interpretation of analysis results for an evaluation according to this criterion

When the user commits an error (seizure of wrong data, wrong actions) but the EVIU corresponding to the display of error messages or the display of error windows does not occur, the evaluator cannot conclude that the system is acceptable according to the "protection against errors" criterion. In the opposite case, this criterion is ensured in the system.

b) Critiques and improvements proposed by the evaluator based on this criterion

After this experiment, using the result of the analysis of module 3 EVIUs, the evaluator may note that the EVIUs corresponding to error message displays never occur when the subjects have seized data; consequently, the evaluator may draw two conclusions:

– the subjects have not committed any errors when seizing data; and

– the principles of error prevention of the IAS interactive system have shown themselves to be effective during the experiment by preventing subjects from committing data-seizure errors during the situations encountered.

In fact, in the IAS, there is one case in which users must seize data. When they wish to send a message to stations or vehicles, they must compose the message, but there are no constraints on the format of the data seized. Thus, evaluation according to this criterion for predetermined scenarios in the IAS system has not allowed this particular problem to become apparent.

5.7. Conclusion

In this chapter, we first presented the principles and criteria for the evaluation of interactive systems as well as a classification of evaluation methods. In section 5.2, we laid out an overview of tools utilizing ergonomic rules by emphasizing their advantages and disadvantages, as well as evaluation assistance tools. An evaluation tool developed in our research laboratory (LAMIH) was described – EISEval. This tool has been used to evaluate an agent-based interactive system prototype as part of the SART (Traffic Regulation Assistance System) project.

The SART project is part of the advanced transport technology program of the regional Nord-Pas de Calais Group for Transport Research, this theme having been explored as part of the CISIT SART project and which aims to create a system to assist control-room staff in improvement of the execution of tasks in the normal and impaired-functioning modes of the traffic network. The IAS agent-based interactive system, one of the three subsystems of the project concerned, was described in detail in this chapter.

An experiment conducted in our LAMIH laboratory with 10 individuals was also presented. During this experiment, the EISEval evaluation environment was applied to evaluate the IAS system. The approach to the evaluation of an interactive system using this environment was illustrated. Finally, we described a group of evaluation results concerning criticisms of the IAS and the improvements proposed, based on some criteria of module 6. In the case of this experiment, we played the role of the evaluator who can operate the EISEval in order to produce a printable document containing these criticisms and improvements by clicking the "see as text" button on the module 6 interface.

This experiment has helped us to detect the problems of the IAS and to test EISEval. Thus, EISEval now possesses the advantages that have been presented. The experiment has also helped to identify the problems of each IAS agent so that the evaluator can suggest relevant improvements. However, EISEval still has disadvantages and needs to be improved.

Research perspectives can involve the IAS system as well as the modules of the EISEval environment, and a more general integrated environment may also be envisioned. The improvements proposed in this chapter should be applied to IAS, and a second experiment should be planned with users who are professionals in the regulation of public transport. The perspectives related to EISEval would be aimed at improving modules 1, 5 and 6 in order to improve the method of event capture, facilitate the evaluator's work, and increase EISEval's level of automation. The perspectives related to a more general integrated environment would involve the proposition of an environmental model that would allow us to combine the evaluation results from different methods in order to obtain a more pertinent and complete evaluation. This integrated environment could be composed of:

– a questionnaire-generated method (in order to gather subjective user data);

– a tool using ergonomic rules (to evaluate the static aspect of the HMI); and

– EISEval (or an extended EISEval with the taking into account of video and oculometric data) in order to evaluate the dynamic aspect of the HMI.

The IEISEval environment would be modular and open; thus, the integration of other evaluation methods is very promising from a more long-term perspective.

5.8. Bibliography

[ABE 98] ABED M., EZZEDINE H., "Vers une démarche intégrée de conception-évaluation des systèmes Homme-Machine", *Journal of Decision Systems*, vol. 7, pp. 147-175, 1998.

[ABE 90] ABED M., Contribution à la modélisation de la tâche par des outils de spécification exploitant les mouvements oculaires: application à la conception et à l'évaluation des interfaces homme-machine, doctoral thesis, University of Valenciennes and Hainaut-Cambrésis, September 1990.

[ABE 01] ABED M., Méthodes et Modèles Formels et Semi-formels pour la Conception et l'Évaluation des Systèmes Homme–Machine, Habilitation à Diriger des recherches, University of Valenciennes and Hainaut-Cambrésis, May 2, 2001.

[AFN 03] AFNOR, Ergonomie de l'Informatique. Aspects Logiciels, Matériels et Environnementaux, No. 9388, AFNOR, 2003.

[APP 92] APPLE COMPUTERS, *Macintosh Human Interface Guidelines*, Addison Wesley, Reading, MA, 1992.

[BAC 05] BACCINO T., BELLINO C., COLOMBI T., *Mesure de l'Utilisabilité des Interfaces*, Hermès-Lavoisier, Paris, 2005.

[BAL 94] BALBO S., Evaluation ergonomique des interfaces utilisateur: un pas vers l'automatisation, doctoral thesis, University Joseph Fourier, Grenoble I, September 1994.

[BAR 88] BARTHET M.F., *Logiciels Interactifs et Ergonomie, Modèles et Méthodes de Conception*, Dunod Informatique, Paris, 1988.

[BAS 93] BASTIEN J.M.C., SCAPIN D.L., Ergonomic Criteria for the Evaluation of Human–computer Interfaces, Technical Report, n° 156, INRIA, Rocquencourt, 1993.

[BAS 98] BASTIEN J.M.C., LEULIER M., SCAPIN D.L., "L'ergonomie des sites Web", *Créer et Maintenir un Service Web, cours INRIA*, pp. 111-173, Pau, France, ADBS Editions, Paris, September 28 - October 2, 1998.

[BAS 01] BASTIEN J.M.C., SCAPIN D.L., "Evaluation des systèmes d'information et critères ergonomiques", in KOLSKI C. (ed.), *Environnement Évolués et Évaluation de l'IHM. Interaction Homme–Machine pour les SI*, vol. 2, pp. 53-80, Hermès, Paris, 2001.

[BAS 02] BASTIEN J.M.C., SCAPIN D.L., "Les méthodes ergonomiques: de l'analyse à la conception et à l'évaluation", *Ergonomie et Informatique Avancée, Ergo-IA'2002*, I.D.L.S., Biarritz, France, October 8-10, 2002.

[BAY 02] BAYSSIÉ L., CHAUDRON L., "Evaluation de la performance d'un opérateur en fonction de sa tâche", *Application aux IHM. In IHM 2002*, Poitiers, France, November 26-29, 2002.

[BEA 02] BEAUDOUIN-LAFON M., MACKAY W., "Prototyping "Tools and Techniques"", in JACKO J.A., SEARS A. (eds), *Human Computer Interaction Handbook*, pp. 1006-1031, Lawrence Erlbaum Associates, London, 2002.

[BEI 04] BEIREKDAR A., A methodology for automating web usability and accessibility evaluation by guideline, doctoral thesis, University of Namur, Namur, August 2004.

[BER 08] BERNONVILLE S., Exploitation des techniques de modélisation du GL et de l'IHM pour la création de supports communs entre intervenants de projet de développement de systèmes interactifs et pour la modélisation des situations de travail complexes, doctoral thesis, University of Valenciennes and Hainaut-Cambrésis, Valenciennes, December 2008.

[BLA 02] BLACKMON M.H., POLSON P.G., MUNEO K., LEWIS C., "Cognitive Walkthrough for the Web", *Proceedings CHI 2002*, vol. 4, no. 1, pp. 463-470, 2002.

[BOE 88] BOEHM B.W., "A spiral model of software development and enhancement", *IEEE Computer*, vol. 21, no. 5, pp. 61-72, 1988.

[BOJ 06] BOJKO A., "Using eye tracking to compare web page designs: A case study", *Journal of Usability Studies*, vol. 1, no. 3, pp. 112-120, 2006.

[BRA 00] BRAJNIK G., "Automatic web usability evaluation: where is the limit?", *Proceedings of the 6th Conference on Human Factors & the Web*, Austin, TX, United States, available at: http://users.dimi.uniud.it/~giorgio.brajnik/papers/hfweb00.html, 2000.

[CAR 83] CARD S.K., MORAN T.P., NEWELL A., *The Psychology of Human Computer Interaction*, Lawrence Erlbaum Associates, Hillsdale, NJ, 1983.

[CHA 01] CHALON R., DAVID B.T., BELDAME M., CHERIEF N., LASALLE J., MOINARD J., "L'oculomètre comme support d'évaluation et d'interaction", in VANDERDONCKT J., BLANDFORD A., DERYCKE A. (eds), *13ᵉ Conférence Francophone sur l'Interaction Homme-Machine*, Lille, France, September 10-14, 2001, Editions Cépaduès-éditions, Toulouse, France, vol. 2, pp. 117-122, 2001.

[CHA 04] CHALON R., Réalité mixte et travail collaboratif: IRVO, un modèle de l'interaction homme–machine, doctoral thesis, Ecole Centrale de Lyon, December 2004.

[COO 69] COOPER G., HARPER B., The Use of Pilot Rating in the Evaluation of Aircraft Handling Qualities, Report TN-D5153, NASA Ames, Moffett Field, CA, April 1969.

[COU 90] COUTAZ J., *Interface Homme-ordinateur, Conception et Réalisation*, Dunod, Paris, 1990.

[DAV 92] DAVID R., ALLA H., *Du Grafcet aux Réseaux de Petri*, Hermès, Paris, 1992.

[DEH 01] DE HAAN G., "Accommodating diverse users in ETAG and ETAG-based design: task knowledge and presentation", *Proceedings of HCI International 2001/1st International Conference on Universal Access in HCI*, New Orleans, United States, August 5-10, 2001.

[DEN 97] DENLEY I., LONG J., "A planning aid for human factors evaluation practice", *Behaviour & Information Technology*, vol. 16, no. 415, pp. 203-219, 1997.

[DIA 89] DIAPER D., *Task Analysis for Human–Computer Interaction*, John Wiley & Sons, Chichester, 1989.

[DIA 04] DIAPER D., STANTON N. (eds), *The Handbook of Task Analysis for Human–computer Interaction*, Lawrence Erlbaum Associates, Mahwah, NJ, 2004.

[DUC 03] DUCHOWSKI A.T., *Eye Tracking Methodology: Theory and Practice*, Springer, London, 2003.

[EAS 84] EASON K.D., "Towards the experimental study of usability", *Behaviour and Information Technology*, vol. 3, pp. 133-143, 1984.

[EZZ 97] EZZEDINE H., ABED M., "Une méthode d'évaluation d'interface homme machine de supervision d'un procédé industriel", *Journal Européen des Systèmes Automatisés*, vol. 7, pp. 1078-1110, 1997.

[EZZ 02] EZZEDINE H., Méthodes et Modèles de spécification et d'évaluation des interfaces homme–machine dans les systèmes industriels complexes, mémoire d'HDR, University of Valenciennes and Hainaut-Cambrésis, December 2002.

[EZZ 03] EZZEDINE H., TRABELSI A., KOLSKI C., "Modelling of agent oriented interaction using Petri nets, application to HMI design for transport system supervision", in BORNE P., CRAYE E., DANGOURMEAU N. (eds), *CESA2003 IMACS Multiconference Computational Engineering in Systems Applications*, Ecole Centrale Lille, Villeneuve d'Ascq, pp. 1-8, Lille, France, July 9-11, 2003.

[EZZ 05a] EZZEDINE H., TRABELSI A., "From the design to the evaluation of an agent-based human-machine interface. Application to supervision for urban transport system", in P. BORNE, M. BENREJEB, N. DANGOUMEAU, L. LORIMIER (eds.), *IMACS World Congress "Scientific Computation, Applied Mathematics and Simulation"*, ECL, pp. 717-725, Paris, July11-15, 2005.

[EZZ 05b] EZZEDINE H., KOLSKI C., PÉNINOU A., "Agent-oriented design of human-computer interface: application to supervision of an urban transport network", *Engineering Applications of Artificial Intelligence*, vol. 18, pp. 255-270, 2005.

[FAR 97] FARENC C., ERGOVAL: Une méthode de structuration des règles ergonomiques permettant l'évaluation automatique d'interfaces graphiques, doctoral thesis, University Toulouse 1, January 1997.

[FAY 03] FAYECH B., Régulation des réseaux de transport multimodal: Systèmes multi-agents et algorithmes évolutionnistes, doctoral thesis, University of Sciences and Technologies of Lille, October 2003.

[GAR 97] GARZOTTO F., MATESA M., "A systematic method for hypermedia usability inspection", *The New Review of Hypermedia*, vol. 3, pp. 39-65, 1997.

[GAW 08] GAWRON V.J. (ed.), *Human Performance, Workload, and Situational Awareness Measures Handbook*, second edition, Taylor & Francis, Guernsey, 2008.

[GIR 07] GIRARD J.M., Contribution à l'évaluation de la charge de travail du conducteur automobile: une approche exploratoire multivariée, doctoral thesis, University of Valenciennes et du Hainaut-Cambrésis, December 2007.

[GIR 09] GIRARD J.M., YOUNSI K., LOSLEVER P., POPIEUL J.C., SIMON P., "Etude du système conducteur-véhicule-environnement sur simulateur avec perturbation de la tâche de conduite", *Journal Européen des Systèmes Automatisés*, vol. 43, pp. 263-294, 2009.

[GRA 00a] GRAMMENOS D., AKOUMIANAKIS D., STEPHANIDIS C., "Integrated support for working with guidelines: the Sherlock guideline management system", *International Journal of Interacting with Computers, special issue on 'Tools for Working with Guidelines'*, vol. 12, no. 3, pp. 281-311, 2000.

[GRA 00b] GRAMMENOS D., AKOUMIANAKIS D., STEPHANIDIS C., "Sherlock: A tool towards computer-aided usability inspection", in VANDERDONCKT J., FARENC C. (eds), *Proceedings of the Scientific Workshop on 'Tools for Working with Guidelines' (TFWWG 2000)*, Biarritz, France, pp. 87-97, Springer-Verlag, London, October 7-8, 2000.

[GRI 96] GRISLIN M., KOLSKI C., "Evaluation des interfaces homme–machine lors du développement de système interactif", *Technique et Science Informatiques* (TSI), vol. 3, pp. 265-296, 1996.

[GRI 95] GRISLIN M., Définition d'un cadre pour l'évaluation a priori des interfaces homme-machine dans les systèmes industriels de supervision, doctoral thesis, University of Valenciennes and Hainaut-Cambrésis, January 1995.

[HAM 84] HAMMOND N., HINTON G.E., BARNARD P., LONG J., WHITEFIELD A., "Evaluating the interface of a document processor: A comparison of expert judgement and user observation", in SCHACKEL B. (ed.), *Human–computer Interaction, INTERACT'84*, IFIP, pp. 725-729, Elsevier Science, Amsterdam, 1984.

[HAY 01] HAYAT S., Amélioration de la Qualité des Correspondances dans les Réseaux de Transports Urbains, Final report on the SART project, INRETS, 2001.

[HEL 88] HELANDER M. (ed.), *Handbook of Human Computer Interaction*, Elsevier Science, Amsterdam, 1988.

[HEL 97] HELANDER M., LANDAUER T.K., PRABHU P. (eds), *Handbook of Human-computer Interaction*, Elsevier Science, Amsterdam, 1997.

[HIL 00] HILBERT D.M., REDMILES D.F., "Extracting usability information from user interface events", *ACM Computing Surveys (CSUR)*, vol. 32, no. 4, pp. 384-421, 2000.

[HOL 93] HOLYER A., *Methods for Evaluating User Interfaces*, School of Cognitive and Computing Sciences, University of Sussex, Brighton, 1993.

[HEW 88] HEWLETT-PACKARD, *Common User Interface Behaviour Guide*, Hewlett-Packard, September 1988.

[HUA 08] HUART J., KOLSKI C., BASTIEN C., "L'évaluation de documents multimédias, état de l'art", in MERVIEL S. (ed.), *Objectiver l'humain, Qualification, Quantification*, vol. 1, pp. 211-250, Hermès-Lavoisier, Paris, 2008.

[HUL 96] HULZEBOSCH R., JAMESON A., "FACE: A rapid method for evaluation of user interfaces", in JORDAN P.W., THOMAS B., WEERDMEESTER B.A., MCCLELLAND I.L. (eds), *Usability Evaluation in Industry*, pp. 195-204, Taylor & Francis, London, 1996.

[IGL 89] IGL TECHNOLOGY, *SADT, un Langage pour Communiquer*, Eyrolles, Paris, 1989.

[IBM 93] IBM, *Object-Oriented Interface Design: IBM's Common User Access Guidelines*, Que Pub, March 1993.

[ISO 98] ISO 9241: Ergonomic Requirements for Office Work with Visual Display Terminals, ISO, 1998.

[ISO 96] ISO, ISO/DIS 9241-10, Ergonomic Requirements for Office Work with Visual Display Terminals, Dialogue Principles, ISO, 1996.

[ISO 01] ISO/IEC 9126-1: Software Engineering – Product Quality – Part 1: Quality Model, (JIS X 0129-1: 2003), ISO, 2001.

[ISO 03a] ISO/IEC 9126-2: Software Engineering – Product Quality – Part 2: External Metrics, ISO, 2003.

[ISO 03b] ISO/IEC 9126-3: Software Engineering – Product Quality – Part 3: Internal Metrics, ISO, 2003.

[ISO 04] ISO/IEC 9126-4: Software Engineering – Product Quality – Part 4: Quality in Use Metrics, ISO, 2004.

[IVO 01a] IVORY M., HEARST M., "The state of the art in automated usability evaluation of user interfaces", *ACM Computing Surveys*, vol. 33, no. 4, pp. 173-197, 2001.

[IVO 01b] IVORY M., An empirical foundation for automated web interface evaluation, doctoral thesis, University of California, Berkeley, 2001.

[JAC 02] JACKO J.A., SEARS A. (eds), *The Human–computer Interaction Handbook: Fundamentals, Evolving Technologies and Emerging Applications (Human Factors and Ergonomics)*, Lawrence Erlbaum Associates, London, 2002.

[JAC 00] JACOBSEN N.E., JOHN B.E., Two Case Studies in Using Cognitive Walkthrough for Interface Evaluation, Carnegie Mellon University, Report No. CMU-CHII-00-100, Carnegie Mellon University, May 2000.

[JAS 06] JASSELETTE A., KEITA M., NOIRHOMME-FRAITURE M., RANDOLET F., VANDERDONCKT J., BRUSSEL C.V., GROLAUX D., "Automated repair tool for usability and accessibility of web sites", *Proceedings CADUI 2006*, pp. 261-272, Bucharest, Springer-Verlag, 2006.

[JOH 96] JOHN B.E., KIERAS D.E., "The GOMS family of user interface analysis techniques: Comparison and contrast", *ACM Transactions on Computer-Human Interaction*, vol. 3, pp. 320-351, 1996.

[KAR 88] KARAT J., "Software evaluation methodologies", in M. HELANDER (ed.), *Handbook of Human-Computer Interaction*, pp. 891-903, Elsevier Science, Amesterdam, 1988.

[KOL 97] KOLSKI C., *Interfaces Homme–machine: aux Systèmes Industriels Complexes*, vol. 2, Hermès-Lavoisier, Paris, 1997.

[KOL 91] KOLSKI C., MILLOT P., "A rule-based approach to the ergonomic "static" evaluation of man-machine graphic interface in industrial processes", *International Journal of Man-Machine Studies*, vol. 35, pp. 657-674, 2001.

[KON 03] KONTOGIANNIS T., "A Petri net-based approach for ergonomic task analysis and modeling with emphasis on adaptation to system changes", *Safety Science*, vol. 41, no. 10, pp. 803-835, 2003.

[KOV 04] KOVÁCS B., GAUNET F., BRIFFAULT X., *Les Techniques d'Analyse de l'Activité pour l'IHM*, Hermès-Lavoisier, Paris, 2004.

[LEC 98] LECEROF A., PATERNO F., "Automatic support for usability evaluation", *IEEE Trans. on Software Engineering*, vol. 24, no. 10, pp. 863-888, 1998.

[LOS 03] LOSLEVER P., POPIEUL J.C., SIMON P., "Analyse de données provenant d'unités temporelles relatives au comportement d'un système complexe. Exemple des mouvements oculaires dans le système conducteur-véhicule", *APII-JESA*, vol. 37, no. 6, pp. 799-824, 2003.

[LOS 08] LOSLEVER P., SIMON P., ROUSSEAU F., POPIEUL J.C., "Using space windowing for a preliminary analysis of complex time-data in human component system studies. Examples with eye-tracking in advertising and car/head movements in driving", *Information Sciences*, vol. 178, pp. 3645-3664, 2008.

[MAH 09] MAHATODY T., KOLSKI C., SAGAR M., "CWE: Assistance environment for the evaluation operating a set of variations of the Cognitive Walkthrough ergonomic Inspection Method", in HARRIS D. (ed.), *Engineering Psychology and Cognitive Ergonomics, 8th International Conference, EPCE 2009, Held as Part of HCI International 2009* (San Diego, CA, United States, July 19-24, 2009), Proceedings, LNAI 5639, pp. 52-61, Springer-Verlag, 2009.

[MAH 10] MAHATODY T., SAGAR M., KOLSKI C., "State of the art on the Cognitive Walkthrough method, its variants and evolutions", *International Journal of Human-Computer Interaction*, vol. 26, pp. 741-785.

[MAH 97] MAHFOUDHI A., TOOD: Une méthodologie de description orientée objet des tâches utilisateur pour la spécification et la conception des interfaces homme-machine, doctoral thesis, University of Valenciennes, June 1997.

[MAR 05] MARIAGE C., MetroWeb: logiciel de support à l'évaluation de la qualité ergonomique des sites web, doctoral thesis, UCL, Louvain-la-Neuve, 2005.

[MIC 95] MICROSOFT, *The WindowsTM Interface Guidelines for Software Design*, Microsoft Press, Redmond, 1995.

[MIL 88] MILLOT P., *Supervision des Procédés Automatisés et Ergonomie*, Hermès-Lavoisier, Paris, 1988.

[MOH 05] MOHA N., LI Q., GAFFAR A., SEFFAH A., "Enquête sur les pratiques de tests d'utilisabilité", *IHM'05, 17e Conférence Francophone sur l'Interaction Homme-Machine*, pp. 115-122, Toulouse, France, September 27-30, 2005.

[MOR 81] MORAN T.P., "The Command Language Grammar: a representation for the user interface of interactive computer systems", *Internal Journal of Man-Machine Studies*, vol. 15, pp. 3-50, 1981.

[MOU 02] MOUSSA F., RIAHI M., KOLSKI C., MOALLA M., "Interpreted Petri nets used for human-machine dialogue specification", *Integrated Computer-Aided Engineering*, vol. 9, pp. 87-98, 2002.

[MUL 01] MULLIN J., ANDERSON A.H., SMALLWOOD L., JACKSON M., KATSAVRAS E., "Eye-tracking explorations in multimedia communications", in BLANFORD A., VANDERDONCKT GRAY J., P. (eds), *People and Computer XV- Interaction without Frontiers – Joint Proceedings of HCI 2001 and IHM 2001*, pp. 367-382, Springer, London, United States, 2001.

[NEN 99a] NENDJO ELLA A., Vers un outil d'aide à la décision en évaluation des systèmes interactifs et la prise en compte conjointe de critères techniques et socioculturels, doctoral thesis, University of Valenciennes and Hainaut-Cambrésis, January 1999.

[NEN 99b] NENDJO ELLA A., KOLSKI C., WAWAK F., JACQUES C., YIM P., "An approach of Computer-aided choice of UI evaluation criteria and methods", in VANDERDONCKT J., PUERTA A. (eds), *Computer-Aided Design of User Interfaces II*, pp. 319-328, Kluwer Academic Publishers, Dordrecht, 1999.

[NIE 90] NIELSEN J., MOLICH R., "Heuristic evaluation of user interfaces", *CHI'90 Conf. Proc.*, Seattle, United States, pp. 349-356, ACM, New York, 1990.

[NIE 93] NIELSEN J., *Usability Engineering*, Academic Press, Boston, MA, 1993.

[NIE 94] NIELSEN J., "Heuristic evaluation", in NIELSEN J., MACK R.L. (eds), *Usability Inspection Methods*, pp. 25-62, John Wiley & Sons, New York, 1994.

[NOG 08] NOGIER J.F., *Ergonomie du Logiciel et Design Web*, Dunod, Paris, 2008.

[NOR 86] NORMAN D.A. "Cognitive Engineerin", in NORMAN D.A., DRAPER S.W. (eds), *User Centered System Design: New Perspectives on Human Computer Interaction*, pp. 31-61, Erlbaum, Hillsdale, NJ, 1986.

[OPE 93] OPEN SOFTWARE FOUNDATION, OSF/Motif Style Guide, Revision 1.2, Prentice-Hall, London, 1993.

[PAG 02] PAGANELLI L., PATERNÒ F., "Intelligent analysis of user interactions with Web applications", *Proceedings of ACM IUI 2002*, pp. 111-118, San Francisco, CA, United States, January 2002.

[PAG 03] PAGANELLI L., PATERNÒ F., "Tools for remote usability evaluation of Web applications through browser logs and task models", *Behavior Research Methods, Instruments, and Computers*, vol. 35, no. 3, pp. 369-378, 2003.

[PAL 97] PALANQUE P., BASTIDE R., "Synergistic modelling of tasks, system and users using flat specification techniques", *Interacting with Computers*, vol. 9, no. 12, pp. 129-153, 1997.

[PAR 00] PARUSH A., "A Database Approach to Building and Using Online Human Computer Interaction Guidelines", in VANDERDONCKT J., FARENC C. (eds), *Tools for Working with Guidelines*, pp. 77-84, Springer-Verlag, London, 2000.

[PAT 97] PATERNO F., MANCINI C., MENICONI S., "ConcurTaskTrees: A diagrammatic notation for specifying task models", *Proceedings Interact'97*, pp. 362-369, Sydney, Australia, 1997.

[PAT 99] PATERNO F., BALLARDIN G., "Model-aided remote usability evaluation", in A. SASSE, C. JOHNSON (eds.), *Proceedings of the IFIP TC13 Seventh International Conference on Human-Computer Interaction*, pp. 434-442, Edinburgh, Scotland, IOS Press, Amsterdam, 1999.

[PAT 00a] PATERNO F., *Model Based Design and Evaluation of Interactive Applications*, Springer-Verlag, London, 2000.

[PAT 00b] PATERNO F., BALLARDIN G., "RemUSINE: a bridge between empirical and model-based evaluation when evaluators and users are distant", *Interacting with Computers*, vol. 13, no. 2, pp. 229-251, 2000.

[PAT 06] PATERNO F., PIRUZZA A., SANTORO C., "Remote Web usability evaluation exploiting multimodal information on user behavior", *Proceedings CADUI 2006*, 285-296, Bucharest, Romania, 2006.

[PAY 89] PAYNE S.J., GREEN T.R.G., "Task-action grammar: the model and developments", in DIAPER D. (ed.), *Task Analysis for Human–Computer Interaction*, pp. 75-107, John Wiley & Sons, New York, 1994.

[PIV 06] PIVEC M., TRUMMER C., PRIPFL J., "Eye-tracking adaptable e-learning and content authoring support", *Informatica*, vol. 30, no. 1, pp. 83-86, 2006.

[POL 91] POLLIER A., Evaluation d'une Interface par des Ergonomes: Diagnostics et Stratégies, INRIA research report, no. 1391, INRIA, February 1991.

[POL 92] POLSON P.G., LEWIS C., RIEMAN J., WHARTON C., "Cognitive walkthroughs: A method for theory-based evaluation of user interfaces", *International Journal of Man-Machine Studies*, vol. 36, pp. 741-773.

[RAV 89] RADVEN S.J., JOHNSON G.I., *Evaluating Usability of Human–computer Interfaces: a Practical Method*, Ellis Horwood, Chicester, 1989.

[RAY 98] RAYNER K., "Eye movements in reading and information processing: 20 years of research", *Psychological Bulletin*, vol. 124, pp. 372-422, 1998.

[REI 91] REIMAN J., DAVIES S., HAIR C., ESEMPLARE M., POLSON E., LEWIS C., "An automated cognitive walkthrough", in ROBERTSON S.E., OLSEN G.M., OLSEN J.S. (eds), *Human Factors in Computing Systems, CHI 91 Conference Proceedings*, pp. 427-428, ACM Press, New York, 1991.

[REI 84] REISNER P., "Formal grammars as a tool for analysing ease of use: some fundamental concepts", in THOMAS J.C. and SCHNEIDER M.W. (eds.), *Human Factors in Computer Systems*, pp. 53-78, Ablex, Norwood, N.J., 1984.

[REY 05] REY G., Contexte en interaction homme–machine: le contexteur communication langagière et interaction personne-système, doctoral thesis, University of Joseph Fourier, Grenoble, 2005.

[ROB 03] ROBERT J.M., "Que faut- il savoir sur l'utilisateur pour concevoir des interfaces de qualité?", in BOY G.A. (eds), L'Ingénierie Cognitive: IHM et Cognition, pp. 249-284, Hermès-Lavoisier, Paris, 2003.

[ROO 83] ROOT R.W., DRAPER S., "Questionnaire as a software evaluation tool", in JANDA A. (ed.), Human Factors in Computing Systems-I, pp. 83-87, ACM, Amsterdam, 1983.

[RUS 86] RUSHINEK A., RUSHINEK S., "What makes users happy?", Communication of ACM, vol. 29, pp. 594-598, 1986.

[SYS 07] Système d'Aide à la Régulation de Trafic du Réseau de Transpor Valenciennois et de ses Pôles d'Échanges, Final report, SART cooperative project, INRETS, France, December 2007.

[SCA 86] SCAPIN D.L., Guide Ergonomique de Conception des Interfaces Homme-ordinateur, Rapport INRIA, no. 77, INRIA, October 1986.

[SCA 89] SCAPIN D.L., PIERRET-GOLBREICH C., "MAD: Une méthode analytique des descriptions des tâches", Colloques sur l'Ingénierie des IHM, 131-148, Sophia Antipolis, Nice, France, May 24-26, 1989.

[SEN 90] SENACH B., Evaluation Ergonomique des IHM: Une Revue de la Littérature, Rapport INRIA, no. 1180, INRIA, March 1990.

[SHE 93] SHEPHERD A., "An approach to information requirements specification for process control tasks", Ergonomics, vol. 36, no. 11, pp. 1425-1427, 1993.

[SID 06] MAHMOUD OULD SIDI M., Contribution à l'amélioration des systèmes d'aide à la décision dans le domaine du transport, doctoral thesis, Ecole Centrale de Lille, 2006.

[SIM 93] SIMON P., Contribution de l'analyse des mouvements oculaires à l'évaluation de la charge de travail mental, Doctorat thesis, University of Valenciennes and Hainaut-Cambrésis, January 1993.

[SMI 86] SMITH S.L., MOSIER J.N., Guidelines for Designing User Interface Software, Report No. MTR-10090, ESD-TR-86-278, MITRE Corp., Bedford, MA, 1986.

[SPE 96] SPERANDIO J.C., "L'apport de la psychologie du travail", in CAZAMIAN P., HUBAULT F. (eds), Traité d'Ergonomie, pp. 165-207, Octares, Toulouse, 1996.

[STA 05] STANTON N., SALMON P., WALKERN G., BABER C., JENKINS D., Human Factors Methods: A Practical Guide for Engineering and Design, Ashgate, London, 2005.

[SZE 96] SZEKELY P., "Retrospective and challenges for model-based interface development", in VANDERDONCKT J. (ed.), Proceedings of Second International Workshop on Computer-Aided interface development CADUI'96, pp. 21-44, Presses Universitaires de Namur, Namur, 1996.

[TAB 01] TABARY D., Contribution à TOOD, une méthode à base de modèles pour la spécification et la conception des systèmes interactifs, doctoral thesis, University of Valenciennes and Hainaut-Cambrésis, January 2001.

[TAR 93] TARBY J.C., Gestion automatique du dialogue homme-machine à partir de spécifications conceptuelles, doctoral thesis, University Paul Sabatier, Toulouse I, 1993.

[TAU 90] TAUBER M.J., "ETAG: Extended Task Action Grammar – A language for the description of the user's task language", in DIAPER D. *et al.* (eds), *Human-Computer Interaction, INTERACT'90*, pp. 163-168, Cambridge, United States, 1990.

[TRA 04] TRABELSI A., EZZEDINE H., KOLSKI C., "Architecture modelling and evaluation of agent-based interactive systems", *Proc. IEEE SMC 2004*, pp. 5159-5164, The Hague, Netherlands, October 2005.

[TRA 06] TRABELSI A., Contribution à l'évaluation des systèmes interactifs orientés agents, application à un poste de supervision de transport urbain, doctoral thesis, University of Valenciennes and Hainaut-Cambrésis, September 2006.

[TRA 07] TRAN C.D., EZZEDINEH., KOLSKI C. "Towards a generic and configurable model of an electronic informer to assist the evaluation of agent-based interactive systems", in CARDOSO J., CORDEIRO J., FILIPE J. (eds), *ICEIS'2007, Ninth International Conference on Enterprise Information Systems* (Funchal, Portugal, 12-16 June 2007), *Proceedings Human-Computer Interaction, INSTICC*, pp. 290-293, 2007.

[TRA 08a] TRAN C.D., EZZEDINE H., KOLSKI C., "A generic and configurable electronic informer to assist the evaluation of agent-based interactive systems", *7th international Conference on Computer-Aided Design of User Interfaces, CADUI'2008*, Albacete, Spain, June 008.

[TRA 08b] TRAN C.D., EZZEDINE H., KOLSKI C., "Evaluation of agent-based interactive systems: proposal of an electronic informer using Petri Nets", *Journal of Universal Computer Science*, vol. 14, no. 19, pp. 3202-3216, 2008.

[TRA 09] TRAN C.D., Vers un environnement générique et configurable pour l'aide à l'évaluation des systèmes interactifs à base d'agents, Application à un Système d'Aide à l'Information voyageurs, doctoral thesis, University of Valenciennes and Hainaut-Cambrésis, July 2009.

[VAN 94] VANDERDONCKT J., *Guide Ergonomique des Interfaces Homme–Machine*, Facultés universitaires Notre-Dame de la Paix à Namur (Belgium), Presses Universitaires de Namur, Namur, 1994.

[VAN 98] VANDERDONCKT J., *Conception Ergonomique de Pages WEB*, Vesale, 1998.

[VAN 99] VANDERDONCKT J., "Development milestones towards a tool for working with guidelines", *Interacting With Computers*, vol. 12, no. 2, pp. 81-118, 1999.

[WHI 91] WHITEFIELD A., WILSON F., DOWELL J., "A framework for human factors evaluation", *Behaviour & Information Technology*, vol. 10, no. 1, pp. 65-79, 1991.

[WIE 79] WIERWILLE W.W., "Physiological measure of aircrew mental workload", *Human Factors*, vol. 21, no. 5, pp. 575-593, 1979.

[WIE 83] WIERWILLE W.W., CASALI J.G., "Evaluation of 20 workload measures using a psychomotor task in a moving-base aircraft simulator", *Human Factors*, vol. 25, no. 1, pp. 1-16, 1983.

[WIL 96] WILSON J.R., CORLETT E.N. (eds), *Evaluation of Human Works: a Practical Ergonomics Methodology*, second edition, Taylor & Francis, London, 1996.

[WIL 05] WILSON J.R., CORLETT E.N. (eds), *Evaluation of Human Work*, third edition, Taylor & Francis, London, 2005.

List of Authors

Amar BENNASSEUR
LGI2A
Lille Nord de France University
University of Artois
Béthune
France

Thierry DELOT
LAMIH CNRS
Lille Nord de France University
University of Valenciennes and Hainaut-Cambrésis
France

Mikael DESERTOT
LAMIH CNRS
Lille Nord de France University
University of Valenciennes and Hainaut-Cambrésis
France

Arnaud DONIEC
Département Informatique et Automatique
Ecole des Mines de Douai
Lille Nord de France University
France

Stéphane ESPIÉ
IFSTTAR
Paris
France

Houcine EZZEDINE
LAMIH CNRS
Lille Nord de France University
University of Valenciennes and Hainaut-Cambrésis
France

Slim HAMMADI
LAGIS CNRS
Ecole Centrale de Lille
Lille Nord de France University
France

Daniel JOLLY
LGI2A
Lille Nord de France University
University of Artois
Béthune
France

Boumediene KAMEL
LGI2A
Lille Nord de France University
University of Artois
Béthune
France

Christophe KOLSKI
LAMIH CNRS
Lille Nord de France University
University of Valenciennes and Hainaut-Cambrésis
France

Mekki KSOURI
Tunis El Manar University
National Engineering School of Tunis (ENIT)
Tunisia

Sylvain LECOMTE
LAMIH CNRS
Lille Nord de France University
University of Valenciennes and Hainaut-Cambrésis
France

René MANDIAU
LAMIH CNRS
Lille Nord de France University
University of Valenciennes and Hainaut-Cambrésis
France

Sylvain PIECHOWIAK
LAMIH CNRS
Lille Nord de France University
University of Valenciennes and Hainaut-Cambrésis
France

AbdelwahebTRABELSI
GIAD, FSEG
University of Sfax
Tunisia

Chi Dung TRAN
LAMIH CNRS
Lille Nord de France University
University of Valenciennes and Hainaut-Cambrésis
France

Hayfa ZGAYA
Laboratoire de Santé Publique-EA 2692
Institut Lillois d'Ingénierie de la Santé (ILIS)
University of Lille 2
France

Index